KT-218-453

The First and the Last

The First and the Last

The Claim of Jesus Christ and the Claims
of Other Religious Traditions

George Sumner

WILLIAM B. EERDMANS PUBLISHING COMPANY
GRAND RAPIDS, MICHIGAN / CAMBRIDGE, U.K.

© 2004 Wm. B. Eerdmans Publishing Co.
All rights reserved

Wm. B. Eerdmans Publishing Co.
255 Jefferson Ave. S.E., Grand Rapids, Michigan 49503 /
P.O. Box 163, Cambridge CB3 9PU U.K.

Printed in the United States of America

09 08 07 06 05 04   7 6 5 4 3 2 1

Library of Congress Cataloging-in-Publication Data

Sumner, George R., 1955-
    The first and the last: the claim of Jesus Christ and the claims of
    other religious traditions / George Sumner.
        p.   cm.
    Includes bibliographical references.
    ISBN 0-8028-2498-6 (cloth: alk. paper)
    1. Christianity and other religions.   I. Title.

    BR127.S89   2004
    261.2 — dc22

                                        2004043407

www.eerdmans.com

Contents

Acknowledgments

This essay is in spirit missiological, in which discipline I learned most from Professor Charles Forman of Yale. Its kernel grows out of my dissertation, and so I am particularly indebted to my *Doktorvater* George Lindbeck for his wise counsel. My friends Rusty Reno, Joe Mangina, Ephraim Radner, and Kathryn Greene-McCreight have provided support intellectual and personal. It was an honor to receive the corrections of Bishop Kenneth Cragg over tea. St. Philip's, Kongwa, Tanzania, and Good Shepherd, Fort Defiance, Navajoland, were my real teachers about final primacy. Trinity, Geneva sheltered me as the project began, and the Jesuits of Regis College gave a way station. At Wycliffe College, Barbara Beatty, Karen Baker-Bigauskas, Andrew Kaye, Mark Bowald, and Chris and Christina Holmes gave technical aid. My classes in African Christianity and other religions gave me a forum to test ideas. My children Marta and Sam provided comic relief. This book is dedicated to my wife, Stephanie Hodgkins, *sine qua non*. Through all these persons Christ, the Alpha and Omega, has shown me his grace, and so to him be all the praise.

GEORGE SUMNER
Wycliffe College
Feast of the Annunciation

1 *Toward a Postliberal Christian Theology of Religions*

A specter hangs over contemporary Christian theology, the specter of pluralism. So might think the defender of traditional Christian claims, for pluralists contend that such claims offend a modern understanding of truth, and stand in the way of harmony between religions and cultures. More specifically, the pluralist claims that the transcendent, the "Real in itself," is expressed by, but is to be strictly distinguished from, the wide array of particular myths, rites, and beliefs of the religious communities of the world.[1] Furthermore, in order to restrain the evil effects of fanaticism, the pluralist advocates that such communities restrict themselves to the moral effects of religious practice, the resulting works of love, and thus evolve away from any exclusive claims for their tradition.

The radical challenge to traditional Christian belief is plain: the primacy of the revelation in Jesus Christ and the uniqueness of his mediating agency in salvation are at stake. Thus traditionalist and pluralist alike can agree on the momentous change acceptance of such a view would represent, indeed a theological "crossing of the Rubicon."[2] Al-

---

1. "We now have to distinguish between the Real *an sich* and the Real as variously experienced-and-thought by different human communities." See John Hick, *An Interpretation of Religion: Human Responses to the Transcendent* (New Haven: Yale University Press, 1989), p. 236.

2. So says John Hick in his "The Non-absoluteness of Christianity," in *The Myth of Christian Uniqueness: Toward a Pluralistic Theology of Religions,* ed. John Hick and Paul Knitter (Maryknoll, N.Y.: Orbis, 1987).

though some might argue that the readers of the works of Knitter, Hick, or Wilfred Cantwell Smith are limited to academes, who can doubt that the effect of such a sea change would ripple widely into the religious populace at large?

This essay offers an alternate, "postpluralist" view of the relationship between Christian belief and the claims of other religious traditions. But precisely because one should take its challenge seriously, a sharper focus on the real significance of the phenomenon of pluralism at the outset is required. Here it is useful to rehearse the chorus of recent retorts to pluralism, all of which may be characterized as attempts to turn the tide by "relativizing the relativizers."[3]

Critics have contended, first of all, that though they seek to widen interreligious horizons, pluralists do not take seriously what practitioners of religious traditions say they believe and think they are doing. When the pluralist claims to see behind particular claims and practices, the mere phenomena of religion, to the universal object of the transcendent, one catches a whiff of paternalism, albeit of a liberal sort. Secondly (and as the converse of the first critique), pluralists fail to see that theirs is one more particular position, emerging from a series of assumptions embedded in a particular tradition, namely that of Western Enlightenment thought. What may appear an objective perspective, a "view from nowhere" from which to judge the truth and falsity of all particular religious traditions, is merely the employment of certain philosophical arguments (prominently those of Kant) to bolster the pluralist position.[4] Pluralism quickly resembles, not a view beyond specific religious traditions, but rather a new religion of reason.

Thirdly, critics have turned the "hermeneutic of suspicion," the questioning of unexamined motives, on the pluralists. The view that religions represent so many choices, suited to the customer, though the specifics of each choice cease to matter much, parallels closely the Western capitalist encroachment on markets and attitudes worldwide.

---

3. For a sociologist with a keen sense of the limits of relativist and reductionist arguments, see Peter Berger, e.g., *The Sacred Canopy: Elements of a Sociological Theory of Religion* (Garden City, N.Y.: Doubleday, 1969), appendices.

4. "The book is about a single problem: how to combine the perspective of a particular person inside the world with an objective view of the same world, the person and his viewpoint included." Thomas Nagel, *The View from Nowhere* (New York: Oxford University Press, 1986), p. 3.

Pluralism is complicit in the commodification of religious traditions. By an insidious genius this process leaves the outward appearances the same, though now the turban, the prayer wheel, and the mantra have been rendered "consumer preferences."[5]

A key distinction here is between the challenge of other religious traditions and the challenge of pluralism itself. While pluralism seems to focus its attention on the plethora of traditions, in fact its main task is the modern, post-Enlightenment questioning of the truth of Christian claims in the light of historical and cultural relativism, of which the non-Christian religions amount to a prime occasion. If one accepts this insight, one can no longer consider pluralism in a vacuum. It must rather be seen as a specific Western cultural and intellectual phenomenon posing its challenge to Christianity. One must then consider pluralism's own historical roots, the particulars of its story, intertwined as they are with Christianity's own intellectual travails in the past three hundred years.

The historical nub of the matter is this: the existence of other religious traditions became a problem for the Christian tradition at the very time that Christianity became a problem to itself. To be sure, Christians have, since the beginning of the church, had contact with, and so formed opinions of, other religious traditions. On this issue one need think only of the attention given to Greek philosophy in the Patristic era, or of the traumatic encounter with Islam in the Middle Ages. The widened horizons of the age of discovery in the seventeenth century also led to intense debate over the status of the "noble pagan" and the value found in other religions. Just the same, the religions came to play a different sort of role in the Enlightenment of the eighteenth century. Then, for the first time, thinkers came to see Christianity and the religions as comparable religious artifacts. Then, for the first time, in a variety of authors like Herder, Rousseau, and Lessing, the example of the religions became the outward occasion for a deeper crisis within the Christian tradition itself.[6]

---

5. See for example Kenneth Surin's "A 'Politics' of Speech," in Gavin D'Costa, *Christian Uniqueness Reconsidered: The Myth of a Pluralistic Theology of Religions*, Faith Meets Faith Series, ed. Paul F. Knitter (Maryknoll, N.Y.: Orbis, 1990), pp. 192ff.

6. Gotthold Lessing's view of the religions can be seen most dramatically in *Nathan the Wise* (London: N. Truebner, 1868). Jean-Jacques Rousseau's view of religions as derived from the diversity of climates and cultures can be seen in his *The Creed of a Priest of*

At the heart of the Enlightenment was an attack on tradition and its presumed authority, and a new emphasis on universal reason accessible to any thinking person. The thinkers of the Enlightenment employed several strategies of critical reason to release authority's grip on the mind. In the rising movement of biblical criticism they sought to arrive at the truth behind what the texts claimed, to arrive at the historical contexts and sources that actually contributed toward the creation of the text. As a result the intellectuals of the Enlightenment came in time to shake the very foundations of Christology, the church's doctrine of who Jesus Christ is.

A common intellectual movement linked this internal doubt and the new attention paid to the plurality of religions. For at the very time that Jesus became a Middle Eastern religious figure fit for scholarly scrutiny, the fact of the other religions appeared distinctly on the horizon. So it is no accident that a figure like Gotthold Lessing was a pioneer both in the criticism of traditional Christology and in the awareness of the religions.[7] Both the particular claims of the Christian tradition over against other religions, and more specifically the particular figure of Jesus Christ for Christians themselves, are simultaneously rendered problematic by the Enlightenment critic.

The great historical religious traditions fell under the same judgment in Enlightenment quarters as Christianity due to their encrustations of tradition, their own uncritical appeals to authority, and their miraculous worldviews. By most accounts they were even more backward and questionable than Christianity. It was, for example, something of a breakthrough when Hegel envisioned a scheme of evolution that included the other traditions as necessary and valuable stages, albeit at a less evolved level. Though more knowledgeable about other traditions, the contemporary pluralist, taking as a starting-point epistemological problems born of the Enlightenment, anticipates a certain predictable evolution and revision in non-Christian traditions. The changes will conform to their insights about "religion," the category associated with a foundation identifiable and

Savoy (New York: Ungar, 1956). Herder's view of the same issue is lucidly analyzed in A. O. Lovejoy's "Herder and the Enlightenment Philosophy of History," in his Essays in the History of Ideas (New York: Capricorn, 1960).

7. See Lessing's Basic Theological Writings, ed. Henry Chadwick (Stanford, Calif.: Stanford University Press, 1956).

definable in all human beings and its priority over all the particulars of tradition.

In sum, the genesis of the "challenge of the religions" was inextricably tied up with the challenge to the Christian faith in the modern West. In order to understand this encompassing intellectual condition several insights of the contemporary moral philosopher Alasdair MacIntyre are helpful.[8] Of particular relevance is first of all, his concept of an "epistemological crisis," a historical moment in which a tradition finds its very existence as an ongoing coherent enterprise called into question by external rivals offering more compelling accounts of the reasons for the extant crisis itself. For MacIntyre, the prime example of such a crisis is precisely modernity's pursuit of a foundation for knowledge independent of the particularity of the Christian tradition.[9]

According to such a diagnosis pluralism is the presenting symptom for a wider epistemological illness in Western Christianity. MacIntyre emphasizes, secondly, the importance of narrative as the underlying form of philosophical argumentation, and thus the mode in which traditions strive to respond to such rivals. Accordingly, traditions prevail in the face of epistemological crises when they manage to tell a more convincing story, one that may comprise retrospectively both re-

8 My application of MacIntyre's philosophy to the question of a theology of the religions (1995) has been pursued more recently in Gavin D'Costa's *The Meeting of Religions and the Trinity* (Maryknoll, N.Y.: Orbis, 2000). His work is especially helpful in its extension of the analysis of pluralism to other traditions themselves in Part I, so that one may see parallel struggles in them. My present work complements and extends D'Costa's treatment, particularly by giving a fuller account of the Christian tradition as a "running argument," to borrow MacIntyre's phrase. This argument finds its condition and boundary in the rule we will elaborate below. Likewise we agree when D'Costa speaks of inculturation as a "continuity" within a larger "discontinuity" (p. 126). The virtue of final primacy is that it clarifies how "continuity" and "discontinuity" normatively relate one to another, since in many cases they are seemingly contrasting answers to different questions.

9. The phrase "epistemological crisis" is employed, for instance, in the title "Epistemological Crises, Narrative, and the Philosophy of Science," in Stanley Hauerwas and L. Gregory Jones's *Why Narrative? Readings in Narrative Theology* (Grand Rapids: Eerdmans, 1989). MacIntyre's interest is moral philosophy, and so he is not interested in defending the Christian theological tradition as such. However, given his advocacy of Thomistic moral philosophy, it would seem fair to say that his arguments, transposed to theology, amount to a defense of the particularity of Christian theology's grand tradition.

buttals of its rivals and, when necessary, internal reformulation of its own beliefs.[10] Such narratives prove powerful in part to the extent that they open themselves to the critique of their rivals and acknowledge their own debatability within the narrative itself.[11] Only in this way can the narrative offered by the tradition in question successfully assimilate the alien beliefs and challenges into the terms of its own intellectual world. In such a process traditions may need to reformulate their beliefs even as they appeal to precedents in their own stream of reflection. Thus MacIntyre distinguishes emphatically between such a dynamic view of tradition as the arena of intellectual contestation and adaptation and what is often thought of as "traditionalism."[12]

There is of course no guarantee that a tradition will succeed in the face of such an epistemological crisis. It could be that it will eventually prove incredible, and gradually wither. It is also possible that (to paraphrase the helicopter pilot in the Vietnam War) in order to save the tradition, it will prove necessary to destroy it. The revisions proposed may be so extensive as to render the tradition unrecognizable. Like so many Trojan horses, criteria unfriendly to the major tenets of the tradition may be imported in such a way that the enterprise as a whole is undone from within. Obviously in many cases it will require a prudential judgment to distinguish between reasonable and excessive revision.[13]

For MacIntyre the intellectual history of the modern West has, thirdly, consisted of a contest between three major schools or types of thought. In the first case his attention has focused on Thomism, though, as the most coherent and encompassing expression of Chris-

---

10. For MacIntyre on "retrospective narrative" see *After Virtue: A Study in Moral Theory* (Notre Dame: University of Notre Dame Press, 1981), pp. 190-209 passim.

11. ". . . no claim to rational superiority, on the view which I am ascribing to the Aristotelean-Thomistic tradition, can be made good except on the basis of a rationally-justifiable rejection of the *strongest* [emphasis mine] claim to be made from the opposing point of view." See MacIntrye, *Three Rival Versions of Moral Inquiry: Encyclopaedia, Genealogy, and Tradition* (Notre Dame: University of Notre Dame Press, 1990), p. 181.

12. For Edmund Burke, e.g., as a "traditionalist" see *Whose Justice? Which Rationality?* (Notre Dame: University of Notre Dame Press, 1988), p. 8.

13. At this point a logically odd and anomalous aspect of this argument should be clear. For I am marshalling the philosophical proposal of MacIntyre in defense of understanding the threat of pluralism in a context-specific way, and, in what follows, in support of arguments located in a manner developed from the Christian theological tradition.

tian theology, it may be taken as a metonymy for the Christian tradition as a whole. The Enlightenment challenge represented by liberalism, supposing as it does an independent and objective norm of reason, he calls "the encyclopedic tradition." Liberalism both critiques the inherited tradition and seeks to place the residue of its claims on a solid rational footing. The subsequent attack on liberalism, epitomized by the thought of Friedrich Nietzsche, based in the reduction of reasons to motives for power, is tagged "the genealogical tradition." Liberalism, by failing to see itself for what it is as one more tradition of thought born of distinctive practices in a particular community, becomes unstable and decomposes into genealogy.

Such an analysis helps to explain several theological efforts to make sense of the claims of the religions in the face of the modern epistemological crisis. Thinkers such as Schleiermacher and Hegel adopt a strategy that begins with a definition of "religion" in general which is followed by a consideration of the history of religions according to which Christianity proves to be the pinnacle, the perfect manifestation of religion's definition, the "absolute religion." Such a strategy is prone to the criticism that the initial definition has imported assumptions from the thought-world of the thinker, thereby biasing the resulting interpretation of the history of religions toward the desired result. Thus by the end of the nineteenth century Ernst Troeltsch, though he continued to think in terms of an "absolute religion," had come to see that such a designation is based on "values" imposed by the thinker, and the force of this awareness caused him, by the end of his career, to reject the argument entirely. He moved instead toward an argument basing the privilege of Christianity simply on the cultural power and sophistication of the West.[14] This is an example of just the sort of slide from the "encyclopedic" to the "genealogical" that MacIntyre would lead us to suspect. One finds something similar in the rising interest that advocates of interreligious pluralism have recently taken in liberation theology as the source of common cause among the religious traditions of the world.[15]

14. Ernst Troeltsch, "The Absoluteness of Christianity and the History of Religions," in *Christian Thought: Its History and Application: Lectures Written for Delivery in England during March, 1923*, ed. Friedrich von Hülge (Westport, Conn.: Hyperion, 1979).

15. See, e.g., Paul Knitter, *One Earth, Many Religions: Multifaith Dialogue and Global Responsibility* (Maryknoll, N.Y.: Orbis, 1995).

By contrast, MacIntyre advocates a return to the particularities of an intellectual tradition aware of its own assumptions, as one contestant for truth among others. The Christian tradition strives to encompass as many as possible of the claims and conditions of its surrounding world into a coherent narrative, and so show itself to be preferable to its rivals. In recent years new voices have been heard in the debate about the place of Christianity among the religions, voices that offer warrants for just such a postliberal, neotraditional alternative. I will term this loosely affiliated yet complementary group of thinkers "particularists." They all share, in contrast to pluralism, an emphasis on the epistemological distinctiveness of religious traditions. For all of them it is misleading to search for a definitional substratum beneath the particularities of the various traditions.

Developing the metaphor of natural languages, George Lindbeck, for example, understands each religion to have its own "grammar" or internal logic, whose rules are expressed in a community's doctrine, in keeping with which it can express itself in a variety of ways.[16] Likewise Joseph DiNoia has shown a "variety of religious aims" in the different traditions, thus making for a truer plurality than the pluralists themselves acknowledge.[17] He goes on to criticize Christian "inclusivists" who conceive of non-Christians as saved by imagining them to be, in the famous expression of Karl Rahner, "anonymous Christians," for he fears such a strategy overlooks how the adherent of the other tradition actually understands his or her own actions and beliefs.[18]

This does not mean that particularists think that Christians should cease to try to make sense of their neighbors, only that they cannot make sense of their neighbors in a single grand move, or by means of an Archimedean point beyond their own tradition. Thus, for instance, the philosopher William Christian focuses on the way in which religious communities employ their distinctive "primary doctrines" to make sense of the claims of "alien communities." So each community

16. *Nature of Doctrine: Religion and Theology in a Postliberal Age* (Philadelphia: Westminster, 1984), esp. ch. 4.

17. Joseph DiNoia, *The Diversity of Religions: A Christian Perspective* (Washington, D.C.: Catholic University Press, 1992).

18. See Mark Heim, *Salvations: Truth and Difference in Religion* (Maryknoll, N.Y.: Orbis, 1995).

must generate its own "doctrines about alien claims" of other communities in a manner consistent with its own beliefs.[19]

Such a particularist position is open to at least two obvious criticisms. First of all, one might ask, as have detractors of postliberal approaches in general,[20] if such a view of religious traditions is not overly isolating or ghettoizing. At an epistemological level, does such an approach overemphasize difference? As a result, from within Christian quarters, particularist proposals may seem overly isolationist. If religions are distinctive "forms of life," and if interreligious understanding is more difficult than often supposed, it might seem to follow that religious traditions should mind their own affairs. What become then of the Christian traditions of apologetics and of missionary activity in general? For example, one wonders when DiNoia emphasizes the "providential diversity of religions" and the possibility that adherents of other traditions are even now being built up in virtues that may contribute to an imagined eschatological "prospective salvation," what room is left for the imperative of Christians to witness to these neighbors and to seek to convince them of the truth of the gospel? For these (among other) reasons, Paul Griffiths, a Christian Buddhologist working from particularist philosophical assumptions, insists on the "necessity of interreligious apologists" (to which he gives the acronym NOIA). The difficulty of the task of making oneself apologetically understood should not obviate its necessity.[21]

Another particularist, from a completely different quarter, making a similar point, is Lesslie Newbigin. A longtime missionary to India, leader of the ecumenical movement, and eminence grise among missiologists, he appealed extensively to the "postcritical" philosophy

19. William Christian, *The Doctrines of Religious Communities: A Philosophical Study* (New Haven: Yale University Press, 1987) on primary doctrines, introduction, and on alien claims, ch. 7-8.

20. See, e.g., James Gustafson's "Just What Is 'Postliberal' Theology?" *Christian Century*, 116, pp. 353-55.

21. See Paul Griffiths, *An Apology for Apologetics* (Maryknoll, N.Y.: Orbis, 1991). Here one may note, parenthetically, that the subject of interreligious understanding is as important to postliberal theological methods as the latter are fruitful for dialogue. For it is in just such an inquiry as this one that the "ghettoizing" criticism is overcome, and readers are reminded that the distinctive grammar of Christianity is useless unless it is employed in "absorbing" surrounding claims into "the Scriptural world" (George Lindbeck, *Nature of Doctrine*, p. 118).

of science of Michael Polanyi to emphasize the epistemological distinctiveness and authority of the Christian tradition. But the particular origin of the Christian claim, growing out of the "fiduciary framework" of Scripture read and interpreted by the church, in no way relieves Christians of the need to make that claim boldly in the public square. The church may be a particular minority, but it confesses a "public truth" believed to have "universal intent" (again to borrow a phrase from Polanyi).[22]

With this second objection in mind, as well as the contributions of Griffiths and Newbigin, one might observe that there is among particularists itself a certain dissonance. They emphasize, in contrast to their pluralist opponents, the irreducible difference between religions; Mark Heim's *Salvations: Truth and Difference in Religion* is a careful, extended exposition of this point about the epistemological conditions for religious knowing. This must not be confused, however, with limitation on the span or scope of things about which a religious tradition claims to know or seeks to interpret in its own lights. The way Christians know may be particular, but the object of their knowledge is universal, since their God is one, as are God's creation and God's truth.

So an unavoidable (creative?) tension resides within contemporary Christian particularism itself. A theological awareness of human nature and culture (not to mention the virtue of humility) require a sense of the finite, limited nature of theological constructions concerning other religious traditions, while a Christian understanding of God's truth, as well as the imperatives to teach and preach, require that Christians stretch their efforts to make some kind of Christian sense of the welter of other traditions and all their claims. The new emphasis on difference may be salutary in the interreligious debate, but a satisfactory account will need to acknowledge that theology invariably implies both particularist self-awareness and universal intent.

One might, secondly, observe an inevitable issue in the cluster of particularist arguments surveyed so far. For there is inherently an irony in defenses of the specificity and uniqueness of traditions that appeal to general observation about the nature of human knowing

---

22. Lesslie Newbigin, *The Gospel in a Pluralist Society* (Grand Rapids: Eerdmans, 1989), esp. ch. 4. Michael Polanyi, *Personal Knowledge: Toward a Post-Critical Philosophy* (Chicago: University of Chicago Press, 1958).

(e.g., that it is tradition-specific) or human community (e.g., about practices embedded in a unique form of life). Put simply, most particularists give general defenses of particularity, and so play the interreligious game continually on the opponents' field. As a result, many accounts sympathetic to interreligious particularism seem to float vaguely. They espouse both the maintenance of distinctive Christian claims tied to communal identity and open dialogue with other traditions, but never go on to say how both are to be accomplished, or in what relation these goals rest. There remains the task of giving a distinctively Christian, explicitly theological, account of how Christians relate their own claims to those of alien communities. That is the task of this essay, which agrees with fellow particularists in large measure, but hopes in this way to make a contribution to their case.

One final methodological explanation is in order. MacIntyre has suggested that traditions, even as they strive to take into account the most trenchant criticisms offered against them, seek to encompass these rival claims in a narrative culminating in their own central beliefs. Christians, faced with rival claims, characteristically do just this, albeit in a variety of ways. The reader will note that this essay is seeking, along the way, as it treats Christian theologies of other religions, to accomplish just such a confrontation with and encompassing of the claims of contemporary pluralist rivals (who remain, remarkably, within the Christian community itself). This treatment of Christian theological narratives seeks to be such a narrative itself.

Proposing a Rule for Christian Discourse about Other Claims

The task then is a normative one, to propose what a Christian theology about other religious claims ought to be. However, a helpful place to begin is with a more descriptive task, to understand how the tradition has tended in the past to make sense of such claims. To be sure, further arguments will be needed to show why such an accustomed pattern ought still to be followed, why it ought not to be changed.

The history of Christian theologies of other religions is often rendered in a parodied form, as a history of sheer rejection and know-nothingism. But proposals made by the tradition have tended to follow a describable pattern, as it has come into contact with other communities and their claims, to size up the extent to which these claims are true and right and to decide how it ought to respond. Such a rule will prove to be suppler than is often supposed, and so its explication will require pluralists to reject tradition at its most potent, and not a parody thereof.

Here it is possible to borrow an approach that has been fruitful in contemporary constructive theology, according to which distinctive rules may be discerned in the way Christians have tended to speak on different doctrinal subjects, much in the way that laws of grammar form an underlying structure for a language. The undergirding rules enable the Christian to maintain the distinctive contours of belief, especially when two simultaneously valid theological goals seem to be at odds. For example, to know how to talk in a Christian way about the identity of Jesus Christ is to know, more often than not implicitly or unconsciously, that one should speak of him using terms descriptive of an actual human being at the same time that his deeds are spoken of in terms appropriate for the agency of God. Or, to take another example, grace enables the Christian to say that humans are free, but that God is sovereign. So one can observe that frequently rules of Christian discourse are applicable precisely when "something Christians want to affirm appears not to hang together very well with what else they want to affirm."[23] Thus Kathryn Tanner has referred to rules of Christian discourse as "qualified transcendental arguments" that provide the condition for the possibility of claims with seemingly divergent objectives being in fact part of a single coherent body of thought.[24]

Rule-theory then allows us to see how reflection on other traditions strives to reconcile seemingly divergent goals, on the one hand consistency with the gospel and on the other openness to the truths found in other traditions. But at the outset one might suppose this to be an unpromising avenue for considering the claims of other religious traditions. Who could claim that the Christian tradition has taken a single stance toward the claims of other religious traditions? This is, however, precisely what a rule-approach to a theological tradition

23. Kathryn Tanner, *God and Creation in Christian Theology: Tyranny or Empowerment* (Oxford: Blackwell, 1988), p. 20.
24. Tanner, *God and Creation in Christian Theology*, p. 25.

does not suggest. In meeting these ends a "grammatical" approach acknowledges that the tradition has indeed generated a wide variety of approaches. Thus such a pattern is better understood as the common ground-rule or parameter for debate and disagreement within the community about assessment of alien claims. To acknowledge that Christianity is a variegated and contested tradition is not to deny the existence of a common rule or pattern, but rather to say that Christians have been able to assess other claims differently at times, but all within an identifiably Christian pattern, as part of a coherent tradition.

One might object that the discernment of a rule is appropriate for "in-house" matters, tasks of understanding how "we Christians" characteristically think and talk about Christian matters, but offers no help on the front line where the Christian apologist or dialogician encounters someone with radically different beliefs and practices. But this dividing wall between matters internal and external to a tradition is a good deal more porous than it at first seems. The tradition must constantly employ ideas from the surrounding culture to rearticulate doctrines "internal," and it must endeavor to make sense on its own terms of "external" claims.

Scripture can serve as a template for Christian theologies of the religions. One can observe how scriptural authors themselves have treated themes and concepts they encountered from their own context. One can find a multitude of examples of biblical authors borrowing and reworking ideas and expressions from their pagan neighbors. Consider the following examples: the pagan idea of an *heiros gamos* ("sacred marriage") is rebuked, then transformed and employed to describe the relationship of Yahweh and Israel in Hosea. Likewise a borrowed concept of the semi-divine king is deployed to describe the relationship between Yahweh and the king in Psalm 2. Hellenistic speculation about the *Logos* finds a new use to describe the incarnation of Christ in John 1, and the Stoic idea of "conscience" in Romans 8 to illustrate the dynamics of grace. In each case a concept or term was borrowed from the surrounding environment and adapted creatively for the purpose of saying something about Yahweh or his people within the terms and confines of the tradition of Israel, old or new. Each such borrowing implies a kind of narrative of its own, an intellectual and semantic process of critique and appropriation to a new end, a movement from a prior toward a reworked stage. The pattern discernible in Scripture is itself deployed in Scripture before it is applied to subsequent, contemporary cases of other claims.

So Christian theologies of religions are best understood as assorted secondary constructions that all derive their (often implicit) narrative or sequential deep structure from their master-template, Scripture. In other words, such constructions imagine other communities and claims as somehow prior to the gospel, though for these communities and claims the gospel may as likely represent judgment as fulfillment. This quality of narrative movement toward the gospel makes it possible theologically to engraft a wide variety of such claims and communities by means of a narrative continuity. Such narrative constructions often find a theological rationale in the doctrine of the divine economy, since they imagine how diverse areas of human thought, practice, and history might be thought of as related to and governed by the divine providential ordering (the *oikonomia*) of God. Theology takes as its goal to show such ordering in as much of human endeavor and history as possible.

Here it is crucial to distinguish narrative continuity from other sorts of continuity, for instance the logical continuity of premise and conclusion or the pedagogical continuity of question and answer. One might say in general that the conclusion of a narrative occupies the primary place to the extent that, in its light, the preceding chapters receive their roles and significance, their places in the whole. In the case of narratives leading up to the culmination in Christ, "earlier" truths are only "partial" with respect to Christ as the "final" truth, "earlier" structures only "paedagogic" (Gal. 3:24) or preservative, in light of what finally arrives, and "earlier" attitudes only "despairing" or "under wrath" from the later perspective of God's grace.

Since theologies of religions are such constructions with an underlying, derivative narrative form, it follows that what is temporally subsequent is theologically prior. It would be fair at this point to ask if the argument has not fallen into the trap mentioned above, of offering general arguments about "particular" theological narratives. It is true that all religions (including Christianity) arrive at their assessment of other traditions "retrospectively." But the argument needs to go further and make the material claim that Christ, the *prima veritas* or "first truth," though born "late in time," orders all that follows and precedes. The way the narratives order themselves backwards conforms to the material claim that the main actor of the last act, Jesus, reigns over the whole tale.

Accordingly, an underlying structure, consisting of a sequence culminating in Christ, is basic and "grammatical" for Christian theologies of religions, though a wide variety of plot-lines, found in Scripture, can conform to this pattern, and a limitless array of alien customs, claims, and stories would make up the stuff of such theologies of religions. But in all cases the revelation of Christ serves as the norm by which reflection on alien claims and communities casts its backward gaze. So the flow of assessment, of affirmation as well as critique, moves backwards, while the flow of narrative is forward. This accounts for the element of irreducible complexity in all constructions in the Christian theology of religions.

One might object that obedience to such a rule would stifle the ability of Christian theology to say something new, especially as it comes to grips with ways of thinking quite unprecedented in its own past. How will the Buddhist idea of "nothingness" influence Christology, for example, or a Native American idea of the earth affect a Christian theology of creation? Here the example of language is instructive, since the relative constancy of grammar is not a bar to, but the condition for, saying new and creative things (although any language also, presumably, leaves some things unsayable as well). To return to MacIntyre for a moment, one can go so far as to say that the power to meet new crises, and in the process to say new things, is constitutive of the very concept of a tradition. To be sure, it is within a particular tradition that the new thing is said, but this is true of any statement. So the search for such a rule cannot be derailed for these reasons at the outset.

The task of arguing for such a pattern is however a daunting one, for Christians have spun understandings of other religions off from a wide variety of their own primary doctrines (to use William Christian's phrase): the Trinity, grace, the economy of salvation, eschatology, creation, etc. Furthermore, the church has cast the religions in a wide variety of roles derived from different biblical types: preparer of the coming of the gospel, ordained restrainer of evil, rod of God's wrath, exemplar of legalism, recipient of secret wisdom or inarticulate faith, etc. In the face of such an admitted profusion, how could one hope to defend a common pattern?

One must look deeper for an answer. The search for such a pattern requires that one consider in a more basic way the shape of the scriptural story and so the manner of the Scripture's witness itself. Assume, as did Christians throughout the pre-modern period, that the story of the relationship between God and his people Israel, and the culmination of that relationship in Jesus Christ, is the overarching, unifying scriptural metanarrative. An implication of this starting-point is that other communities are tangentially related to the metanarrative, to the extent that Israel emerges out of "the nations," is attacked or aided by them, witnesses to them, etc.

Theological reflection on the status of the nations and their teaching must be consistent with that metanarrative, while at the same time it maintains a derivative and secondary status. To be sure, Scripture does have many words of judgment and hope for the nations. But theology is the task of ordering these statements theologically in relation to the primary witness about God and Israel, and the further, specific task of relating them to the alien claims of Gentiles encountered during the history of the church. To fulfill these tasks Christian theologies of religions are required, varied and contestable though they may be.

From the master-template of Scripture, a variety of subnarratives tie the lives of the nations in to that of Israel, the elect. Consider the following, among numerous other possibilities: In Acts 17, a period of worshiping "an unknown God" precedes the moment of hearing the gospel proclaimed. In John 1 the Word is at work before becoming flesh. In Romans 1–2, the pagans have some knowledge of "the law written in their hearts," but still they are under God's wrath, awaiting redemption in Christ. In each case reflection on the role of the Gentiles involves some kind of transition or narrative, however truncated, as if the theological construction were endeavoring again and again to graft the subnarrative into the biblical story. It seeks to tell a story moving likewise from "before" to "after," from a "Gentile" to a "gospel" stage in imitation of a pattern borrowed from Scripture. Just as the backbone of Scripture is a narrative, so these derivative accounts tend also to mimic this narrative shape.

The pattern described above may be called the "final primacy" of Jesus Christ. It consists in the fact that, in narratives generated from the scriptural narrative, by which theological constructions imagine alien claims and communities somehow engrafted into the divine economy, Christ is the One toward whom the narratives run and from whom their truth (to the extent that they are true) derives. He is at once the *finis legis* (the end of the law) and the *prima veritas* (the first truth).

"Final primacy" is the pattern common to all appropriate Christian theologies of religions. It is important here to reiterate that the pattern gleaned follows formally from the narrativity of Scripture and materially from the doctrine of the divine economy, precisely to the extent that it is a gloss on the innate shape of that narrative. As such it does not predetermine the precise sort of narrative we are to imagine linking alien claim and gospel, and so it allows ample room for the variety of narratives with precedents in the Scripture.

Such a finally primary narrative will lie implicit behind the Christian theologian's actual treatment of the other claims. "Final primacy" amounts to a kind of deep structure beneath a variety of competing and often conflicting accounts. In each case, however, the author finds value in the other claim as it sets the stage for the Christian truth, as well as grounds for criticism as the light of the gospel shines back in judgment. The normative Christian treatment brings this other truth into relationship with the final, hence norming, truth of Christ. Assumed then by every treatment that discriminates between valuable and worthless is this same undergirding narrative moving toward that truth which serves as first principle.

Not only is such a pattern discernible in the historical mainstream of Christian theologizing about other communities and claims, but it should also act as a norm in any such theologizing. Several different sorts of arguments conspire to support this latter assertion. First, the pattern subserves the goal of preserving the position of Jesus Christ as the *prima veritas*. The great and definitive battles in the history of Christian theology have shared the defense of such an assertion about the Lordship of Jesus Christ, that he is "the First and the Last," though they have done so on different fronts, with respect to different doctrinal loci (the doctrine of God, the nature of Christ, the doctrine of grace, etc.). For Athanasius, for Luther, for Barth too, whatever the "presenting diagnosis" theologically, this was the real matter at stake. In other words, there is a fundamental link between the finality of Christ and Christian identity which a variety of doctrinal crises have attested to.[25]

---

25. Edward Lohse, *Short History of Doctrine: From the First Century to the Present* (Philadelphia: Fortress, 1978), p. 22.

The next section will show how the major sorts of theological formulations about other claims have shared this underlying narrative structure. Obviously this will not constitute any sort of proof, but the process of analysis aims to convey a sense of aptness. Taken together they suggest a kind of trajectory, a pattern of similarity able in the past to address a variety of crises. Following on this will be the argument that formulations which have overlooked or violated this pattern have resulted in serious theological problems. If the pattern of final primacy serves an ordering function, so disorder, where the pattern is neglected, should not be surprising. But again, this is not a logical proof, but rather another piece of evidence in a cumulative case.

A word of clarification here may head off a misunderstanding. The pattern of final primacy is not intended to suggest that every claim of every other tradition must be measured against the Christian doctrine of Christology, in contrast to the doctrine of creation, or sin, or eschatology, etc. In many cases another locus may be a more natural conversation partner with a particular claim on another tradition. For example, if one were discussing the Hindu concept of karma, the Christian doctrines of anthropology, sin, and providence would be the natural interlocutors. Final primacy is a structure assumed by and undergirding all the doctrinal claims, all the loci, namely that other truths are judged by and rendered coherent with the Christian truth in a pattern shaped after the coming of Christ in the economy of salvation.

But the concept of final primacy also carries an implied claim that the teaching about Jesus Christ does in fact occupy the central place among all Christian doctrines, such that "Christ" can serve as a shorthand for them all. For doctrinal loci are not discrete quanta, but are better understood as different yet related points of entry into understanding "the Christian thing" as a whole.[26] Thus, no matter what locus may serve as a better point of comparison for another claim, that locus stands in immediate relationship to the claim about Jesus Christ, in relationship to which the other claim then must also stand.

One may now note several implications of a general, formal nature, which will be true of a range of scripturally derived constructions. First, the telos of all such narrative sequences is Christ and not

---

26. See David Yeago, "Memory and Communion," in Ephraim Radner and George Sumner, eds., *Reclaiming Faith* (Grand Rapids: Eerdmans, 1993).

the church, though obviously the latter is the herald, sacrament, or servant, of the former. One might say that the church as medium is formally implied but not materially decisive. So the narratives construed, and the alien claims and communities about which they speak, always stand in a complex relationship to the church. The church witnesses to the goal, but must not be confused with it. In other words, the church must, in any such theological construction, retain some sort of kinship with its non-Christian neighbors, since it too is under judgment. It fallibly and imperfectly reflects God's revealed truth, while at the same time it has an ambassadorial role on behalf of Christ the goal. Any theology of religions must somehow retain this cognizance of kinship between the proclaimers and those "who are far off" (Eph. 2:17).[27]

All the religions, secondly, present an element of ambivalence. This is most clearly true in a relationship of fulfillment, for the idea of the other religion as a "partial truth" implies some admixture of falsehood or ignorance. But even when Christian theologians have seen the religions as predominantly idolatrous, or as "works of the law" evoking divine wrath, they combine truth and falsity, since these assessments entail the idea of a corruption of a true knowledge or of a right relationship with God. While some constructions stress the positive assessment of the religions, and others the negative, some element of ambivalence remains, if only in the background.

Here one must remember that even a theologian as chary about non-Christian religions as Calvin insisted that the *imago Dei* could not be erased, though it remained in fallen human beings, whose prolific idolatry, especially evident in the religions, served only to condemn them manifestly.[28] This ambivalence may be observed at its source in the argument in Romans 1, where Paul affirms at once "[God's] invisible nature . . . has been clearly perceived" so that "they are without excuse" (v. 20). Similarly in chapter 2 "what the law requires is written on [the Gentiles'] heart," but this means that "all . . . without the law will perish without the law." Much reflection on the religions in the

27. This point was perhaps made most emphatically in Karl Barth's insistence that Christianity too is religion and hence *Unglaube* (in *Church Dogmatics* I/II, paragraph 17), but all constructions must make some kind of allowance for such a distinction. (On Barth and religions, see Chapter 3A.)

28. *Institutes of the Christian Religion* (Grand Rapids: Eerdmans, 1971), Book I, ch. 1, pp. 3-4.

Christian tradition has reverted to these passages, and so the ambivalence of Paul's view has had a pervasive effect. Paul's clearest references to a "natural knowledge of God" are, by no mistake, coupled in the same passage with resounding condemnation of the religions as idolatrous and unsalvific.

A third implication is that Christian reflection according to the pattern of final primacy in no way prohibits one from deeming other beliefs and practices true and right, though they be in themselves altogether different from and unrelated to Christian beliefs and practices, so long as they do not contradict the latter.[29] At the same time, it remains incumbent upon Christian theology to take the further step and to imagine how these truths and practices might be brought into relation with and so narratively engrafted into Christian truth. The latter task will remain ever contestable and provisional, since their traditions are epistemologically distinct and the rule of final primacy itself is patent of varied constructions. Such engrafting does require as accurate as possible knowledge of the other community in question, but it involves no claim that the other community sees itself in this finally primary way.

A fourth implication is that final primacy can address a number of different, though related, questions. The possibility of divine revelation in the alien tradition is one frequently posed question, and the possibility of saving truth is another. Since the answers a theologian might give may depend on other systematic decisions, constructions that are close kin in their type of conformity to final primacy may actually arrive at different answers. At the very least, one should pay close attention to which question is being posed in any particular case.

Fifthly, if it were true that Christian efforts to come to terms with alien claims normatively follow the pattern of final primacy, then the basic contrast for Christian theology between the challenges of integrity with past tradition and openness to new truths must be seen in a new way. For, according to final primacy, the presupposition of Christ as the *prima veritas* is the condition for the ongoing pursuit of openness to the truths in alien traditions rather than the cause for the abandonment of such a pursuit. These goals reside in a distinctly Christian relationship to one another shaped according to the pattern of final pri-

---

29. William Christian, *The Doctrines of Religious Communities*, esp. ch. 7.

macy itself. To set these goals over against one another only follows from the dissolution of a robust understanding of what the Christian has to say.

Assume that, formally, Christian theology is a tradition in the sense in which MacIntyre uses the term, a coherent, ongoing realm of discourse in which different constructions contend to make sense of external challenges. Then assume, materially, that Christian tradition has been (and should be) characterized by a rule of final primacy in its evaluation of other claims. What sense could one then make of other religious traditions, and how could one maintain the dual goals of integrity to the gospel and openness to other truths? The rest of this essay will be devoted to explicating and illustrating the answer to this question.

A Typology of the History of Christian Theologies of Other Religions

This chapter presents four types or "families" of application of the rule of final primacy which Christian theologians have characteristically employed. The types will be presented in roughly chronological order. In each case assessments of the claims made by other religious traditions may be understood as corollaries of the assertion of Christ as *prima veritas*, or they may be understood as "free-standing" truths, detached from the context of a narrative moving from such a Christological presupposition. In the former case the Christian tradition is performing its appointed task, namely to seek to order and affirm as many truths as possible, and so to understand the world as widely as possible, in a manner consistent with its own first principle. In the latter case the tradition has become disordered, and these corollary truths begin to undercut and confuse the affirmation of Christ as the *prima veritas*. This is because the sense in which alien claims are true as they are located in an encompassing Christian narrative is lost, and openness and integrity are set against one another. As a result first principle and corollary are reversed, and the theological tail wags the dog. This corruption will be called an "inversion."

The first great answer to the problem of alien claims is the *Logos solution* of the Patristic period, which was initially articulated by Justin Martyr in the second century A.D. It became the standard approach in theologians such as Origen and Gregory of Nyssa, and is still employed by Eastern Christian theologians. The idea itself is straightforward: God made himself known in partial and fragmentary ways, until the "fullness of time" when the Word itself *(Logos)* was incarnate and God was fully known. So the knowledge of God prior to Christ was preparatory of the incarnation, even when the bearers of this knowledge were pagans. The apologetic object in this approach was to answer charges that Christianity was a novel religion with dubious philosophical underpinnings. By means of the *Logos* theology Justin could enlist established philosophical authorities like Socrates and Plato for the Christian cause.

Justin himself worked this approach out by contrasting the *Logos spermatikos* ("seedling Reason"), a Stoic term used over against *Logos endiathetos* ("inwardly ordered Reason"), to the incarnate Word Christ. Thus the implied narrative sequence proceeds from the era of the "spermatic" to the era of the incarnate. This solution proved so useful that it continued to be employed even after multiple problems with the *Logos* approach to Christology were laid bare. These problems included a tendency toward a subordinationalist trinitarianism and a difficulty in explaining why, if God's objective was the revelation of the *Logos,* an incarnation per se should be necessary.

One should note that Justin himself made modest claims for his *Logos* theology of other communities, since he supposed that the *Logos* was at best only sporadically identifiable prior to Christ. In fact, the concept was employed to show that all the truths philosophers boasted of already belonged to Christ. Likewise Origen could acknowledge that there were a variety of mediations of the Word, but subordinated others to the incarnate form in Jesus Christ. At the same time one can note that this distinction between prior, unincarnate forms of the *Logos* and the incarnate Christ can become potentially problematic when it is coupled with Origen's cosmology, according to which an eternal and heavenly realm has ontological priority over the temporal realm. Origen can at times mention an eternal gospel, and even a heavenly passion, over against their corresponding temporal realities.[30] In a similar vein M. Harl has made the case that Origen insufficiently emphasizes the

---

30. See *On First Principles* 3.6.8 and 4.3.13, as cited by Douglas Farrow in *Ascension and Ecclesia* (Grand Rapids: Eerdmans, 1999), p. 91.

uniqueness of the incarnate form of the *Logos*, and this weakness is at-tributable to the neo-Platonic substructure of his thought.[31] In fairness, Origen was able to keep Jesus Christ incarnate at the center of his theo-logical vision, in spite of such a built-in tendency.

One can see the rifts possible in the *Logos* type, and the resulting problems, if we consider the Arian controversy of the fourth century that grows out of the Origenist theological environment. The Arians opened a gap between the by-nature-unincarnate Godhead and the in-carnate and creaturely Jesus Christ. To be sure, the controversy never touched on interreligious questions, but just the same the Arian vision allows one to speak of the Trinity and of the Word in a way effectively disconnected from Jesus Christ. This in turn has profound implica-tions for the question of how the Word might be at work in other tradi-tions. To reiterate, both Justin's and Origen's proposals do succeed in maintaining the proper ordering, even where the incarnate and unincarnate forms of the Word should be simultaneously observable in the world. But one can see how, following a problematic trajectory of a *Logos* theology, the incarnate Christ might become a mere option, one way in which the *Logos* reveals itself, and separate, balkanized economies of salvation would be established.

One can observe both the strength and weakness of this approach to the theology of other claims in Nicholas of Cusa's fifteenth-century mas-terpiece, "On the Peace of the Faith," *De Pace Fidei*.[32] The background for Nicholas's approach is the Patristic idea that one may find traces of the Trinity in triadic forms of thought in pagan writers who thereby antici-pate the full revelation of the inner being of God (note here the confor-mity to final primacy). Nicholas claims that the other religious traditions in question, Judaism and Islam, also include the depth of God, its ratio-nal expression, and their unity, and so the Trinity in embryo. Christian-ity thus differs from her monotheistic siblings by making these claims more explicit and by understanding more fully the nature of that expres-sion in Jesus Christ. Nicholas in effect shows the "Reason" of God to have a trinitarian structure (and so may be seen to offer a more sophisti-

---

31. See her *Origène et la function revelatria de verbe incarne* (Paris: Editions de Seuil, 1958). I am indebted to Professor Rowan Greer of Yale Divinity School for this reference.

32. Nicholas of Cusa, "On the Peace of Faith," in *Toward a New Council of Florence: Writings of Nicholas of Cusa*, trans William F. Wertz Jr. (Washington, D.C.: Schiller Insti-tute, 1993).

cated version of the *Logos* approach). For him it follows that other traditions should see in the Christian gospel their own fulfillment. The "peace of the faith" will be achieved as they make this acknowledgment, though they should at the same time be allowed to keep their own rites and customs, so that they become in effect (though Nicholas does not say this) "Jewish" and "Muslim" rites within the church. Thus Nicholas helped a culture weary of interreligious conflict[33] to imagine an open-minded yet doctrinally faithful cessation of hostilities.

It is natural for such an argument to evoke several reactions in the contemporary reader. One is struck by its remarkable prescience, verging as the argument does on the "consciousness" type to be discussed below. At the same time one can identify serious problems. On the one hand Christianity's rivals are reduced to a single (somewhat arbitrary) metaphysical thread in such a way that everything else is relegated to the status of cultural accouterment (cf. John Hick!). On the other hand Nicholas says precious little about the relationship between this trinitarian structure and the incarnation of Jesus Christ, so that one is left with a decidedly Nestorian impression that the *Logos* of God may be considered adequately in separation from Jesus himself. In other words, the proposal seems at once to say too little and too much.

One can put these apparent deficiencies in their proper perspective, however, if one thinks of the proposal in relationship to the grammar of final primacy. For Nicholas isolates this one strain of the other traditions precisely because it seems to him to anticipate the telos of religious truth, the doctrine promulgated by the church in which he was a cardinal. The thicker Christological explication can be omitted precisely because it is assumed, since it comprises for him part of the "subsidiary awareness," the background of assumptions that he brings to the argument. The complaints of an outsider, that Nicholas brings Christian assumptions to his case, may be answered, if one considers the work as an act of generous Christian imagination, expanding on the *Logos* model. Just the same, internal deficiencies, related to certain faults in the *Logos* model, remain.

The second major family of proposals for a theology of religions emerged from the doctrine of salvation. It characteristically has re-

33. See R. W. Southern, *Western Views of Islam in the Middle Ages* (Cambridge, Mass.: Harvard University Press, 1962), ch. 4, "Moment of Vision."

flected on the nature of faith, and has employed the key Augustinian terms "nature" and "grace."[34] These terms are properly applied to the person who comes to explicit faith in Jesus Christ, to explain how the one God who both creates and redeems is at work throughout the process. The terms are correlative, for both derive from God in such a way that nature is open to grace, and grace presumes nature, though grace exceeds and thereby also stands in contrast to nature. Terms like "nature" and "grace" are originally designed to explain conversion and sanctification in the Christian. In other words, they have originally to do with explicit faith. But they come to be employed to imagine how God's salvation might be wrought in cases of implicit faith.[35] It is by virtue of this last point that the nature-grace model can be more subtle than, and should not be simply identified with, the concept of fulfillment (though by some authors it will be used to this effect).

The most sophisticated expression of this position may be found in the *Summa Theologiae* of St. Thomas Aquinas.[36] He wants to think through how nature and grace are to be understood in cases of implicit faith, and with respect to the latter he moves deliberately from clearer, more biblically warranted cases, whose relation to explicit faith is stronger, to cases that are less clear and require a wider imaginative leap. Thus his reflection moves deliberately from the faithful Israelites who did not yet know Jesus Christ, to the analogous case of "holy pagans" of the Old Testament, and on finally (in the most tentative and hypothetical way, in the "subjunctive," as it were) to comparable Gentiles who may have lived or do live after the time of Christ. The receptivity of nature for grace emboldens the theologian to infer that

---

34. While the nature-grace option tends to be Catholic, a recent evangelical deployment may be found in Clark Pinnock's *The Wideness in God's Mercy: The Finality of Jesus Christ in a World of Religions* (Grand Rapids: Zondervan, 1992).

35. The term "implicit faith" has its own history, for its original context is a reflection on the salvation of faithful Catholics who by ignorance or mental incapacity (*imbecilitas*) cannot consciously understand the *fides quae creditur*, but who can simply assent to whatever *ecclesia mater* teaches, and so have implicit faith in its actual doctrinal assertions. When this analogy is used for pious pagans, their likeness to the mentally deficient serves to render their ignorance nonculpable. In a very different vein one may compare Calvin's reflection on the possible salvation of the unbaptized children of Christians, who die in infancy, as another "case at the margins" of nonculpable ignorance. (See *Institutes of the Christian Religion*, Book IV, ch. 16.)

36. See, e.g., *S.T.* II/II, q.12, a.7-8.

God may be savingly at work, creating here too implicit faith in some such Gentiles.

Of course there are certain constraints implied by the contrast between knowing something implicitly (and thus partially or "from afar") and knowing something explicitly. In other words, a "nature-grace" argument depends on the priority and distinctive features of explicit faith in the saving God fully known. This kind of extension of the logic of salvation steps "back" from Christian to Israelite, to holy pagan, to pagan ignorant of the gospel at this very moment. It thus depends, as a background belief, on the salvation-historical scheme, and so presupposes the doctrine of the economy of salvation. Within these constraints such thinking "back" from grace clearly fulfilling nature to the possibility of such fulfillment of an analogous but more hidden kind conforms precisely to the pattern of final primacy.

The further one's imaginative construction marches from the "home base" of the revelation in Jesus Christ, the more tenuous and hypothetical its results become. Far from being a flaw in Thomas's presentation of the possibility of implicit faith, this quality of increasing vagueness in speculation about the possibility of saving grace at work in the present-day idolater confirms the wisdom and balance of his approach. In other words, to distinguish between more certain statements about the economy of salvation in Jesus Christ, and less certain statements about how that grace might be at work "prior" to Christ, is to use the categories of nature and grace in a manner consistent with the grammar. One finds just such a commendable, "subjunctive" vagueness in Thomas: "If, however, some were saved without faith in a mediator, for . . . they did, nevertheless have implicit faith through believing in divine providence. . . ."[37]

But quickly the danger of such a theory becomes apparent, namely that the speculative flight will overwhelm and distort the central doctrines on which it is based. For the category of implicit faith can be so extended as to attenuate faith proper (i.e., faith in Jesus Christ as Lord) of its meaning and content. When this occurs, the categories of nature and grace are no longer ordered sequentially according to the final primacy of Christ, and one forgets that one talks of faith in the unbeliever only in an extended sense. Such talk becomes

37. S.T. II/II, q.2, a.7, ad.3.

dislodged from the larger sense of the economy of salvation and assumes a life of its own.

One can see such a loss of original order and purpose in the late medieval theological use of the expression *facere quod in se est,* "to do what one is able."[38] In order that one might be saved, Thomas Aquinas agreed that to the one who did what he could, "God would not withhold grace" *(non denegat gratiam);* but here one should bear in mind that for Aquinas the *facere* itself is by grace. In other words, the Christian grammar of grace and works requires that we think of God himself enabling us to do what we are able, and so required, to do.

But where this understanding is lost, the *facere* is soon seen as compelling the resulting grace, and this latter way of thinking is applied in turn to pagans who have never heard the gospel, but simply "did what was in them." To reiterate, the problem here is not that one employs the theological categories of nature and grace in order to imagine how such a pagan might be saved. Rather the problem is that one ceases to think about how the saving grace one knows might also be at work there, and one begins to think in terms of the salvific efficacy of the works of the pagan themselves.[39]

In post-Reformation Catholicism, the seventeenth-century Spanish Jesuit Juan Ripalda reflected on what he called *fides late dicta,* "faith broadly understood," in just this way. In his thought the act of faith was by this theological device abstracted from any specific content understood in relation to Christian salvation-history. The extraordinary case becomes central and normative. Speculation that had begun with the concrete question of making sense of a whole continent of the unevangelized in the New World came to redefine the nature of faith itself in a classic example of inversion. The emphasis came to rest on the capacity or achievement called "faith" within the human person, rather than on faith as a response to what the God of Israel and of Jesus Christ has done. In this case, as in the earlier case of *facere quod in se est,* the emphasis soon lands on nature and works rather than on grace and faith.

38. See for instance Alister McGrath's *Justitia Dei* (Cambridge: Cambridge University Press, 1986), pp. 85, 89, 145, 170.

39. Here see Louis Caperan's magisterial *La Problème du Salut des Infidèles* (Toulouse: Grand Séminaire, 1934), vol. 1, ch. VIII, Art. III, "Les Théologiens du XVII siècle."

The third model employed widely in Christian theology to understand other claims and communities is the distinctively Reformation
categories of *law and gospel*. Here too reflection on the possible status of
nonbelievers emerges from the central doctrine of soteriology. However, with law and gospel one finds a shift away from the cognitive,
i.e., the contrast between those who have and those who lack saving
knowledge of the truth, and toward the relational and volitional, toward the believer's relationship to what he or she knows, to the question whether one stands in a relationship of self-justification or trust-
ing surrender to God. In this family of theological constructions the
religions are indeed understood to have some knowledge of God, but
they can only know the *Deus nudus*. For the self-justifying human being, this naked God turns out to be a God of wrath.

Still, the law-gospel perspective is not totally negative about the
role of religions. They may be seen, constructively, to maintain societal
order and to inspire such despair as may conduce to the acceptance of
the gospel message when it is preached (the first and second uses of
the law, respectively). At the same time, proponents of the law-gospel
solution emphatically deny that any bridge of continuity, however tentative and imaginative, can be built from the religions of humans' own
constructing toward the scandal of the gospel.

Law-gospel solutions, according to which the religions represent
prime examples of human works-righteousness, conform to the pattern of final primacy precisely by precluding the notion of any smooth
transition from the religions to the gospel. To live under the gospel is
to lack the power to gain for oneself access to the true and living God.
This emphasis on the preclusion of a smooth transition serves to emphasize the first corollary to the rule of final primacy, namely the abiding theological priority of Christ in distinction, though not separation,
from the church. In this family of solutions there must be some sense
on the part of the theologian that the church is at one with the religions
under law even as it provides voice for the gospel. While on the one
hand this family of solutions emphasizes the solidarity between the
church and other traditions, it shows on the other most clearly that final primacy is not to be mistaken for the idea of fulfillment.

Once the final primacy of Christ is in place, however, the law-
gospel family of arguments need not preclude the possibility of finding individual elements of continuity between alien claims and prac-

tices and the gospel. The same God creates, gives the law, and redeems in Christ.[40] It is human sinfulness that makes God's work appear complex and dialectical. One may discern claims that are traces of an awareness of the Creator from the perspective of the gospel, though the religions themselves remain, as totalities, broken mirrors of the divine image, themselves unable to convey salvation.

The nature of this family of proposals comes clearer with several examples that will in fact demonstrate the surprising suppleness of the terms. Indonesian Lutheran Christians were converted to the gospel from their old religious allegiances. But when they reflected on the ordering of their new life, they recognized the value of many elements of *adat* (traditional custom and law) to preserve society, not least so as to make possible their eventual conversion. These elements in turn deserved preservation and reintegration into their new Christian life and society.[41] Among modern theologians in the West, Carl Heinz Ratschow[42] has sought a fresh approach to the religions, one free of the debate over the presence or absence of revelation therein. He has done so by turning to the "first use of the law," according to which the law serves the useful purpose of ordering sinful human society and restraining evil. So Ratschow thinks of the religions of *"Weltwalten Gottes,"* worldly powers from God, given for the orderly maintenance of the world. Such an assessment of the religions assumes that the world "waits in eager longing for the revealing of the sons of God" (Rom. 8:19), in other words that the world is being preserved for something, namely the proclamation of the gospel. Such an assumption only makes sense from the perspective of that gospel. It stands in contrast to the religions' own claims to truth. Just the same, the category of *Walten* allows a qualifiedly positive view of the religions.

Another example of the law-gospel pattern may be found in the writings of Lesslie Newbigin. Central to his view of religion, influ-

---

40. The relationship between creation and law is affirmed in the Lutheran theologian Gustav Wingren in his *Creation and Law* (Edinburgh: Oliver & Lloyd, 1961).

41. See especially Lothar Scheiner's *Adat und Evangelium: zur Bedeutung den altvolkischen Lebensordungen für Kirche und Mission unter den Batak in Nordsumatra* (Gütersloh: G. Mohn, 1972).

42. *Die Religionen* (Gütersloh: G. Mohn, 1979), especially C.II.3, "Thesen zur Theologie der Religionen," by Carl Heinz Ratschow.

enced by the theology of Karl Barth, is the crisis that Jesus Christ precipitates for all human endeavors. Religions as high human achievements become occasions for "a claim on our own behalf." The cross is the "the historic deed in which God exposed himself in a total vulnerability to all our purposes and in that meeting exposed us [as] the beloved of God who are, even in our highest religion, the enemies of God."[43] Newbigin relies here on the cruciform theory of German missiologist Walter Freytag, in which religions do not ascend in their gifts, but rather descend together to that lowest point of desolation, the cross, there to find their unity. So the religions here too represent human pretension, and yet, insofar as they lead to a crisis before the cross, play the classic role of law as the occasion for grace.

In the previous families of argument, the *Logos* and nature-grace patterns, the attendant danger was inversion — that the subsidiary affirmation would come to overwhelm the rule itself. The danger of the law-gospel pattern lies elsewhere, namely that the theologian might lose track of the real elements of continuity, however isolated and impotent they may be on their own. The theologian may forget that the religions are real witnesses to the Creator, if only in such a way as to leave the adherents "without excuse" (Rom. 1:20). So the theologian of law-gospel runs the risk of holding on to the scandal of the gospel, and thus proclaiming the primacy of Christ, in such a way as to forget the inevitable, preceding stage, and so of neglecting the parallel theological task of explicating that coming to Christ, however hard and contrary it may have been. Distortion too has a way of witnessing to what is true. Furthermore the theologian of law-gospel must recall that elements of the religions might be spiritually healthful, once they are no longer put at the service of human self-assertion, but offered to the triune God instead. In these ways the theologian avoids supposing that this pattern represents pure negation.

For a fourth family of arguments the root metaphor is that of *human self-consciousness*. As one might expect, this is the model most popular in modern times. In this subsection are found all solutions which emphasize that in Christianity is found an experience (of the infinite, for instance), an awareness (for example, of a compelling symbol), or a kind of knowledge that is uniquely and particularly

---

43. Lesslie Newbigin, *The Open Secret* (Grand Rapids: Eerdmans, 1978), pp. 199, 205.

evoked by the consciousness of Jesus as it is presented to us in the biblical story. The theologian then perceives a similar experience, awareness, or knowledge to be partially or latently present in other religious communities.

The theologian with whom to start in this family is Friedrich Schleiermacher, who treats the religions at length in the Fifth Speech of his *On Religion: Speeches to Its Cultured Despisers*. There he praises the varied, sometimes crude, even chaotic, feelings of the Infinite found in the religions. These feelings in adherents of other religions are authentic and legitimate experiences. But in these experiences one may still notice a conflict between the limited and finite point of view of each religion and the Infinite itself. Only when one comes to Christianity, the religion of the incarnation, does one find this tension between finite and infinite resolved, for God-in-the-flesh is the requisite symbol of that relationship truly understood. Schleiermacher speaks of the "intuition of Christianity" as "more glorious, more sublime, more worthy of adult humanity, penetrat[ing] deeper into the spirit of systematic religion and extend[ing] itself further over the whole universe."[44]

One may find a similar type of argument in other thinkers who would otherwise differ from Schleiermacher on a number of other counts. In the case of the idealist philosopher G. W. F. Hegel, Schleiermacher's contemporary, the contrast is between "positive" (historically contingent) religions and the "absolute religion" of Christianity (properly understood). Paul Tillich could similarly speak of other religions as "latent" church, since the same ontological structure of Spirit was at work there, but not yet clearly.[45] Perhaps most famously, Karl Rahner could speak of the religions as providing their adherents with a form of "anonymous Christianity." This stands in obvious contrast (and also relationship) to conscious or concrete Christianity represented by the presence of the church. Common to all these examples is the movement from latent to patent, from unconscious to self-conscious.

One may also note a special relationship to the types that have preceded in this chapter. For this fourth construction characteristically

---

44. Friedrich Schleiermacher, *On Religion* (New York: Harper & Row, 1958), p. 241.
45. Paul Tillich, *Systematic Theology* III (Chicago: University of Chicago Press, 1963), IV.II.B.4.b, pp. 152ff.

borrows from its predecessors and so recapitulates the earlier solutions. Now, however, the terms have been transposed into a new, distinctively modern, anthropological and epistemological key. So one may see a similarity between Tillich's construction and those of a *Logos*-theology, since the former's system is built on the resolution of the ambiguities and conflicts at the depth of what he calls "Reason." But now the *Logos* in question has to do with the structure and struggle of the individual with his or her own existential guilt. Likewise Rahner borrows freely from and builds upon a Thomist foundation of nature and grace, but his Thomism is filtered through the analysis of human consciousness derived from modern philosophers like Marechal and Heidegger. Nature and grace have been transposed in terms relating to states of human consciousness.

In this fourth family of arguments one can see most clearly the danger of inversion. For here one finds at the outset the weakest commitment to the unique finality of Christ. One may ask of these theologies what truly necessary and indispensable relationship exists between Christ, rendered narratively, and the consciousness found in the church, much less the partial form found in the other religions.[46] In other words, if the final primacy of Christ is not clear at the outset with respect to Christianity, its loss when claims are made on behalf of the consciousness of other religions should be no surprise. Still, it would be a mistake to suppose that there are not examples of theologians of this type who do speak "grammatically" of the gospel in relationship to the religions. Certainly Rahner and Tillich intended so to speak, though one may point out that Tillich's later writings about the religions reveal just the sort of gradual slide into a quasi-pluralism that confirms a sense of the faultiness of this type of solution.[47] Various theologians of this family have treated the subject grammatically, but still there lurks within this kind of argument an internal fault tending toward the disorder here identified.

What then is the lesson of this typology? First, one can clarify what the different types do and do not share. They all present a common se-

46. See Bruce Marshall, *Christology in Conflict: The Identity of the Savior in Rahner and Barth* (Oxford: Blackwell, 1987).

47. For the contrast in Tillich, compare his views in *Systematic Theology* III with that of *Christianity and the Encounter of the World Religions* (New York: Columbia University Press, 1963).

quential feature, a "before" and an "after," by which the religions have narrative location defined by where the story is going, Christ. By this feature each remains close to the underlying biblical template. So each type comprises something "continuous" as well as something "discontinuous" between the Christian tradition and other traditions. These shared features are ingredients in such narrative-shaped constructions. At the same time the types do not share a single view of the role or value of the religions. They cannot be subsumed under a single thematic banner, for example as "fulfillment" or "judgment." This too is fitting, since the Bible, the text generating these types, offers a variety of images and roles for the Gentiles.

Furthermore one should not mistake these types for the myriad of actual theological proposals about the relationship between the Christian truth and any specific religious tradition. The types are generalizations about common ways in which specific theologies tend to execute the master pattern of final primacy. The pattern is only a helpful observation about how orthodox Christians tend to speak. For example, a particular Lutheran Batak confession may evince a law-gospel pattern, but what remains truly primary is the particular confession itself, and not this second-order generalization about it. Furthermore there could well be more than the four types considered here; this would in no way endanger, but only enrich, this argument.[48]

---

48. An impressive proposal for a theology of religions, Joseph DiNoia's *The Diversity of Religions,* may represent its own type, the eschatological-typological. (There are some precedents, among them John Wycliffe's and Uthred of Boldon's visions of posthumous meeting with Christ. See Southern, *Western Views of Islam.*) To be sure, DiNoia's view has strong affinities with the nature-grace type. He creatively uses a Wittgensteinian concept of the "form of life" to show how other communities may instill virtues and expound truths that, while not readily comparable to those of the Christian community, are quite possibly complementary to the Christian faith.

DiNoia's proposal is a grammatical use of final primacy, since it involves the idea of preparation beyond the church but moving toward a meeting with Christ (albeit beyond the grave). In effect he has constructed an expanded narrative by appeal to the doctrine of purgatory, so that his narrative is inclusive of the diversity of histories of other traditions and of the consummation. But one worries when he criticizes the temporal ordering of the status of the unbeliever before and after hearing the gospel (p. 77). This essay would argue that his proposal subtly relies upon just such a temporal ordering. He also tends to de-emphasize the practice of witness. Our essay seeks to show how these added elements in fact complete and strengthen a proposal like DiNoia's.

The reader comes away from this quick tour of types with a general impression that when the rule of final primacy is neglected, and so when statements about other traditions are torn out of their natural habitat in the larger matrix of claims about Christ, distortions result. A more careful assessment of the nature of the disordering we have called "inversion" is appropriate. The reversal ripples through Christology, the economy of salvation, and finally the practices of the church. First, Christ is no longer seen as finally primary, so that cases to be explained in his light come to serve as the norm, and the theologian tries to explain Christ in the light of the alien circumstance, doctrine, or practice.[49] This error then tends to ramify into one's understanding of the economy of salvation. More specifically, it tends to balkanize that domain. While there can be different dispensations or actions, theology must convey the sense that they are the consistent work of the one God. If, for example, the Son were at work in one locale of the economy and the Spirit in another, or if the *Logos asarkos* and *ensarkos* had different spheres, then an ungrammatical division would have occurred. This disorder in turn tends to spawn a problem within the practices of church, more specifically in the relationship between theologizing and witnessing.[50]

This chapter has in no sense offered a proof; the critic can always object that we have but assumed what is to be shown. In the end such a claim will depend on its enduring explanatory power and elasticity, by the sense, in its wake, that Christian approaches to the religions from different places and eras hang together. Only with a sustained display of explanatory coherence can one make the transition from description to normative claim.

---

49. My account of the relationship between the Christocentric rule of final primacy and other claims is consistent with the careful treatment of the logic of justification and truth in Bruce Marshall's *Trinity and Truth* (Cambridge: Cambridge University Press, 2000). Final primacy is, in Marshall's terms, an "essential doctrine," itself entailed in the classical doctrines of Trinity and Christology. His warning about using external norms to evaluate essential doctrines buttresses our argument. The main point of distinction between this work and his may be found precisely in the notion of the rule of final primacy, for we are suggesting that it is an "internal," if implicit doctrine — in Christian's terms a "doctrine about alien doctrines" — that provides a pattern for the treatment of alien claims consistent with the great essential doctrines about God and Christ. It provides in effect the ruled bridge between essential beliefs and (to use the term Marshall has borrowed from Lindbeck) "assimilative power."

50. We will treat this question in more detail in the coming chapter.

Through such a display, as one looks back on these historical precedents for the rule of final primacy, one may note that the descriptive blurs imperceptibly into the normative. Talk about how theologians in history have tended to speak slides easily toward an assertion about how Christian theologians should speak. Such an argument is only convincing as it conveys a general impression made up, pointillistically, of a number of examples. Furthermore the argument hinges on a sense that failure to follow the rule has often led to the loss of certain crucial theological emphases. This in turn depends on the assumption that one such emphasis, the centrality of the person Christ for salvation and revelation, is doctrinally "the one thing needful."

Here one may be tempted simply to dismiss the question of the relationship between descriptive and normative claims by what one might call "the anthropological appeal." One might observe, like an anthropologist amidst a local tribe, that to change certain intellectual habits, deeply engrained, would be so profound a disruption as to render the communal identity unrecognizable. By analogy one might say that if baseball were now to be played with a basketball and fifty bases, the game might be entertaining, but might not resemble the national pastime enough to be called "baseball." In this vein, Paul Griffiths has argued that, to borrow an expression from George Lindbeck, "reading the world into Christ"[51] is constitutive of being a Christian.

---

51. The question of the descriptive vs. the normative status of doctrines as rules echoes a debate about George Lindbeck's proposal. Many have accused him of abandoning truth. For example Brevard Childs, in spite of the compatibility of his own project, has criticized the "Yale School's" views as "functional." (See, e.g., *Biblical Theology of the Old and New Testaments: Theological Reflection on the Christian Bible* [Minneapolis: Fortress, 1992].) To cite a recent example, Trevor Hart, writing expressly about religious pluralism, has worried that doctrines in Lindbeck's view become customary, and so undercut a realist view of theological claims. (See his chapter "Karl Barth, the Trinity, and Pluralism," in *The Trinity in a Pluralistic Age: Theological Essays in Culture and Religion*, ed. Kevin Vanhoozer [Grand Rapids: Eerdmans, 1997], p. 130.) Since this essay is indebted to Lindbeck's concept of doctrines as rules, this challenge strikes at this proposal as well. Several answers can be offered. First, Lindbeck is fighting on other fronts, namely foundationalism and an experiential-expressivist view of religion, and so only seeks to avoid the wrong sort of truth-claiming. So, most of the time, one could reply that Lindbeck is answering a different question. Lindbeck's primary interest is in how religious talk means. In answer to this question, a formal question, one can say that grammatical talk gives rise to statements about the gracious, sovereign God of the gos-

He explains his point this way: "Christ is the axis of the cosmos and the means through which all meaning is given."[52] This is assumed to be both descriptive and normative for Christian belief. Griffiths makes just such a point when he suggests that the abandonment of the Christocentrism of the tradition would be like "the abandonment of the rule governing noun-verb agreement for the writer of Latin . . . what results would be sufficiently different from what we knew before that it is hard to see what sense there might be in calling it the same thing."[53]

Griffiths' contention agrees with final primacy, and this essay of-

---

pel. But, considered in a different light, materially, God is obviously not the result of discourse or rules or communities or practices. On the contrary he is the agent and condition for all of these. Second, one should note that in *The Nature of Doctrine: Religion and Theology in a Postliberal Age* (Louisville: Westminster/John Knox, 1984) he includes a strong claim to referential truth, though he claims it for systems as a whole, and eschatologically (pp. 63ff.).

Just the same, the question about the descriptive and normative status of rules (and so of final primacy, for example) is a real issue for Lindbeck, one that has been clearly delineated by Lee Barrett in his "Theology as Grammar: Regulative Principles or Paradigms and Practices?" *Modern Theology* 4 (January 1988): 156-72. Barrett explains the tension in this way: "On the one hand, Lindbeck tends to treat doctrinal rules as having some sort of specificity, significance, and self-identity quite apart from their particular applications to the motley circumstances of human life. On the other hand, Lindbeck often does talk as if the very meaning of a doctrinal rule is tied to its particular uses in regulating the actions, passions, and attitudes of Christian living" (p. 159). Surely Lindbeck wishes to hold together both a stable grammar on the one hand and the elements of communal consensus and practice on the other. But what happens when they show the strain of moving in opposing directions? To this possibility Kathryn Tanner is pointing, on the "left wing" of the children of the Yale school, in her *Theories of Culture: A New Agenda for Theology* (Minneapolis: Fortress, 1997). In this study the emphasis is on the other side, on the continuity of a stable grammar through history, a consistent skeletal structure making movement possible. The negative effects of the kind of internalist Hegelianism (a phrase from him in private conversation) Barrett worries about are mitigated in several ways. The first is the actual performance of theological application, where the practice-oriented and contextual features are held up to view. The second is the realization that Lindbeck is not ultimately interested in some abstract algebra of doctrine, but rather his argument is an "ad hoc apologetic" for the Nicene reading of Scripture in the Christian community. So, implicitly, Lindbeck is assuming both the rule and the paradigmatic case in close interdependence on one another.

52. "The Properly Christian Response to Religious Plurality," *Anglican Theological Review* 79 (Winter 1997): 15.

53. "The Properly Christian Response to Religious Plurality,"21.

fers intends to show a "Christocentrism" that should order Christian theology's relationship to other traditions. Still, his contention only goes so far, and even if one assumes the grammar of Christocentricity, several tasks remain. In particular one needs to show how coherence results where the norm is followed, and how incoherence results where it is lacking. His suggestion spells the beginning, not the end, of the task. Second, his argument, and this one as well, will remain unconvincing to someone whose starting-point is a "hermeneutic of suspicion" toward the tradition per se, or to a pluralist who can happily take up received doctrinal affirmations and then redefine them in a new way. Just the same, an "anthropological" argument from identity such as Griffiths' is helpful, for it reinforces the line here drawn between two radically different ways of understanding the relationship between the Christian tradition and its neighboring traditions. To understand better that sharp difference, and so to clarify the nature of a theological tradition itself, is the next task.

Excursus: Final Primacy and the Church's Relationship to Israel

A clear implication of this argument is that the church's relationship to Israel is unique and complex, not only for contingent historical reasons, e.g., the legacy of Christian persecution that renders the task of witnessing peculiarly problematic, but also for reasons internal to and constitutive of the Christian theological tradition. All retrospective narratives are derivative analogues of the "*Ur*-narrative" in the New Testament, according to which the hopes of Israel meet their goal surprisingly in Jesus the Messiah. While the task of exegesis remains, in this one case an act of "analogical imagination" is not required. Romans 11 addresses the question of the enduring place of Israel in light of the Lordship of Christ with a directness unparalleled in the case of any other religion (with the possible exception of the now extinct case of Greek paganism).

One should also recall that the rule requires one to differentiate Christ and the church. On this score too the situation of Israel is unique, since they have no need of the mission of the church to tell them of the messianic hope of Isaiah or the visions of the Son of Man in

Daniel. If then by "supersessionism" one means the dominance of the church, it is categorically ruled out. But if by the term one means the Lordship of the Jew Jesus, crucified and risen, over Israel first and then the whole world, one finds here the most inalienable belief in the whole panoply of doctrine, one immediately comprehensible, if not acceptable, to Israel.

Contemporary Judaism's relationship to Christianity is related to, but not identifiable with, that of first-century Israel. So final primacy can be applied to Judaism qua contemporary religious tradition. By the rule's criteria construals of the relationship between Christianity and Judaism in the "Two Covenants" mode, whether proffered by Christian or Jew, are problematic.[54] For example, Franz Rosenzweig's *The Star of Redemption*, according to which a more circuitous route to the Kingdom is offered to the Gentiles through Christ, neatly sets the rule on its head. As a Jewish doctrine about another tradition, Christianity, it is, however, most appropriate, comprising as it does its own kind of retrospective narrative.[55] Likewise proposals for the cessation of witness by Christians to Jews can be criticized as contrary to the grammar of the faith on the same grounds as with other traditions.

At the very least one can conclude that Israel represents a most complex case: the rule seems at one moment superfluous, at the next paradigmatically applicable. The relationship in question is not only complicated, it is also of the greatest importance. These factors taken together impel us to leave this case aside to await a fuller consideration.

54. Here, amidst his brilliant critique of the Creeds for their myopia about Israel, one may see, with the help of final primacy, the Achilles' heel of Kendall Soulen's *The God of Israel and Christian Theology* (Minneapolis: Fortress, 1996), especially where the role of Christ is reduced to that of proclaiming an eschaton, as opposed to being himself identifiable with the End.

55. (Boston: Beacon, 1972). For a study of a Jewish tradition of "retrospective narratives," see David Novak's *Jewish-Christian Dialogue: A Jewish Justification* (New York: Oxford University Press, 1989), esp. his treatment of the "Doctrine of Noachide Laws" in ch. 2.

2 *Christian Theology as Tradition*

Lessing: Tradition Inside Out

The first chapter of this essay offered a rule or pattern, according to which Christians have tended to reflect on and assess the claims and practices of other religious traditions. But it would be all too easy to come away with a negative impression of such a proposal. It might seem first of all as if the resulting vision of Christian thought and practice would be a constricted and parochial one. Why should theology impose this seemingly arbitrary restriction on itself? Does it not rule out of court any conceptions of the faith that are radically bold? Most tellingly, doesn't a norm so "imposed" from without render the tradition ultimately irrational, to the extent that it immunizes Christian reflection from critique and from the rough-and-tumble of competing, conflicting ideas?

Second, the straining of a rule out of the thicker stuff of the history of Christian theological discourse may seem disappointingly abstract. The critic might suggest that religions ought to attend with at least equal care to their behavior. Claims and practices ought to be held together in a single vision of the way, the *hodos* or *via*, that is a particular religious tradition. George Lindbeck, in proposing that doctrines be understood by analogy with grammatical rules, himself insists that Christian discourse should not be separated from the practices native

39

to it, and he memorably offers the example of the Crusader who cried "*Christus dominus*" as he raised his sword to lop off the infidel's head. In such a case the accompanying act would have rendered the discourse false, however proper it may have sounded. In a similar way, the critic can rightly press the advocate of a rule for the assessment of alien claims to show what practices must accompany these Christian theological constructions, and how claim and practice should interact.

But it is the third critique that is, in the present era, most frequently and tellingly heard. To imagine that the beliefs of others culminate in the truth of Jesus Christ strikes many as intellectual imperialism, the absorption of the ideas of others into one's own sphere in imitation of the manner in which customs and lands were, and sometimes still are, expropriated. Here the rule of final primacy seems not so much false as pernicious. It would seem to lack the virtue of attentiveness, so that the Christian cannot hear what the other actually thinks. This seems tantamount to a violation of the ninth commandment. The rule of final primacy seems hubristically short of the virtues of humility and charity. While this same salvo has been aimed in the direction of pluralism as well,[1] this does not diminish its potential damage for particularism.

According to MacIntyre, a tradition facing an epistemological crisis must respond to its strongest objections. Pluralism precipitates just such a crisis, and questions like the three listed above bitingly articulate that challenge. So it is incumbent on proponents of final primacy to offer responses to these questions. In the process, they may reap an added benefit. For the answers to these very questions will render an account of Christian theology as tradition which is endowed with greater richness and complexity. The goal is to show what it truly means for the tradition to work to meet a new challenge, in what sense it can be perceived as rational, how its practices must bolster its claims, and how humility and charity can and must coexist with assertion. Only as these questions are answered has one shown what it means for the Christian tradition to follow the rule of final primacy.

Here pluralism the intimate enemy can aid in clarifying the orthodox position. For the questions of rationality, practice, and humility

---

1. See Kathryn Tanner's "Respect for Other Religions: An Antidote to Colonialist Discourse," *Modern Theology* 9 (January 1993): 1-18.

constitute the heart of the pluralist attack on traditional Christian doctrine when it comes to the relationship with other religious traditions. So more detailed attention must first be paid to that attack. It was suggested in the previous chapter that pluralism is no new phenomenon, but rises up with the advent of the Enlightenment. We should listen first to one of pluralism's first and most artful advocates, Gotthold Lessing himself. For Lessing sets forth the pluralist case in its main contours, offering as he does a vision of religion revised so as to be, to his lights, rational, practical, and humble. It will turn out that pluralists since his time have followed these contours with remarkable consistency.

The premise for Lessing's account of the sense in which Christianity is true was the very crisis described in the opening chapter. His contention, in the phrase made famous by Kierkegaard, that between the "contingent truths of history" and the "necessary truths of reason" there is fixed an "ugly ditch," represents one dramatic expression of his view that the claims of orthodoxy were no longer tenable.[2] But Lessing did not see this situation in a negative light. On the contrary, at the end of "The Education of the Human Race" he offers a vision of a dawning "third age," the emergence of a new religion of modernity characterized by that heightened awareness by which the enlightened can see through the errors of their native religions to the truth to be found behind the traditions themselves.[3] For Lessing such "gnostics" have no need to attack their particular religious traditions, since they can see through them easily. These same traditions may render aid to the less mature. At one point Lessing remarks that the rising of the sun does not make it one's business to blow out all the candles that may still be burning.[4] Thus the third age of which Lessing speaks is a state of mind, well salted with irony, an intellectual distance from particular religious traditions, by which one may continue one's allegiance to one such tradition.[5]

---

2. "On the Proof of the Spirit and the Power," in Lessing's *Basic Theological Writings*, ed. Henry Chadwick (Stanford, Calif.: Stanford University Press, 1956), p. 55.

3. Lessing, "On the Proof of the Spirit and the Power," pp. 82ff.

4. This passage is cited in Helen Zimmern's *Gotthold Lessing: His Life and His Works* (London: Longmans, Green and Co., 1878), p. 431.

5. It is possible that this attitude, in which one held secretly to a supposedly higher and esoteric religious insight, had a connection in Lessing's mind with his flirtation with

So, consistent with such a view, Lessing can acknowledge that the doctrines of "positive religions" can contribute to the "education of the human race." To be sure, history is for him a winding path of return to an original, pure insight, by contrast with which the religions are degenerations, "childish systems . . . [of] rewards and punishments," or vacuous speculations.[6] At the same time doctrines can prove valuable to the extent that the unmasking of their errors can render the concept of God more profound. Lessing offers the example of the Trinity to show how doctrine can serve as a creative error that, like a faulty mathematical hypothesis, can stir up thought. He makes his point in typically cryptic fashion: "and what if it were as good as proved that the great, slow wheel, which brings mankind nearer to its perfection, is only set in motion by smaller, faster wheels, each of which contributes its part to the whole?"[7]

This ironic contribution of the particular religious traditions to historical progress may be illustrated by Lessing's famous play, *Nathan the Wise*. Set during the Crusades, it portrays the religions as dangerously prone to a destructive *Schwämerei*, "emotional fanaticism," though beneath their roiling emotions they consist merely of *toten Zeichen*, "dead signs." In this they stand in contrast to the true liveliness and immediacy of human dialogue.[8] For Lessing the real miracle lies not in some superstitious past, but rather in the simple kindness of everyday life expressed across sectarian lines and so undercutting serious allegiance to a particular religion.

In keeping with his subtler view, Lessing did not advocate the elimination of the religions, for they are a necessary concession to the human need for *bürgerliche Bände*, "social bonds."[9] Furthermore they can actually contribute to the very process of the elimination of fanaticism and the elevation of a higher consciousness. Here Lessing employs the famous fable of the rings, borrowed from a tale of Boccaccio, to espouse a new, sublimated competition between the religions in the

freemasonry. See, e.g., the Masonic dialogue "Ernst und Falk" in *Gessammelte Werke in Zehn Bände*, VIII, pp. 554ff.

6. "Education of the Human Race," Lessing's *Basic Theological Writings*, p. 84.

7. Lessing, "Education of the Human Race," p. 92.

8. *Nathan the Wise*, ed. Peter Demetz (New York: Continuum, 1994), act 4, scene 4, line 1335.

9. 4.2.2580.

field of good works and toleration. In Lessing's version of the story there is no ring, but the irenic pursuit of the ring, among those who still inhabit the old, hollowed-out shells of the particular religions, itself leads to the sought-after prize. Thus, ironically, each religion proves its respective worth to the extent that it guts its own particular claims and thus tames its own passions.

The final irony of Lessing's vision is that, in spite of the past blood on its hands, Christianity may prove uniquely capable of ushering in the emerging interreligious process. Here Lessing distinguished between Jesus himself, the exemplar of a purified natural religion, and Christianity, which represents its corruption.[10] It would seem to have been providential that the emerging crisis of historical consciousness emerged in the midst of Christian culture. For, to the needed revision Christianity could contribute Jesus himself as the exemplar of natural religion, the heuristic value of the Trinity for a monistic vision of God, and the apt (if heterodox) concept of the third age of the Spirit. Standing in this unique relationship to the dawning era of religions, Christianity, by obeying John's exhortation to "love one another," may prove superior in this charitable competition of self-evisceration.

Consider now this vision of Christianity and the religions, first and most eloquently offered by Lessing. It passes, in its own way, the three tests posed to traditional Christian theology at the outset of this chapter. It offers a norm of rationality, oriented in large measure to a series of Enlightenment assumptions about history, reason, and dogma. It proceeds to conceive of religious claims as properly competing to conform to this norm. At the same time, Lessing's vision places a strong emphasis on ethics, and in particular competition in works of tolerance and charity. This emphasis in turn arises from a perception of the hubris of exclusive claims to superiority and to the imperative for each religion to exhibit humility in the face of the ultimate mystery of divine things (embodied in the fable by the uncertainty about the genuine ring). On its own terms, then, Lessing's vision can make its claim to be rational, practical, and humble.

But Lessing does not simply debunk the "positive" religions. On the contrary he aims to mine them for the resources to accomplish

10. "The Religion of Christ," Lessing's *Basic Theological Writings*, p. 106.

their departicularization. It is this more subtle and complex goal that demonstrates his intellectual power. Here one may borrow terms from a contemporary philosophical theologian, Ingolf Dalferth, who has offered two alternatives for understanding the relationship between any theological system and the main philosophical terms and assumptions amidst which it is situated. He contrasts theological *externalism,* which finds its norm for truth outside the tradition itself, with *internalism,* which finds its norm within its own realm of discourse.[11]

Lessing is a clear and strong example of externalism. But his position may be characterized as "nuanced" externalism, since he searches the tradition itself for internal warrants to advance his goal of departicularization. By contrast one might imagine a "nuanced" internalism, seeking to build a theological case normed from within by the first principles of the tradition itself, while at the same time it appropriates and applies external, contextually available philosophical concepts and terms to bolster its case.

One should not be surprised, then, that Lessing expresses both interest in and support for Christian doctrine, for in his version of nuanced externalism the Christian religion, in its competition with other traditions, seeks to divest itself of its particular and tradition-specific claims by means of arguments derived from its own storehouse. The elegance and irony of the process, the quiet palace coup, is worthy of Lessing.

If the pattern of argumentation, and the accompanying vision of the relationship of the religions, were unique to Lessing, and if it had died with him, not to return, then antiquarian interest would not suffice to spend time on them here. But in fact the pattern has perdured, and it may be readily identified in most contemporary theological writings described as "pluralist." Though one cannot offer exhaustive proof, a catena of citations and illustrations should suffice to illustrate how Lessing's pattern of argumentation is very much alive.

The first element isolated in Lessing was the historicist consciousness encapsulated in the anxiety about the "ugly ditch." To see all phenomena of particular religions as sheerly historically conditioned

---

11. See *Theology and Philosophy* (Oxford: Blackwell, 1988), ch. 1, "The Rationality of Theology."

phenomena is to be disbarred from privileging any one religion. The *second* element is a perception of the evolutionary shape of religious history, not, to be sure, as a continuous spiral of increased insight, but rather as a growing awareness of precisely its limited condition. So, within each or any religion, the evolution is toward an awareness of this condition. To perceive this is to enter the "third age," "the new global situation," etc. But how are the religiously enlightened to make progress in this situation? They must strive, *thirdly,* in the evacuation of their outdated and tradition-bound claims. Where the claims of the tradition can help in a "nuanced" way in this task, they should be affirmed, but precisely in their capacity to turn themselves inside out. In Lessing's case this evacuation was accomplished, for example, in his idea of doctrine as "creative error." Under the enduring shell of the particular religions, each moves toward a more thinned-out form more closely approximating his goal of a simple monotheism of natural religion.[12]

This idea of interreligious competition is a dangerous idea, even in this attenuated form, and so the enduring pluralist paradigm makes it clear, *fourthly,* that doctrinal evacuation must be accompanied by competition in good works. This is an ironic form of competition, since here too, the religions, like Alphonse and Gaston, strive in giving way to one another. Since Lessing's time, charity has provided a clear and universally accessible criterion for evaluating religions. It consists prominently in works of peace and material kindness. Since the strife of doctrines, even here, has not been altogether left behind, this charity also includes, *fifthly,* an emphasis on the suppression of fanaticism. This is necessary, since, from the Enlightenment perspective, the latter is destructively entailed especially in doctrinal and institutional particularity.

The classic pluralist case imagines that the harmful contention of traditions must be overcome as participants in interreligious dialogue come to see themselves and one another, *sixth* and finally, as simply human, as, in Lessing's terms, *blosse Menschen.*[13] So it is basic to the

12. Compare John Rawls's "thin" account of pluralism as described in Richard Mouw and Sander Griffioen's *Pluralisms and Horizons: An Essay in Christian Public Philosophy* (Grand Rapids: Eerdmans, 1993).

13. "Ernst und Falk," conversation 2.

pluralist case that in dialogue human beings discover a level of communion deeper than the particularities of their traditions. In Lessing's *Nathan the Wise,* conversation at the end melts doctrinal rigidity and leads to the wordless embrace as the ultimate form of communication that concludes the play.

Historicism, evolution, doctrinal evacuation, competition in good works, suppression of fanaticism, and dialogue: these elements comprise the enduring shape of pluralism, discernible in Lessing's position in the late eighteenth century and discernible with equal ease in a variety of pluralist writers today. Illustration of this *Gestalt* can be readily offered from works of prominent contemporary pluralists. Such a presentation implicitly calls into question pluralism's contention that it represents some dramatic new departure of the late twentieth century.

The pluralist project of Wilfred Cantwell Smith is built on the assumption of historicism. The central contrast is between "faith," which is the correlate of transcendence, the vertical dimension of reality, found uniformly and equally everywhere, in and beyond history, and "belief," in which faith works itself out in what Smith calls "cumulative traditions." The latter are encrustations of faith relevant only to a single, limited temporal context. Though the principle is most explicitly programmatic for Smith, the same historicist assumption may be found throughout a variety of pluralist authors.

The awareness of this very quandary for particular religions constitutes the condition for a higher state of religious consciousness. Pluralists are not shy about applying the language of conversion to this new awareness. Leonard Swidler speaks of a "radical openness" that now makes possible a "universal theology of religions." Smith again speaks of being on the threshold of an "exciting new stage of global self-consciousness." Krieger says that a "transformation of human consciousness" is afoot, and Knitter terms it a "new global situation" involving an "evolutionary shift in Christian consciousness."[14]

14. Key passages for this mosaic argument are the following: Leonard Swidler, "Interreligious and Interideological Dialogue: The Matrix for All Systematic Reflection Today," in *Toward a Universal Theology of Religions* (Maryknoll, N.Y.: Orbis, 1987), pp. 20ff., 36ff.; Smith, *Toward a World Theology: Faith and the Comparative History of Religion* (Philadelphia: Westminster, 1981), p. 124; David Krieger, *The New Universalism: Foundations for a Global Theology* (Maryknoll, N.Y.: Orbis, 1991), pp. 47ff.; Paul Knitter, *No Other Name: A Critical Study of Christian Attitudes Towards World Religions* (Maryknoll, N.Y.: Orbis, 1985),

Raimundo Panikkar, in a manner most reminiscent of Lessing, refers to the time of pluralism as the "third stage," the time of the symbol of the Ganges.

On this new evolutionary plane contemporary pluralists conduct their business of evacuation using warrants internal to the Christian tradition in the service of conformity to an external norm. In this the third element of the pluralist paradigm, Christ himself becomes a symbol of the very "creative transformation" by which the pluralist conversion itself is enacted.[15] This subversion can take a variety of other forms, as it appeals to a series of traditional Christian narratives and doctrines.

The ordinary sense of the terms from the Christian tradition comes to be neatly inverted. Wilfred Cantwell Smith accomplishes this boldly as he insists that what has been called "idolatry" in the past should be reinterpreted as the revelation of the transcendent in a finite medium. The term should actually be reserved for claims to unique finality such as is attributed to Christ by traditional Christians. Similarly Paul Knitter offers an evacuative doctrine of the atonement. When Knitter insists that "the more the particular mediator's efficacy is realized, the more its relativity is recognized"; what Christ mediates is pluralism itself. Thus he can understand the story of the cross as expressive of "a process . . . of fuller life from the pain of letting go of the present to trust and move into the mysterious future."[16]

A more prominent strategy of Christological evacuation, employed for instance by both John Hick and Paul Knitter, is to cite the familiar contrast between "the Jesus of history" and "the Christ of faith" (and hence of the church), between Jesus proclaiming the reign of God and Jesus proclaimed as Lord. These authors then identify the "real," historical Jesus in his uniqueness with his "universally relevant manifestation of theocentrism." The inversion again is complete: Jesus' unparalleled power is to communicate in all times and places how he is not unique and final.

In light of such evacuation pluralists can profess, in all honesty, an

---

"The Jordan, the Tiber, and the Ganges: Three Kairological Moments in Christic Self-Consciousness," in *The Myth of Christian Uniqueness: Toward a Pluralistic Theology of Religions,* ed. John Hick and Paul Knitter (Maryknoll, N.Y.: Orbis, 1987), pp. 102ff.

15. John B. Cobb, *Christ in a Pluralistic Age* (Philadelphia: Westminster, 1975), pp. 44-61.

16. Knitter, *No Other Name,* pp. 202, 230.

appreciation for the differences in traditions and the contribution of each to the global interreligious community. They can do so precisely because theirs is a nuanced externalism, according to which each tradition will conform to the pluralist norm in its own way. So John Cobb envisions "inner appropriations," specific to each tradition, though what is being appropriated is a common, universal "openness." Yet more subtle is Langdon Gilkey's advocacy of a "relative absoluteness." Gilkey recognizes that doctrinal claims may have an absolute claim within the confines of a particular tradition. But his contrast between their authority within these "local" confines and outside of them constitutes a denial that any particular claim could be privileged vis-à-vis the absolute.[17]

The remaining characteristics of pluralism comprise its ethical counsels, those practices that it enjoins on all religious traditions. We have mentioned three sorts of practices: charitable works, the extinguishing of fanaticism, and the encouragement of dialogue. But in pluralist writings the three tend to blur into one another, since the preeminently charitable act is the elimination of fanaticism, and the preeminent means for the latter is dialogue. In a well-known example of such works, John Hick offers the universally valid imperative of the Golden Rule, and he suggests that each religion may be judged by its capacity, as it pursues this ideal, to produce saints (though, in the best spirit of Lessing, the outcome is a perennial draw).[18] However, an

17. One must handle this proposal most delicately, since one is here agreeing with Gilkey that the claims of a tradition must be understood within the confines of that tradition. Each tradition has the task of making its case about the nature of things, a case it must make with "universal intent" (Polanyi). In other words, the difference lies in the way in which "the absolute" functions within one's vision of the religions. Gilkey, however skittish he may be about tracing its contours, employs "the absolute" as the final arbiter, as trump, which determines the relativistic and pluralistic relationship between the religions. He gives the traditional Christian claim its due, but within the confines of a defining concept of the absolute consistent with the pluralist paradigm. Hence his is a most nuanced externalism. By contrast, if the center of gravity is within the Christian tradition, then the contrast between the relativity of Christian claims and the absolute maintains a place within the orbit of Christian theological claims, more specifically as a (highly traditional) material contrast between human knowledge and capacity and the transcendence of God. See "Plurality and Its Theological Implications," in Hick and Knitter, *The Myth of Christian Uniqueness*, pp. 37ff.

18. See *An Interpretation of Religion: Human Responses to the Transcendent* (New Haven: Yale University Press, 1989), ch. 18.

increasingly popular alternate formulation of the universal imperative is drawn from liberation theological discourse: the promotion of
freedom for the powerless and oppressed.[19] (Few pluralists have been
troubled by the wrenching shift here from the rhetoric of tolerant relativity to the confident universal imposition of an ethical norm.)
Whether expressed in terms of love or liberation, pluralists all lay a
significant portion of the blame for past oppression and present fun-
damentalism at the doorstep of claims to uniqueness on the part of
particular religious traditions. Once this connection is in place, the
cause of charity is closely linked to the suppression of fanaticism, and
finally, both these goals are furthered by the practice of interreligious
dialogue.

It is not so much in what is said that these ethical goals are advanced, but rather in the very process of the talking itself. One can
find no more dramatic example of this notion than David Krieger's
The New Universalism, where both the meaningfulness and truth of religious traditions may be defined in terms of their capacity for what
he calls a "diatopical hermeneutics," i.e., the suppleness with which
participants can "jump in between" themselves and their dialogical
partners. The boundaries between traditions, serving to maintain the
distinctiveness of each, now make up the problem, challenge, or bar-
rier, and the very traversing of those boundaries constitutes their
truth. Krieger goes on to find in this practice the "foundation" for the
meaningfulness and truth of religions, in what he calls the "prag-
matics of cosmotheandric solidarity."[20] The truth of religions as the
evacuative activity of the *Illuminati,* the central point of Lessing, is re-
stated eloquently.

Taken together, these elements form a single constellation or system, as if they were together the moving parts of a single mechanism.
Pluralism constitutes itself as a tradition, which, when working
properly, continually shifts its weight from internal to external. It envisions a process of conversion, whereby the formal boundaries of
the religious tradition remain, but the dynamic of the system works

19. See, e.g., Paul Knitter's "Toward a Liberation Theology of Religions," in Hick
and Knitter, *The Myth of Christian Uniqueness*, ch. 11. A Gandhian version of the same argument can be found in Krieger, *The New Universalism*, pp. 150ff.

20. Krieger, *The New Universalism*, p. 46.

to conform traditional claims to an external norm, with the help, ironically, of appeal to internal claims themselves. In the case of pluralism, this "external" norm is the view of the transcendent inaccessibility of the Ultimately Real to the religions as described in the opening chapter.[21]

The "nuanced internalism" of orthodoxy and the "nuanced externalism" of pluralism, then, are both traditions. Together they stand in a starkly inverse relationship. Pluralism is to orthodoxy as its *Döppelgänger*, its mirror image. Pluralism and orthodoxy present themselves as the two major alternative approaches to the question of a Christian theology of other religious traditions, as opposed to the oft-repeated threefold typology of pluralism, exclusivism, and inclusivism. The major claim of this essay is that the decisive watershed between the two alternatives is final primacy.

Once this difference is understood as central, then one can see that the two positions differ with respect to the order, position, and weight assigned to different theological functions. Both would, for example, acknowledge that Christians have throughout history assimilated the views of other philosophical and religious traditions. But the decisive issue has to do with the norm to which claims are being assimilated, whether the gears of tradition are moving in an inward or outward direction.

If orthodoxy and pluralism stand in such a stark relationship, it becomes clear that the two are not simply offering different answers to the same question, posed from the same assumptions. On the contrary, each defines a distinct field of interpretation, a distinct league within which theologians struggle to offer the best account of the world of the religions, though this stronger distinction between orthodoxy and pluralism is veiled by the fact that each may describe itself as "Christian." Each employs a combination of warrants from sources internal and external to the tradition itself. Each seeks to offer

---

21. While this norm is "external" relative to the Christian tradition, when considered in relation to pluralism itself it is obviously "internal."

One ironic spin-off of this view is that it allows one to see the pluralist project in a more charitable and coherent light. It is a tradition with a governing rule derived from the Enlightenment, which renarrates other traditions retrospectively. It ceases to be some "perspective from nowhere," but is one tradition native to Western intellectuals alienated from the Church.

a comprehensive, rational, realistically and practically grounded, and charitable account. But each moves in pursuit of the end in the precisely opposite direction.

On the orthodox side of the watershed there is still plenty of room for considerable disagreement. Is veneration of the ancestors allowable for converts in Ricci's China? Can unbelievers be saved? Was sacrifice to the Yoruba *orishas* preparatory of Christ's coming? The diverse answers will straddle the fence previously separating "inclusivist" and "exclusivist." The shared background commitments of orthodoxy will make a comprehensible "running argument" possible, and the intractable nature of the debates will make it inevitable. The reality of such intra-orthodox conflict refocuses our attention on one of the questions posed at the outset of this chapter. Can a tradition, "ruled" by a pattern such as final primacy, be considered rational? The "litmus test" for a rational enterprise would be a free contest of opinions for mutual testing and criticism. Can the traditional view claim these features?

Here one may have some sympathy for pluralism's desire for a direct, "equal-access" standard of interpretation and comparison between the religions, an independent bar for the rational adjudication of dispute. But a more careful consideration of the epistemological nature of religious traditions in general and Christianity in particular reveals such a bar to be chimerical. Rationality does require contestation, but this can and must be found within each tradition, and not above or outside them, as pluralism would imagine. For, as described above, the pattern of final primacy not only allows, but assumes and requires, a wide variety of different construals of the claims and practices of an alien tradition, each of which will grate against the other.

But how can there be real rational challenge in intellectual traditions hermetically sealed one from another? Christian theologians may well spar over the proper assessment of alien claims, but what good is this "running argument" if it is artificially confined within the cloister of a predetermined final primacy? Such an imagined criticism misses the point, for the combatants are struggling over the proper understanding of external and alien claims. Rationality is more accurately thought of as the orderly argument about the sense to make of repeated expeditions outside that cloister.

So, within the orthodox confines themselves, the matter never can be settled, and the argument will run on continually and inconclusively. The coherence and power of the tradition shed light along the way in the process of the arguing itself. To borrow terms from the work of Nancey Murphy (and the philosopher of science Imre Lakatos),[22] while the inner band of commitments — including one to final primacy — are preserved, the outer band of theological constructions following from the inner band remain contestable, varied, and changeable. Such a view of rationality does allow for comparisons and debates between traditions. But it also means that there is no neutral ground for such a comparison, nor "knock-out" arguments that settle the conflict between traditions once and for all.

Does this mean that traditions do not compete with one another? Of course they do in the realm of human history, each seeking credibility and converts. Still, in what sense can one understand different religious traditions to be directly competing intellectually with one another? MacIntyre asserts that religious traditions which over the long haul fail vigorously and creatively to respond to the strongest arguments of opponents during epistemological crises fall into decrepitude. And likewise, Lindbeck can appeal, in equally holistic fashion, to traditions as constituting in their entirety massive claims, made over the whole course of their history. In both senses internal intellectual adequacy is a significant factor in survival and thriving in history.[23] One tradition's grammar and vocabulary may be more adequate to reality than another's.

At the same time both MacIntyre and Lindbeck have in mind increased *explanatory* power and advancement in charitable vision, which may look very different from thriving in terms of worldly power. Any smuggled notion of religious Darwinianism or an overarching Hegelian schema of history would badly misunderstand the matter. Any such interpretation would itself be one more externalist construction subject to debate. So it is no accident that Lindbeck appeals finally to an eschatological sense in which the religions finally will be sufficiently transparent one to another to be easily compared, and in which the correspondence to the *veritas* who is Christ can be

22. See especially Nancey Murphy, *Theology in the Age of Scientific Reasoning* (Ithaca, N.Y.: Cornell University Press, 1990).

23. Alasdair MacIntyre, "Epistemological Crises, Narrative, and the Philosophy of Science," in *Why Narrative?* ed. Stanley Hauerwas and L. Gregory Jones (Grand Rapids: Eerdmans, 1989); George A. Lindbeck, *The Nature of Doctrine* (Philadelphia: Westminster, 1984), pp. 77-90.

seen face to face. Such talk about the epistemological status of religions on that Day on the one hand draws a limit for our present epistemological condition, and on the other hand, makes a claim altogether internal to the bounds of Christian theology.

Not Three Types, but Three Distinctive Christian Practices

What practices are distinctive of Christian tradition as it reflects on the claims and practices of other religious traditions? To answer this question requires a short detour. For it has become a standard trope in recent writings about the religions to speak of three models, options, or types of approach: exclusivism, which asserts the sole truth of a single tradition; inclusivism, which seeks to assert its own truth even as it reinterprets, and so includes, other claims under the wing of its own; and pluralism, which affirms in some way that religions are different paths up the same mountain.[24] But even as this typology has come to be used widely, its inadequacy has become clear. One problem is that the typology conflates answers to different questions of revelation and salvation. For example Karl Barth, who affirms forcefully that other religions are "unfaith," also insists on seeing all humans as *Christiani designati in spe* ("Christians designated by hope"). Whether one thinks of him as a rigid exclusivist or an expansive inclusivist depends on the question one is considering. Likewise the line between inclusivism and pluralism can be a blurry one, especially when theologians begin to espouse weakened senses of "uniqueness" to be attributed to Jesus.[25]

One may justifiably have a sense that each alternative offers a measure of truth, the trick being how coherently to imagine their relationship. Wolfhart Pannenberg states this sense that each type should be given its due in the following way: "The elements of exclusivism in the Christian truth claim, the inclusivism of the Christian faith in the

24. The classic citation here is Alan Race's *Christians and Religious Pluralism: Patterns in the Christian Theology of Religions* (Maryknoll, N.Y.: Orbis, 1983).

25. See Schubert Ogden's argument for a "representatively" "true religion" in *Is There Only One True Religion or Are There Many?* (Dallas: Southern Methodist, 1992), ch. 5, "Beyond the Usual Options."

revelation of the one God of all human beings, and the acknowledgment of a factual pluralism of different belief systems and conflicting
truth claims belong together in the Christian self-understanding. If
these conceptions of exclusivism, inclusivism, and pluralism fall apart
into alternative conceptions and descriptions of the relationship of
Christianity to other religions, the results will be a one-sided and truncated account of the situation of the religious encounter."[26]

In a similar way prominent theologians such as Gavin D'Costa[27]
and Newbigin have reconceived the theology of religions in part by
reconfiguring these three terms. Newbigin, like Pannenberg, has also
suggested that they be taken to refer not to three types, but rather to
three dimensions of any way: "The position which I have outlined is
exclusivist in the sense that it affirms the unique truth of the revelation in Jesus Christ, but it is not exclusivist in the sense of denying
the possibility of salvation of the non-Christian. It is inclusivist in the
sense that it refuses to limit the saving grace of God to the members
of the Christian Church, but it rejects the inclusivism that regards the
non-Christian religions as vehicles of salvation. It is pluralist in the
sense of acknowledging the gracious work of God in the lives of all
human beings, but it rejects a pluralism which denies the uniqueness
and decisiveness of what God has done in Jesus Christ."[28] This essay
will follow the same trajectory as Pannenberg, Newbigin, and others,
that the exclusivist, inclusivist, and pluralist should be considered as
denoting three necessary dimensions of the Christian life.

Assume then that there are two major alternatives, and that the
nuanced internalist, orthodox side must itself be conceived as a field of
contestation. How might one still imagine the threefold alternatives of
the exclusive, the inclusive, and the pluralist? They can be understood
as three interrelated practices, distinctive to the Christian tradition's

26. "The Religions from the Perspective of Christian Theology and the Self-
Interpretation of Christianity in Relation to the Non-Christian Religions," *Modern Theology* 9, no. 3 (July 1993): 297.

27. See, e.g., "Revelation and Revelations: Discerning God in Other Religions: Beyond Static Valuation," in *Modern Theology* 10 (April 1994): 165-83.

28. *The Gospel in a Pluralist Society*, pp. 182-83. Another important example of the
desire to move beyond the inherited typology is Joseph DiNoia's *The Diversity of Religions* (Washington, D.C.: Catholic University Press, 1992), ch. 2, "Beyond Exclusivism,
Inclusivism, and Pluralism."

relationship to other traditions,[29] all of which should be present and in good "working order" for the Christian life to assume the requisite seriousness and depth truly to make and mean its claims vis-à-vis other traditions.

In order to grasp these three distinct practices, imagine a small church living amidst non-Christian neighbors, indeed in many cases amidst its own non-Christian relatives, say in India. Those Christians are enjoined by the New Testament first of all to proclaim their faith, be it by word or by example, in the hope that some may encounter their witness, accept Jesus as Lord, and come to be catechized and baptized. This may be called the practice of proclamation, and its occasion the conversional moment. This practice, leaving aside all questions of mission strategy or logistics, is warranted by a wide variety of New Testament passages. It corresponds to the exclusivist type. It commences from the particular authority of Jesus proclaimed, and it hopes that the hearer will turn from whatever he or she pledges allegiance to, and will accordingly turn toward Christ's Lordship. Where this practice is present, discourse conformed to the rule of final primacy serves to offer diverse maps for the ground it is hoped the neophyte will traverse.

This practice will in turn raise a myriad of questions: What of those who have died before the proclamation? How can we tell if the converts have "really" converted? What is the relationship of their new belief to what they formerly held? and so forth. These sorts of questions offer a second purpose for theological accounts according to final primacy, namely to resolve the conundra consequent on the proclamatory practice. The main point here is that such questions, and in turn the various, contending answers, presuppose for their cogency the preceding practice. Where the practice of witness is absent, there the motive for the questions and answers is considerably changed.

---

29. Edmund Schlink in his *The Coming Christ and the Coming World Church* (Philadelphia: Fortress, 1966) speaks of "basic forms" of the Christian life in relation to which theological statements should be considered, and we are suggesting something similar here.

One can readily imagine a pluralist objecting that such a "correlation" undercuts the truth-claiming capacity of theological constructions, since the arguments have become rhetorically subservient to some practical end. But all ideas have some kind of traditional context, and are accompanied by some kind of distinctive practices, and noting such does not eliminate the capacity to make (or not to make) a claim to truth.

Then the questions may even become rationales not to proclaim. The witnessing practice, like the rule of final primacy itself, may fulfill a sorting function, differentiating the larger purpose and intent of theological constructions

Such answers fall under the second practice, that of offering what MacIntyre called "retrospective narratives" that seek to take in as much as possible of history, belief, mores, etc. of the neighbors' faith into a consistent account whose concluding chapter is Christ. Such narratives may be formed for a variety of reasons, either evangelistic purposes for outsiders, perhaps in apologetic efforts, or else to meet the theological need of insiders when questions arise. This essay has already offered a series of types or subpatterns these narratives may follow, and in theory there could be many more, the common denominator being simply the tradition's need to account for as much of its environment, their neighbors' world, as possible. One can call this the assimilative practice and moment. To be sure, these narratives may not have the same purpose as the projects usually termed "inclusivist," e.g., they may have a more stringent view of the salvific possibilities of unbelievers. Just the same, such constructions cannot help but articulate some kind of narrative continuity by the very telling of the story of the relationship of prior belief and Christian faith.

Final primacy lends itself to imagined practices of proclamation and narrative assimilation corresponding to the exclusivist and inclusivist types, but what then is the practice that corresponds to pluralism? Here one can reiterate the suggestions of Pannenberg and Newbigin cited above, that the Christian tradition must frankly recognize the thoroughly pluralistic situation in which it lives, whether or not adherents of other traditions are in the immediate environs or not. This includes, but exceeds, an acknowledgment of the historical and social fact of pluralism. It has an intellectual dimension as well, for it involves admitting the irresolvable and irremovable reality of the church in contention amidst its religious peers. It involves the admission that the church is unable to prove its case and so remove itself from the fray. It must see itself as a social creature among its fellow creatures, existing as it does as one religious community with the same sociological, political, and psychological, and epistemological limitations and conditions as its neighbors.

All this is undoubtedly true, but what practice does it then involve? One can characterize a number of different practices under the rubric of "neighborliness," the recognition that the church is a fellow creature, taking a share in the larger human community of religious communities. (Here too one may note that the invocation of terms like "neighborly" and "creaturely" assumes specifically biblical warrants for such a cluster of practices.) This rubric of "neighborly practice" includes on the one hand joint service or political action, and on the other dialogue,[30] conversation aimed at knowing the other better. At this point a self-conscious Christian theological particularism can stand in common cause with pluralists in its affirmation of such forms of neighborly practice. It too insists that only as Christians listen carefully to their neighbors in dialogue can they obey the commandment not to bear false witness against that neighbor. It will give specifically Christian reasons for acts of solidarity with those in need, the very same acts that Christian pluralists would urge on the church.

If these three practices of proclamation, theological retrospection, and neighborliness are requisite for any Christian theology of other religious traditions, then one can imagine correlative theological virtues,[31] forming the mind and heart, which make their performance fruitful. "Faith, hope, love, these three endure, but the greatest of these is love" (1 Cor. 13:13).[32] For Paul all three are required, but as parts of

---

30. A strong case is made for dialogue by David Lochhead in his *Dialogical Imperative* (Maryknoll, N.Y.: Orbis, 1988). The main thrust of the argument, that Christian theology must think how other religious traditions' perspectives can be seen to cohere with the unique status of Jesus Christ, bolsters our argument. We do, however, think that his contrast between dialogue and evangelization may mislead. They are distinct according to our argument, but they also require one another.

31. Recently this idea of moving from three types to three Christian virtues has appeared in Michael Barnes's *Theology and the Dialogue of Religions* (Cambridge: Cambridge University Press, 2002), especially p. 184. His work is a thoughtful reflection on interreligious dialogue in relation to postmodern philosophy. Certainly his recurrent theme of "seeds of the Word," as old as Justin, is consonant with this essay. One wonders, however, for all the talk of "Telling the Christian Story" (ch. 5), why his treatment of mission has so little evidence of actual witnessing in the name of Christ to the end that others might be converted. To be sure, the emphasis on the conversion of the missionary's own heart, e.g., in the case of de Nobili, is right and good. But squeamishness about the actual practice of proclamation is the telling feature of faulty theologies of mission, one that neither Ignatius nor de Nobili would have evinced.

32. It is worth noting, as an aside, that in this passage Paul does sound the note of humility, for what we can know of God is in our present condition limited: "for now we

one reality, love of and obedience to the risen Christ present in us, in the church, and in the world. The virtues are not separable, but rather cohere as they conduce to the one end of communion with him. This remains so as Christians address and serve other traditions.[33]

First of all, the gift of charity toward our religious neighbor must precede our other religious activities. Only with humility and solidarity toward this neighbor can one perceive and confess the truth of Christ without distorting such a confession into a boast, in some sense, about ourselves. But real charity must lead to truth-telling and witness-bearing.[34] So one may understand the gift of the theological virtue of faith to empower us for the practice of proclamation. There is no way for the disciple of Jesus Christ permanently to subordinate or lay aside this obligation.[35] But part of this proclamation is, as cited above, the task of making the Christian case as cogent, as winsome, and as explanatorily compelling as possible. The Christian theologian does in this sense "compete," but part of this competition will often be the demonstration of the Christian tradition's power charitably to include the truths of other traditions and their adherents into the economy of God's grace.

When the Christian theologian must work to resolve conundra that may result from faithful response to proclamation, the theological virtue of hope may be paired with the practice of retrospective explanation. For these narratives point in a variety of ways toward Christ as the end, the *telos*, of human religious communities. Such narratives are affirmations of Christ's final reign over all truths and communities, and so such narratives are expressions of Christian eschatological hope. But insofar as such claims are fallible, contested, revisable constructions, one is led back to the point of departure, the necessary per-

---

see in a mirror dimly, but then face to face. . . ." This note is one sweet to the ear of the pluralist. But Paul's uncertainty is how the realities of the world will be conformed to the prime reality of Christ. It is precisely in this sense that the particularist can join the pluralist in admitting the severe limits of our knowledge, and can at the same time not allow this admission to undercut his or her confession of Christ.

33. Citing Aquinas, *S.T.* I.II.62, 63; 2/2,4.3,23.8.

34. Ephesians 4:15: "speaking the truth in love, we are to grow up in every way into him who is the head. . . ."

35. See especially Paul Griffiths' *Apology for Apologetics: A Study in the Logic of Interreligious Dialogue* (Maryknoll, N.Y.: Orbis, 1991).

ception of the Christian community's submission to the very same creaturely and sinful conditions as other religious traditions. So all three practices, and their respective virtues, stand in a close and interdependent relationship one to another.

The initial questions in this chapter quizzed particularism about its credentials with regard to rationality, practicality, and charity. In response, first, contestation within the Christian tradition attests to its internal rationality, as does its ongoing commitment to explanation of as many outward claims and challenges as possible. Now it is further clear such a commitment to contestation presupposes a series of practices that help to give a richer picture of the Christian tradition, its claims and practices making up the thick warp and woof.[36] Of course one might come to the conclusion that the particularists are wrong, and so one might situate oneself within the pluralist tradition. But, even if wrong, one could, and should, acknowledge the rationality, practical depth, and charity of the orthodox tradition.

This defense of the Christian theological tradition, conceived as an instance of what we have called "nuanced internalism," has been buttressed by arguments taken from contemporary philosophy, especially from the work of MacIntyre. Our argument has then been, itself, an example of what it defends, since it has offered selected external (in this case philosophical) arguments in support of the coherent rationality of a particular, "internal" tradition. But more may fairly be demanded of the Christian theologian. What "internal" warrants from Scripture or tradition should also be offered for these practices? Distinctly kerygmatic proclamation and distinctly Christ-centered reinterpretation hardly need apology. But how might one supplement, in a distinctly Christian theological way, the reasons given so far for the practice of neighborliness?

God has submitted the Christian church to the condition, intractable until the consummation of God's kingdom, of epistemological uncertainty, according to which it cannot prove its case. This limitation is linked with its dependence on particular texts, relating accounts of particular events, for the sake of a particular community. What is the reason for the scandal of ecclesial particularity, so bothersome to pluralists?

36. Cf. Ninian Smart's seven dimensions of religious traditions in *The Religious Experience of Mankind* (New York: Scribner's, 1969).

One may offer as many reasons as there are loci in the traditional theological compendium. Submission to epistemological limitation follows as a condition of creation, within whose bounds all God's creatures, including the social creature called the Christian community, must learn to live. From this perspective the pluralist desire to overleap the limits of particular traditions bespeaks pride. But the church shares in this pride, sinful institution that it is, and so the church must accept its own submission to epistemological conflict and uncertainty, as a condition well fit for contrition. At the same time, as it hears of the election of Israel in the Old Testament it may discern the form of its own designated place as a particular and humble tradition among its neighbors. A warrant more specific to the New Testament accompanies this perception. For this submission has in it an element of *kenosis,* an echo of the divine condescension in Christ Jesus apt for its witness to him.

But even as the church is conformed to Christ, the doctrine of the church requires that it be distinguished clearly from him. As it recalls with Aquinas that all its claims are straw, it maintains the proper distinction between disciple and Master. Paul captures both aspects of the condition of submission: "But we have this treasure in earthen vessels, to show that the transcendent power belongs to God and not to us. We are . . . always carrying in the body the death of Christ" (2 Cor. 4:7, 10). Finally, the condition of epistemological submission means that theology reminds itself that it is "faith seeking understanding." In this act of rational faith, the theologian, and indeed the church, are built up in the theological virtues,[37] as we have seen, virtues that are the work of the Holy Spirit and as such promised tokens of the clarity that is the quality of the End alone. In other words, only in relationship to the whole *cursus* of theological loci can one render an adequate account, on Christian theology's own terms, of the condition of epistemological submission underlying all that theologians say about their religious neighbors.

These final loci, having to do with the church in the Spirit anticipating the End, help to put all this talk about practices in its proper light.[38] For the first and last true end of the church is simply praise, the one activity that shall endure even after the form of this world has

---

37. Aquinas, *ST* I,1.2, "Sacred doctrine is a science of the latter kind, depending on principles known through a higher science, namely the science of God and the blessed."

38. This paragraph has the Rt. Rev. Dr. Kenneth Cragg to thank for its main point.

passed away for those who are gathered around the throne and the Lamb (Rev. 5). For the true motive of proclamation is doxology, the conversion of every Gentile being an occasion of joy among the angels and a sign of the reign of God real in Christ.[39] The true motive of renarrating is that a thousand tongues might tell, in a thousand ways, the dear Redeemer's praise. Neighborliness expresses thanks for the One who was a real Neighbor to humankind on the cross. Doxology is the antidote to thinking of these activities as if they were mainly judged by their utility or worldly result.

To be sure, there is a single truth that every religion strives most adequately to express. For Christians this affirmation is bound to the very oneness of God who is truth. Christians believe that, on the Last Day, that one truth will be made clear to all. Philosophers remind us that one must distinguish between the truth itself and the warrants offered for it, the latter springing as they do from particular traditions with their own premises and histories. Christians have reasons of their own why they must make their case alongside their religious neighbors. They have Christian reasons to expect the contention of claims, the "strife of systems,"[40] and they must humbly acknowledge and accept this condition, for it is the one under which God calls the church to witness.

These first two chapters have aimed to present the conditions for Christian theologies about the claims and practices of other religious traditions. The first chapter offered a *material* condition, namely that the many constructions, responding to a myriad of situations and interlocutors, all show the pattern here called "final primacy." This second chapter has offered a *formal* condition, namely that these constructions emerge in the midst of a tradition of inquiry, fostering contestation between rival constructions, and bolstered by the requisite practices and virtues. When Christian theologies of other religious traditions are understood in this way, challenges to their rationality, practicality, and charity can be met.

39. See my "Light and Twilight" in *Reclaiming Faith* (Grand Rapids: Eerdmans, 1993).

40. The phrase is from *The Strife of Systems* (Pittsburgh: University of Pittsburgh Press, 1985) by Nicholas Rescher, from which I have benefited. Owen Thomas is responsible for drawing my attention to it; Mark Heim develops its implications for a theology of the religions in his book *Salvations*.

What do these material and formal conditions help one to do? It is a truism that the meaning of what one says depends on where and when one says it, i.e., on the larger context, the flow of arguments and the background of assumptions in which and against which a claim is made. Consider the following sentence, which was the substance of the title of a famous book about the encounter between two great religious traditions: "There is an unknown Christ already present in Hinduism."[41] Some will hear that sentence and take it to mean that Christ embodies the truth, and so the Christian is able to look at the world of Hinduism and see various elements as *praeparationes evangelicae,* "anticipations of the gospel." Such a view is readily consistent with the rule of final primacy. On the other hand one might read such a sentence and take it to mean that "the christic principle" is actualized as readily in Hinduism as it is in Christianity, and this view would seem to slide easily into pluralism. Yet others might seek to split the difference and talk of "Christ as norm" for Christians, and the hearer is not quite sure what this amounts to. Such a sentence then does not mean one thing that one can either affirm or deny. On the contrary everything hangs on how the sentence is meant, and this in turn depends on the nature of the larger theological project in which the sentence is embedded. In contexts where final primacy is not presumed, and where communities do not engage in the requisite practices, such statements cannot be properly understood. Bearing in mind the material and formal conditions of final primacy enables one to understand what such an ambiguous sentence means in a particular use, and so when that use is theologically appropriate.

Talking about such a theological tradition, just the same, cannot suffice. This essay must now proceed to demonstrate how the rule of final primacy, at work within the Christian theological tradition, can make cogent sense of the questions and quandaries commonly encountered as Christians reflect on other religious traditions. So, to test the proposal, the next two chapters will contend in the field of systematic theology. Can the rule of final primacy help one better to understand tensions within the writings of prominent modern theologians on the

41. Cf. Raimundo Panikkar, *The Unknown Christ of Hinduism* (London: Darton, Longman and Todd, 1967) with *The Cosmotheandric Experience: Emerging Religious Consciousness* (Maryknoll, N.Y.: Orbis, 1993).

subject of the religions (Chapter 3)? Then, in light of the great contemporary systematic interest in the doctrine of the Trinity, can final primacy serve to test the helpfulness of new, consciously trinitarian proposals about the religions? Moving from assessment to construction, can one, with the help of our rule, offer a coherent answer to the contemporary systematic question of the "providential diversity" of the religions, which often follows from the trinitarian debate (Chapter 4)?

Finally the usefulness of our rule will be tested as it engages two external traditions. The point of departure will be the seminal debate about Christianity and other traditions at the missionary conference in Tambaram, India, in 1938, the reconceiving of whose debate will suggest a new way, consistent with final primacy, by which one may understand the different disciplines that engage alien claims (Chapter 5). Tambaram also leads naturally to the specific case in point of Christian reflection on Hindu claims (Chapter 6). A second methodological starting-point, the popular discussions of "contextualization" in missiology, can also be the occasion for the use of final primacy. The rule is then tested in a case in point, African Christian theology (Chapter 7). The conclusion of this essay will then seek to sum up the essential practices, now fully on display, as constituting a cumulative shift from a relationship of "dialogue" with other traditions to one of "disputation." On each of these varied subjects, amidst bewildering arrays of proposals, can final primacy help to locate where the telling differences lie, and can it help to provide articulately "nuanced internalist," bold yet charitable, judgments?

3 Testing Final Primacy in Modern Theology — Barth, Rahner, and Pannenberg

This chapter will consider the theological treatment of the religions in three of the greatest systematicians of the twentieth century, voices of lasting effect: Karl Barth, Karl Rahner, and Wolfhart Pannenberg. For all three the major challenger and interlocutor for Christian theology is the atheistic humanism of modern European society. To be sure, all three, and especially Rahner and Pannenberg, recognize the deep pluralism of that scene, including a greater awareness of the religions. But even so, the religions serve for them as a problem in the very way identified in Chapter 1, a problem typical of the modern predicament. In spite of this fact, they each offer distinctive and influential views of the religions that grow out of their systematic commitments as a whole. "Religion as Unbelief" and "Anonymous Christianity" in particular have powerfully formed Christian reflection on the religions in modern times. Thus Gavin D'Costa, for example, setting out the standard typology discussed in the preceding chapter, offers Barth as the classic case of "exclusivism" and Rahner as the classic case of "inclusivism" (though a goal of this essay is to show how and why such designations are not helpful).

But together with this notoriety has come strong criticism. Both Barth and Rahner have repeatedly been accused of imposing evaluations on other religions with little or no attention to the actual details of religions themselves,[1] or of their self-understandings. This has

---

1. This is so in spite of Rahner's repeated distinction between his project and a posteriori studies, which he always insists are necessary.

seemed to many to impose a kind of intellectual imperialism. How can these approaches seem at once compelling and problematic? This chapter will construe these views anew according to the rule of final primacy, so as to show how each is a "grammatically" Christian understanding of the religions. It will also point in the direction by which the weaknesses of each construction can be best overcome.

The preceding chapter offered three distinctive and mutually implied practices: proclamation, inclusive assimilation, and neighborliness. Each of the three theologians to be considered places one of these practices front and center, so that the perspectives of Barth, Rahner, and Pannenberg may be seen to convey complementary emphases. Barth's stress on the primacy of the revelation of Christ and Rahner's perception that Christ is the final cause of all religions, even "anonymously," correspond to the proclamatory and inclusive moments. Pannenberg's emphasis on the real, historical plurality of religious communities in conflict and competition brings the awareness of pluralism entailed in neighborliness to the fore. Their arguments are different, but in no way contradictory, and in a wider sense mutually enriching.

Barth and the Religions

In considering the theologian of the "triumph of grace,"[2] a good place to begin is with the logic of that doctrine. For grace enables, indeed requires, one to imagine that God could have done otherwise. His election must not be thought of as necessary, for then it would no longer be free and gracious. This feature of grace, namely that it could theoretically have worked in a different manner, was not lost on the Reformers, nor was its immediate implication for the status of adherents of other religions completely lost.

The prime example is Ulrich Zwingli's *On Providence*,[3] where he reflects on the possibility of God's secret election of exemplars of wisdom and virtue from classical Greece and Rome, figures of importance in the era of the Renaissance.

2. G. C. Berkouwer, *The Triumph of Grace in the Theology of Karl Barth* (Grand Rapids: Eerdmans, 1966).
3. See *Selected Works*, ed. Samuel M. Jackson (Philadelphia: Westminster, 1972).

At the same time Zwingli himself, and even more so his fellow Reformers, were aware how such assertions might undercut the trustworthiness of God's unique and particular saving acts, biblically narrated. The other parameter of the grammar of grace, God's freedom precisely to do something with distinct historical contours and lasting repercussions, could be imperiled by speculation about salvation outside the bounds of the saving history. The sobering instance of just such ungrammatical speculation and its deformation of the grammar of grace is found in nominalism, with its distinction between the *potentia absoluta,* everything God could have done, and the *potentia ordinata,* the more limited domain of things God did decide to do. In the former one would find, for example, nominalist speculation about whether God could have been incarnated as a cucumber.[4] Such speculation came to be tied to views of human effort and divine grace unmoored from the specificity of the economy of salvation. Thus the grammar of grace, both in its assertion of freedom as non-necessity and freedom as divine particularity, points toward the necessity of a corollary grammar about the possibility of grace outside of the Christian dispensation. By this grammar any such speculation must be subsequent to the scriptural narrative and its account of salvation, to ensure that two separate accounts, in two separate domains, do not result. Such a corollary grammar amounts to a restatement of the rule of final primacy itself, with the attendant worry about balkanization.

Barth would assert, however, that one should not start in so abstract a mode.[5] Grace is indeed systematically central to *Church Dogmatics.* But Barth's project is equally an extended effort to think through the freedom and concreteness of grace only and always in relationship to the specific name and person of Jesus Christ. Generalizations about grace are only true to the extent that they are glosses on, and lead back to, a recognition of his Lordship. In other words, to think about Jesus Christ is to learn to use the categories of freedom and necessity, generality and specificity, in new, distinct, and normed ways in relationship to him. One must distinguish the ways these terms are

---

4. Alister McGrath, *Iustitia Dei: A History of the Christian Doctrine of Justification* (Cambridge: Cambridge University Press, 1989), p. 126.

5. For a critique of the abstract see George Hunsinger, *How to Read Karl Barth: The Shape of His Theology* (New York: Oxford University Press, 1991), pp. 32, 38, 68.

used in themselves from the proper way they are used to describe God in Christ.

There is an asymmetry and nonreciprocity between Christ's relationship to us and ours to him. Barth himself makes this point in his treatment of religion: "The religion of revelation is indeed bound up with the God of revelation, but the revelation of God is not bound up with the religion of revelation."[6] Conceiving of God's covenant trustworthiness so as to leave God free means constantly revealing the contrast between his freedom and humanity's willful misconception of real freedom. The grammar of grace for Barth can only be expressed by this sharpened, ongoing, thoroughly theological contrast between freedom as human sin and freedom as divine election.

This is the perspective from which to consider Karl Barth's view, first and primarily of the Christian religion, and only then of religion in general. When he categorizes religion as *Unglaube*, "disbelief," he does not have non-Christian religions primarily in mind, nor their presumed corruptions or defects, but rather Christian religion, even at its best. Christian religion is here considered under its "formal object" as human religion. By the grammar delineated above, a sharp contrast must be maintained between the human perspective on the Christian religion and the divine perspective, accessible to humans in the revelation *pro nobis* in Jesus Christ. By its very nature, the Christian religion inevitably consists, from the first perspective, of a human effort directed at a deity, humanly conceived, albeit in this case with the help of the traditions of Scripture and the church.

Barth stresses that religion as *Unglaube* is the highest possibility for the human spirit: "In religion this final passion becomes conscious and recognizable as experience and event. Can there be any affirmation of passion that outstrips the passion with which Prometheus robs Zeus of his fire . . . if then by the consciousness of religion we make human thought and will and act to be the thought and will and act of God, does not human behavior become supremely impressive, significant, necessary . . . ?"[7] In contrast, religion from the perspective of the gospel requires that one think of the life of the religious community — the

---

6. *CD* I/2, p. 329.

7. *Epistle to the Romans*, ch. 7, "The Reality of Religion," trans. E. Hoskins (London: Oxford University Press, 1972).

church — as the result of a gracious initiative of God. At the climax of his treatment of religion Barth straightforwardly asserts: "True religion is an event in the act of grace of God in Christ."[8]

Between these two perspectives on religion there is a thorough asymmetry. If one attempts in any way to combine divine and human perspectives so as to coordinate divine and human wills, one ends up with some sort of division of labor, or some synthesis, such that the divine will no longer overrules all. But the doctrine of God who is Creator requires that one attribute all to God in so encompassing a way as to include, transcend, and empower human action. Only divine action ensures that the "direction" of priority moves from God to humans, so that what God can and does make of human religion takes precedence over what religion amounts to on its own.[9]

One can come to the same insight about Barth's view of religion from a more historical-theological perspective. Barth is employing the central Lutheran category of the human person as *simul justus et peccator*, "at once justified (before God) and also a sinner." For Luther this formula indicates a relationship that is irreducibly dialectical, i.e., two perspectives on the human — one in the human's own light, and one in the light of Christ. This dialectic must be maintained without resolution or progress. Barth applies this same view explicitly to the Christian religion as a whole, for it too is sinful (in itself) and justified (by the action of God in Christ). It is only in this dialectical sense, and not by virtue of any claim or quality of its own, that the Christian religion is the "true religion,"[10] and so set apart from all other religions.

In a similar vein Barth can use other terms to express the human incapacity that God uses for his purpose. He can speak of the Christian

---

8. *CD* I/2, p. 344.

9. Here the major themes identified in George Hunsinger's recent analysis of the *Church Dogmatics*, titled *How to Read Karl Barth*, prove helpful and illuminating. One theme is "actualism," the insistence that God's presence is to be understood in relation to humans as an event initiated by God. This should be coupled with his emphasis on "particularism," the actual event of Jesus Christ that establishes what is really real, and explains all other, general human phenomena, and not vice versa. These formal criteria serve elegantly to summarize the very approach to the category of religion that we are considering. They provide the grounds for the dialectical view of the church that lies at the center of his view of religion.

10. *CD* I/2, esp. p. 325.

religion as "resurrected" from the dead by Christ, or of the Christian religion, taken up into relationship with God, as an *assumptio carnis* analogous to the incarnation itself (though the door to the dangerous next step of making the church an *incarnatio continua* is checked by return to the concept of *simul justus* . . .).[11] Finally, in a more philosophical vein, Barth can speak the *Aufhebung* of religion in the case of the gospel. Barth intends both implications of this Hegelian term, religion's cancellation as well as its elevation.[12] All these terms are employed to express the dialectical nature of the church in keeping with the grammar of grace.

One metaphor dominates Barth's treatment of the religions in both *CD* I/2 and IV/3. He imagines a darkened globe before the sunrise — all regions of the earth are equally benighted. Then the sun dawns, and one region is illumined while other regions remain in darkness. In no sense does one region have any "claim" on the light, nor any superiority over another region. Furthermore the illumination is an event, though it may easily be taken for granted as part of the order of things. The shining of the light actually changes the objective condition of the region. Between the light and the region enlightened there remains an asymmetrical relation, in spite of their connection. This metaphor of the rising sun is one of location; similarly Barth understands Christianity to be, not the possessor, but rather the locus of divine light and grace. Likewise, by the grammar of grace, the action of God in Christ is clearly and properly seen in the Christian religion, but Christ could also bring himself into relationship to anything he chose, and so also to other kinds of religious words (as we shall see in *CD* IV/3). This enables one consistently to maintain that all religions are in themselves equally darkness, and that the light of the Christian faith remains only Christ's.

Such is the main thrust of Barth's argument. One can understand it better if one considers its context of modern intellectual history in general and modern theology in particular. Barth explicitly prefaces his argument with an account of the stages of degeneration of the term "religion" in early modern Protestant scholasticism. In this semantic shift Barth finds the evidence of just that reversal of emphasis from revela-

11. So *CD* I/2, p. 101.
12. So the subtitle of I/2, paragraph 17.

tion toward religion against which he inveighs. In Calvin the term is simply used as a synonym for Christianity itself. Among orthodox scholastics like Hollaz *religio vera* is contrasted with *religio falsa*, i.e., that of non-Christians. While valid enough, this use already shifts attention to Christianity per se. Next, in Buddeus, under the influence of Descartes, Christianity is the *religio vera*, needed to complete innate religious sense. Christianity is still superior, but as religion, understood in relationship to human capacity. The process is finally complete with Schleiermacher, and the reversal of gospel and religion has been in effect ever since. Even when Barth is dealing specifically with other religious traditions, it is in the context of this Christian struggle and defeat that the term "religion" is used.[13] The term "religion" as a prime category is so matted together with the modern turn to the subject as to make it complicit in harm caused to the doctrine of the divine initiative of grace.

In Barth's more explicit treatment of other religions, the accounts given are resolutely theological. Christ is the first reality, and so there is no room for fencing the religions off in some pre-resurrection room and considering them "on their own terms." For they are first and foremost the places where the true light has not shined. But this also means the religions are themselves on a par with Christianity *qua* religion. Barth may lambaste natural theology, but for this very reason the religions can assume a status for him analogous to natural theology itself. Furthermore one may consider the religions on other, purely immanent grounds, so long as the other disciplines are not confused with theology. In fact, for Barth the distinct and incomparable nature of revelation creates space for a "science of religions,"[14] where with openness and sympathy one can consider what he calls the "phenomenon of the religions."[15] But as soon as these phenomena assume the status of a worldview, a potential rival claimant to allegiance with the Christian gospel, they have transgressed their bounds. In such a science, properly understood, one is free to find areas of similarity, or even superiority in comparison to the Christian religion. Theology can find in

13. See Garrett Green's "Challenging the Religious Studies Canon: Karl Barth's Theory of Religion," *Journal of Religion* (1995): 473-86.

14. See *CD* I/2, p. 335.

15. See *CD* I/2, p. 295.

such a discipline value, since it is fitting to show respect for human greatness,[16] and so to reflect on the greatness of the Creator.[17]

It should be no surprise that Barth is most interested in religious traditions that are also considered "religions of grace." Doesn't this similarity undercut the very theme that sets Christianity apart? Barth adamantly insists that the perception of such a similarity is a misunderstanding, a category confusion. To repeat, "grace" is simply another, more soteriologically oriented way to speak the name of Jesus Christ. By contrast, to conceive of Christianity as a "religion of grace," even the premier one, is to turn grace into a general concept, to disconnect it from the distinctive Christian grammar of grace, and so to return Christianity to the status solely of a religion.

With these caveats in mind, Barth entertains his most serious and sustained interreligious comparison, between Christianity and Pure Land Buddhism, *Jodo Shin Shu*, the simplified, popular sect whose teaching was developed by Shinran in thirteenth-century Japan. This reform movement emphasized the rejection of efforts at holy works in favor of the repeated invocation of the name of the Amida Buddha, and sheer reliance on his goodness. But, for Barth, faith is altogether determined by its object, Jesus Christ himself. Lacking him, Pure Land can only invoke itself, and this involves not grace, but rather the human concept of gratuity. So the practice of this sect attains only to the level of the highest human possibility. For grace presupposes the Giver in his freedom; and so where he chooses to give that grace is of primary importance. Again, this argument is not meant to disparage Pure Land, or Buddhism in general; on the contrary, it is precisely its excellence, its seeming isomorphism with Christianity, that gives the comparison importance. It is precisely as the "Lutheran heresy" that Pure Land[18] serves to illustrate how nothing, not even "graciousness," sets Christianity apart except the presence of Christ himself.

So far our analysis has focused on Barth's treatment of religion in *CD* I/2, but there exists a second *locus classicus*, his treatment of

16. Article by Joseph DiNoia, "Religions and Religion," in *The Cambridge Companion to Karl Barth*, ed. John Webster (Cambridge: Cambridge University Press, 2000).

17. See *CD* IV/3, pp. 143ff.

18. See *CD* I/2, p. 341.

"other lights" reflecting the true light of Christ in *CD* IV/3. How do these two treatments comport with one another, since, by a cursory reading, the second seems to take a more sanguine view of the value of the religions than the first? It would be a mistake to attribute to Barth any "softening" of his position. On the contrary Barth in fact maintained his critically dialectical view of human religion consistently from his early *Epistle to the Romans* on to the end of the *Church Dogmatics* project.

Since Christ is the "true Light," one may fairly ask about the status of other, subsidiary, peripheral, reflecting lights. Is there a way in which the true Light might be reflected in other claims, traditions, practices, etc.? What sort of knowledge do these "other lights" provide? At the same time one must answer the corollary question: If the light does so extend, how can one be sure not to end up with a second light separated from and independent of Christ, a theological possibility diametrically at odds with what we have seen in *CD* I/2? The section on "other lights," consistent with the grammar of grace, seeks to answer these questions. As such, it is compatible with what has preceded, but also serves as an extension of the treatment in the earlier passage.

The relevant section in *CD* IV/3 contains a strong echo of Barth's great Reformation teacher, John Calvin. In the opening sections of his *Institutes of the Christian Religion,* Calvin returns periodically to Romans 1:20.[19] In light of this verse Calvin insists that the pagan, though lacking a saving knowledge of God, does indeed retain a distorted knowledge of him, a knowledge rendering him "inexcusable" before God. The judgment of God itself presumes a broken knowledge of God. Barth exploits this same implication as he seeks to find the legitimate way, consistent with the Lordship of Christ, in which one could say that "other lights" do shine. There is a knowledge of God, shrouded and dark, that does not leave the human innocent. On the contrary it bespeaks the faithless turning of the human away from God, even as it whispers something of him: ". . . we have to admit that the knowledge of God the Creator is concealed, wrapped in the great darkness which is due to man's unfaithfulness and lack of perception . . . the knowledge of God as Creator is a hidden one which is not defi-

19. See the discussion in Chapter 1.

nitely apprehensible and which cannot be unequivocally established in its law and continuity."[20]

In the Bible the religions serve as the rod of Assyria, or Balaam's voice, or the wisdom of Job. Here the "other lights" shine as they come to play roles, however small, in the plot or drama of salvation. So these creaturely "other lights" make up the stage on which the drama of redemption can be performed.[21] This argument presumes a larger, supporting girder, namely Barth's understanding of creation as the outer basis of covenant and covenant as the inner basis of creation. In tying creation and covenant together in this way, Barth assumes that creation as a whole must be "read" with the lens of Christ's Lordship too. "It speaks of the *theatrum gloriae Dei,* and therefore of the creaturely world as the setting or background . . . of the . . . revelation of reconciliation. . . . It draws attention to the lights or words or truths which also and already shine in God's creation as such, to the indications of the constant factors in cosmic being and occurrence as chosen, willed, established, and overruled by God."[22]

Barth also sets out more deliberate criteria, derived from that Lordship of Jesus Christ as the true light. Here Barth's premise is straightforward: Christ rules the whole world already, and so he must also rule over the wider realm of claims and practices, including those of the religions, in the modes of both judgment and of approval. This Lordship of Christ as true light may order these "other lights," and how they in turn may lend aid, as concomitant virtues or prophetic words, for the hearing of the Word himself. This ordering is grounded, first and foremost, Christologically. "Our statement is simply to the effect that Jesus Christ is the one and only Word of God, that He alone is the light of God . . . it is in this sense that it delimits all other words, lights, revelations, prophecies, and apostolates, whether of the Bible, the church, or the world."[23] Implicit in this quotation, and in Barth's treatment as a whole, is the image of a center, Christ, defining its periphery in concentric circles, which, in an ordered fashion, trail off from the center itself. Closest to the Word, but not identi-

---

20. Karl Barth, *The Christian Life* (Edinburgh: T. & T. Clark, 1981), p. 123.
21. See *CD* IV/3, p. 137.
22. See *CD* IV/3, p. 151.
23. See *CD* IV/3, p. 136.

cal to it, is the Word in the Bible, and then the words of the church, and then the occasional words that may be found in this divinely determined order.

Barth is anxious throughout to ensure that the status of other lights not be ossified, nor that abstract principles somehow arise as independent arbiters of where the Word is or is not found.[24] Here one may return to his insistence, found in *CD* I/2 as well, that Christ as active agent must be the One who brings himself into conjunction with such words, though they possess no such status on their own.[25] Any systematic or independent means of determining when and where and to what extent such knowledge may be found, could lead back into the dangerous territory of natural theology understood as knowledge available without Christ: "The 'other lights' cannot be 'coordinated or compared,' on their own, to the one Light."[26] Hunsinger summarizes Barth's point this way: ". . . his truth can do any of these things, as is appropriate for them: complete them, defeat them, combine itself with them, or transcend them."[27]

Given this ordering, it is not surprising that the other ways in which Barth describes these "other lights" are dominated by the analogy of commentaries on or extensions of the scriptures themselves. Only by analogy with the way that Scripture conveys the Word can we imagine the Word elsewhere conveyed. So these other instances assume the status of "parables of the Kingdom."[28] But how do we know when we are beholding an "other light"? So Barth makes explicit what is implied in the notion of a confirmation or commentary on Scripture, that nothing repugnant to Scripture can be esteemed to be such a light. Conformity to the creeds, and the test of the fruits these lights bear can be considered lesser tests as well.[29] The claims of other religions may

---

24. One might ask if our rule of final primacy is such an "independent arbiter." (Such is the criticism of David Demson, from private conversation.) But this is not fair, for the rule precisely does *not* presume a single pattern, but rather a plethora of patterns, sharing only the feature that Christ must be the One around whom the patterns are ordered.

25. See *CD* IV/3, p. 151.

26. See *CD* IV/3, p. 97.

27. Hunsinger, *How to Read Karl Barth*, p. 248.

28. See *CD* IV/3, p. 101.

29. *CD* IV/3, p. 117.

indeed be true and right on their own, so long as they do not contradict Scripture.[30]

How are we to assess Barth's treatment of the claims of other religious traditions? First of all, Barth is the most eloquent of exponents of the unique finality and Lordship of Christ, and so of one side of final primacy. An example of the law-gospel type, he is the strongest opponent of systematizing or codifying these relationships, lest bridges move directly from other claims to Christ. In his own way Barth acutely sees the danger of inversion. As to the typology set out in Chapter 2, his view may be classified as an example of the law-gospel type. Still, Barth's theology taken as a whole demonstrates both sides of the grammar of final primacy. While his treatment in *CD* I/2 emphasizes Christ as ever prior in the order of truth, his treatment in *CD* IV/3 shows the possibility of a variety of narratives moving toward him as end. Insistent first on the theological primacy of Christ, he is confident of the possibility that Christ might then come to be the final chapter of many stories into which he chooses to enter.[31]

Before concluding, one should, however, make note of one feature of Barth's treatment. Barth does not allow any room to privilege or separate the religions from ideologies or "worldviews" in general. All

30. *CD* IV/3, p. 133. Cf. William Christian, *The Doctrines of Religious Communities: A Philosophical Study* (New Haven: Yale University Press, 1987), pp. 212ff. There Christian uses Barth as an example of a "doctrine about other doctrines," derived from a governing doctrine.

31. We take it as confirmation of the argument of this essay that Eugene Rogers in his *Thomas Aquinas and Karl Barth: Sacred Doctrine and the Natural Knowledge of God* (Notre Dame: University of Notre Dame Press, 1995) observes that those two theologians have more agreement on "natural theology," which is to say, truths of other traditions, than is widely recognized. Final primacy would lead one to expect them to be different but noncontradictory, in keeping with the shared doctrinal framework. Rogers puts it this way: "For both Thomas and Barth, the Scripture witnesses, whether as the Word's secondary form, or as *scientia's* propositional aspect, to Jesus Christ, as the argument that trumps or absorbs all others. True human words from the secular sphere are true in their supposed and implied, if not always immediately apparent, correlation with the totality of Jesus Christ and his prophecy and therefore as they directly point to this or as this indirectly declares itself in them (*CD* IV/3, p. 123)" (p. 201). Rogers points out that the overarching unity of the *Summa Theologiae* provides just the larger Christological framework to show this coherence between Barth's ultimate goal and Thomas's. The strong difference between the two may be accounted for as different types, as well as emphases on different aspects of the rule.

are equally wrong in their presumption, but all are possible pools of helpful fragments, suggestions, and correspondences. Religions are no more or less sinful, or hopeful, by coming under the rubric called "religions." Religions, taken as entities, are problems, like all other such human systems and projects since Babel. At the same time *CD* IV/3 reminds us that religions as bundles of claims and practices might, in a variety of unpredictable cases, be useful to the Word. In keeping with this view, Barth has neither a sanguine nor a pessimistic view of those entities commonly called "religions" *qua* entities.

Rahner and the Religions

To consider Karl Rahner's theology of the religions is to interpret and assess the catchphrase with which he is associated: "anonymous Christianity." What exactly does he mean by this expression? The place to start is with the philosophical scaffold for Rahner's theology, the universal structures of the human person that condition the human reception of divine communication, in keeping with the Thomist maxim that such communication can only take place "according to the mode of the recipient." Such structures, which together constitute the transcendental dimension of human existence, are called "existentials." They include freedom, openness to mystery, etc. Human beings do not simply possess these, but rather such structures must come to expression concretely in human history. This is what he calls the "categorial" dimension of existence, though as essence and expression the two dimensions are inseparable.

The categorial and the transcendent might be taken to correspond to what in traditional Catholic theology are denoted "nature" and "grace," the latter understood to derive from the specific action of God. But at the heart of Rahner's vision is the belief that God has embraced the whole of human life, and that he as Creator has bestowed grace on it from within. Creation itself yearns for and moves toward God, so that it is his own even as he comes to it — one thinks of Augustine's famous opening to *The Confessions,* that our "hearts are restless until they rest in [God]." Rahner seeks so to conceive of the gracious act of God as to avoid the sort of conceptual separation of nature and grace that has been blamed for making the work of grace seem "extrinsic" and so for spawning an autonomous and atheistic modern world. The conceptual tool Rahner devises to give voice to this intimate relationship of nature and grace is the "supernatural existential." Already in human "nature" God's "grace" is at work so that humans themselves are beings open to the mystery of God, but never in such a way as to make that mystery become an innate and necessary extension of themselves. In other words, the only "nature" humans know is one already "graced," and so both "nature" and "grace" speak of God's free yet intimate work in all human persons.

When Rahner speaks of nonbelievers as "anonymous Christians," he is identifying the "anonymous" part of the claim with the transcendental dimension of the structure of the human person. For all human beings have this "non-thematic, non-objective" awareness, a built-in openness. But Rahner is asserting more than that all human beings *qua* human could be Christians. Since the transcendental and categorial go together, Christian faith as personal acceptance of God's acts in Israel and Christ is precisely the giving of specific content and definition to that encompassing reality which is assumed already "transcendentally." Since this transcendental "toward-ness" must have expression in the categorial realities, their adherence to other faiths expresses this openness toward and acceptance of the divine mystery. Rahner goes yet another step, citing Catholic teaching (for example in Vatican II)[32] that gives grounds for the belief that supernatural grace, already at work in nature, not only could be working in nonbelievers but in fact is actually so at work.

Let us step back for a moment and consider an underlying assumption of Rahner's argument as a whole. He emphasizes the inner dynamic of human history, "searching" or "questing" toward that absolute savior whose perfect expression is Jesus the Christ. In this regard, he asserts that Christ is the "final cause"[33] of all human history, both before and after Jesus' days on earth, for all human existence moves toward that decisive assumption by God to which Christians give the name "incarnation." It is the moment when God's gracious

32. On Vatican II's teaching on this subject, see Mikka Ruokanen, *The Catholic Doctrine of Non-Christian Religions according to the Second Vatican Council* (Leiden: Brill, 1992).

33. Karl Rahner, *Theological Investigations* (henceforth TI) (London: Darton, Longman & Todd, 1966-74), XII, p. 173.

turn toward humankind becomes "irreversible" in the life and death of Jesus.[34]

Rahner finds this inherent movement in history confirmed elsewhere as well. Several times he cites the Christians in Acts who receive the Holy Spirit prior to baptism, since they are already open to and moving toward baptism.[35] Likewise he cites the Patristic tradition that catechumens preparing for baptism, if martyred, have already received the grace of baptism by their longing (votum) for it. Along the same trajectory, in medieval scholastic tradition the contrition that precedes penance already brings its own spiritual benefit.[36] In the movement toward a goal humans are already defined by the goal. This cord of strands from the tradition support his claim about "anonymous Christianity."

Having rehearsed the major relevant features of Rahner's project, the frame into which the argument for "anonymous Christianity" should be placed, a summary of the argument itself can be offered.[37]

1. Christianity is the "true and lawful" religion intended by God for all humankind at all times.
2. The saving event of Christ came at a definite time and place, and likewise its proclamation has not been "chronologically simultaneous for all men, cultures, and spaces of history."[38]
3. Non-Christian religions are mixtures of elements resulting from human sin and divine grace.
4. "Until the moment when the gospel really enters into the historical situation of an individual," by grace that religion can be his or her lawful religion (Rahner's second thesis). Here Rahner argues that the role of the non-Christian religion may be seen as analogous to that of the Old Testament, whose religion was, as the prophets remind one, also just such an admixture.
5. Thus when Christianity does confront adherents of other religions,

---

34. *Foundations of Christian Faith in an Introduction of the Idea of Christianity* (New York: Seabury, 1978), p. 194.

35. TI, XII, p. 171.

36. TI, XII, pp. 166, 173.

37. See Joseph DiNoia's chapter on Rahner in David Ford's *The Modern Theologians: An Introduction to Christian Theology in the Twentieth Century* (Oxford: Blackwell, 1989).

38. TI, V, p. 119.

they stand before it as "anonymous Christians," that is to say, its proclamation does not come as something "absolutely unknown."[39]

6. When the status of the nonbeliever is understood in this way, the church's missionary task remains.

However, (a) now the church must be seen as the "historical vanguard" of a "hidden reality" lying outside of the church.[40] Furthermore, those who hear this explicit proclamation have a "still greater chance of salvation."[41]

But (b) the church will combine this proclamation with acceptance of the pluralism of its modern situation, hope for his or her non-Christian neighbor, and humility before them (since grace is not to be equated simply with church membership).[42]

Rahner's proposal about "anonymous Christianity" has been submitted to sustained criticism, and the attacks may be sorted into three interrelated groups. The first is the *particularity critique*. Other religious traditions are in themselves every bit as "particular," as "categorially" specific, as is Christianity, for each is made up of its own unique mix of religious practices, moral ideals, narratives, doctrinal claims, etc. What Rahner has done, albeit in the interest of appreciating and affirming these other traditions, is to give an account that understands these particular traditions in a general way (in his case, "transcendentally") so as to conceive of them as in a sense "on their way" to something particular, namely Christian faith.

The problems here are several. From the perspective of Christian theology itself, one can argue that such an argument renders essential elements of the Christian faith itself superfluous. According to Bruce Marshall, the transcendental argument for an "absolute savior" is inconsistent with the Christian insistence on, not a particular savior, but this particular, unsubstitutable Jesus of Nazareth as that savior.[43] Con-

---

39. TI, V, pp. 131-32.
40. Rahner himself lays the argument out in TI, V, pp. 115ff.
41. TI, V, p. 132.
42. TI, V, pp. 133ff.
43. Bruce Marshall, *Christology in Conflict: The Identity of the Savior in Rahner and Barth* (Oxford: Blackwell, 1987).

sistency with a general understanding of the human person and its yearning nature requires that one surrender this Christian obsession with the unsubstitutable finality of Jesus.[44] In other words, the center will not hold; the general and particular elements of the argument militate against one another, and one must fall off either in abandonment of such an argument in the interests of Christian particularity, or else in a more frank pluralism.

As part of this defense of the particularity of the other religions, we may turn to a "particularist" (in the sense we used the term in Chapter 1). Consider the following quotation from Joseph DiNoia: "Inclusivist positions [of which Rahner's is exemplary] imply that the affective and intellectual dispositions fostered by different religious communities in fact promote the attainment and enjoyment, not of the aims of life they commend to their members, but of the aims of life commended by the Christian community."[45] "Anonymous Christianity" elides the distinctive particularity of the other religions in question. This critique is only strengthened by Rahner's employment of organic metaphors, as when he insists that other religions have seeds of the final form of faith, Catholic Christianity. The particularist immediately objects that there is no reason at all to imagine that any specific religion is in its actual historical detail so "inclined."[46]

Perhaps the most trenchant expression of this critique, coming from within the fold of modern Catholic theology, may be found in Hans Urs von Balthasar's *The Moment of Christian Witness*. Von Balthasar claims that, by prominently employing his evolutionary schema and the "transcendental" method, and by including the particulars of Christ's life and death only "categorially" at the end of his argument, Rahner relativizes the difference between explicit and im-

---

44. So contends Maurice Wiles in *Christian Theology and Inter-Religious Dialogue* (London: SCM, 1992), p. 58.

45. Joseph DiNoia, *The Diversity of Religions: A Christian Perspective* (Washington, D.C.: Catholic University Press, 1992), p. 55.

46. To Rahner's credit, when he was criticized for his "anonymous Christianity" idea by means of the suggestion that one could equally call a Christian an "anonymous Buddhist," he heartily agreed. This response was consistent with William Christian's idea that religious communities should have doctrines, related to their own central doctrines, that make sense of alien claims.

plicit faith. As a result there remains ultimately no difference between the Christian and the non-Christian. The Rahnerian argument tends toward the erasure of this important line, especially when the idea is received and reused by others "in crude poster-like form." Even in the latter case Rahner must be held responsible, not only for what he says, but also for that toward which his argument drifts. This blurring in turn has other negative consequences in important areas of Christian life. As the crux of his argument von Balthasar claims ". . . the doctrine of an anonymous Christianity . . . involves a proportionate devaluation of the theology of the cross and, correspondingly, of the theology of Christian living in terms of the *Ernstfall.*"[47] For von Balthasar, Rahner's argument diminishes faith as a decision of enormous consequence that brings in its train a willingness to suffer with Christ and a sense of urgency in witnessing to him. All the sharp edges of doctrine and practice are sanded down by the idea of the anonymous Christian.

This leads naturally to the second critique to which the theory of the "anonymous Christian" is open, the *critique of mission*, which too has several forms. One worries that Rahner might be too successful, that he might so persuasively represent adherents of other religions as "anonymous Christians" as to cut the evangelistic nerve that stimulates Christian mission. If grace is already at work, why bother? Why not declare victory and stay home? An assumption in the critique of mission is that the practice of proclamation has a close connection to the unsurpassable finality of Jesus Christ, which Rahner as a faithful Roman Catholic theologian is committed to defend. Conversely, if there is no need for a Christian mission, then talk of finality and uniqueness will ring hollow. Rahner himself acknowledges the problem in the following quotation: "Admittedly any such theology of the possibility of a true and saving faith even in the 'pagan' must be so formulated as to avoid obscuring the importance of an explicit Christianity with its concomitant of gospel and church and the necessity of the missionary preaching of Christianity."[48]

In reply Rahner offers two rebuttals. First, he argues that mission

---

47. Hans Urs von Balthasar, *The Moment of Christian Witness*, trans Richard Beckley (San Francisco: Ignatius Press, 1994), p. 65.
48. "Observations on the Problem of an 'Anonymous Christian,'" TI, XIV, p. 286.

is constitutive of the church and intrinsic to its life.[49] This argument endeavors to survey a vista wider than the fate of individuals. Here Rahner reasserts his theme of the inner, Christ-ward dynamic of history, so that the church as God's instrument in history is blown by the Spirit in a mission-ward direction. It is only right that the church should proclaim so that the true nature of history and its goal might take categorial form. Rahner refers to this as the "incarnational" nature of the church,[50] that it is impelled to follow the flow of the Spirit in world history driving toward fulfillment and the expression of God's irreversible decision for the human being.

Though this argument is consistent with Rahner's theological vision as a whole, it seems to leave him dissatisfied. For if the church is fulfilling only what we might consider a symbolic or dramatic role, giving expression to an inner dynamic already at work, then one might easily suppose that the actual work of grace goes on in the religions in actual history separately from this churchly mission. So, after having distinguished his view of mission from the traditional emphasis on the salvation of the individual, he himself returns, in a second argument, as if by the back door, to the issue of individual salvation. Rahner speaks in his original argument, as well as in later elaborations, of a "still greater chance" of salvation that explicit, as opposed to implicit, faith offers.[51] The trouble of course is that Rahner's starting-point for the entire argument was God's universal saving will. To the extent that he emphasizes the "still greater chance," the critic might raise anew the very issue of fairness he intended to address.

Yet a third critique might be called *the critique of religious concreteness*. Rahner emphasizes that human life in its categorial nature has an inevitably "social and historical character," so that the salvation of the Hindu involves those social structures we call "Hinduism." Here

---

49. It may be observed here that most arguments for missionary motive in our century, which have sought to avoid the traditional idea of saving souls from perdition, have resorted to some kind of "intrinsic" argument: the church is "triune" hence "missionary," the church is a symbol of universality, hence must reach every people, etc.

50. TI, XII, p. 176.

51. A classic expression of this may be found in TI, XII, essay 9, but here we encounter one of the weaknesses of Rahner's approach. Rahner speaks of the nonbeliever "freely achieving the fullness of himself" (p. 157). The blurring of self-realization and divine transformation, in spite of Rahner's objections, is a real danger of his approach.

Rahner's careful distinction may seem an unsatisfactory half-measure to some. For he has included the social reality of Hinduism in his account of anonymous Hindu salvation, but he has not said that Hindus are actually saved *qua* Hindus. Here we should recall one of our initial observations, that Rahner begins with a concern for the possible salvation of the morally conscientious European atheist. Rahner's view of the salvific possibilities of the Hindu is consistent with his view of the atheist European. In fact Rahner has gone as far as the teaching of Vatican II goes.[52] But one can still press him on this point: To what extent is Hinduness or Muslimness involved in salvation? Rahner's position limps between two opinions.

It is at this point that other Catholic theologians, both before and after Rahner and sharing common assumptions with him, have pushed the argument further. In so doing they have broken the bounds of the grammar of Christian theologies of religions and become examples of inversion. The most prominent theologians to mention here are Hans Küng and Heinz Schlette. Both join in Rahner's affirmation of a graced humanity whose salvation can be worked out in the concrete reality of the religions. And both are willing to take, at first gingerly, a further step.[53] For both the religions are themselves the "ordinary" mode of salvation, while the "extraordinary" way, St. Paul's "more excellent way" (1 Cor. 12:31), is now the explicit path of following Christ in the church. Schlette can "ground" his argument in the Rahnerian claim that what tends toward salvation in the human being is found generally and universally in human nature. Küng in his earlier writings included the Rahnerian caveat of validity "until" the gospel comes, but proceeded to emphasize in later works the religions' validity in and of themselves.[54]

Note the subtle but real reversal at work here. The possibility of salvation for the adherent of the other religion is for Rahner an imagined extension of the reality of the grace of Christ expressed in the proclamation of the church. In an author such as Schlette it has become itself a "free-standing" and general principle. To be sure, even for

52. Mikka Ruokanen, *The Catholic Doctrine of Non-Christian Religions*.

53. Jacques Dupuis, *Toward a Christian Theology of Religious Pluralism* (Maryknoll, N.Y.: Orbis, 1997), p. 153.

54. See, e.g., *Christianity and the World Religions: Paths of Dialogue with Islam, Hinduism, and Buddhism* (London: Collins, 1987).

Rahner this possibility might in fact be statistically more likely (and so in a sense "normal"), but the case of salvation explicitly in Christ remains logically and theologically "normative."

At the climax of his argument Schlette makes the following assertion: "The non-Christian religions appear as normal ways of salvation which . . . God has expressly recognized."[55] In support of his reversal of "ordinary" and "extraordinary," Schlette draws a warrant from the phenomenology of religion, namely that all the religions offer a thematization of the experience of the holy. This general argument has now assumed center stage, relegating the "extraordinary" grace of Christianity to an honored, cameo role. Clearly, starting with premises like Rahner's, one can slide easily into a position resembling pluralism.[56]

If one considers the strengths of the Rahnerian argument for "anonymous Christianity," the criticisms cited, and its "fragility" with respect to its "development" by other theologians, what light can the rule of final primacy bring to bear on the question of "anonymous Christianity" as a whole? One should note first that in both the later developments of Rahnerians as well as in the popular accounts of the argument that sometimes accompany critiques, the careful qualifications, the "until," the "in spite of," and the "still greater" often drop out. If they were asked, one could imagine Rahner's critics wondering why Hinduism should be lawful only until the coming of the gospel, why it should be salvific only in spite of its "sinful elements," and why, if grace is truly there at work, there should be a still greater chance of salvation in the church.

But the rule of final primacy helps to highlight these qualifying elements and to show their appropriateness and helpfulness. Far from

55. Heinz Schlette, *Toward a Theology of Religions* (Freiburg: Herder, 1966), p. 102. Schlette does acknowledge that the religions may yet be "far from God and wrapped in darkness." But this concession has no force to affect his prevailing judgment. Later in his argument, on p. 104, he wants to claim that these "normal" ways of salvation are by "the grace of Jesus Christ too." Here we see the vestigial evidence of final primacy, though the claim does not manifest itself in the attempt to show how that grace is operative there. In other words he does not offer the requisite narrative, and in fact the whole thrust of the argument is now in the contrary direction.

56. See for example Küng's offering of general criteria to judge religions: the *humanum,* "authenticity," etc. The only specifically Christian note is the criterion of "the Spirit of Jesus," which in turn can be resolved readily into general ethical and existential terms. See Dupuis, *Toward a Christian Theology of Religious Pluralism,* p. 155.

being back-pedaling addenda, these qualifying elements ensure that the argument starts from explicit faith in Jesus Christ, and then works "back" to imagine how grace may be understood to be more widely at work among humankind. In other words, these qualifications are tools to make sure that, theologically, first things remain first. This is clearly what Rahner intends for the reader to do, since he works explicitly from a series of dogmatic assumptions, namely that Christianity is the "one, true lawful religion" and that the fullness of God's grace is found as one cleaves in faith to Jesus Christ. Such a perspective of the retrospective narrative helps us to realize that critics who see Rahner as disrespectfully imposing his reinterpretation on other traditions are wide of the mark. He is engaged in the normal activity of a Christian theologian, namely to create doctrines about other doctrines, based on the scriptural narrative, to make charitable sense of their neighbors and to come to terms with their claims. Far from aiming to aggrandize the church, Rahner's own stated intention for his "anonymous Christianity" is to dislodge the church from the position of privilege and to ensconce the triune God there: "It [his proposal] is a profound admission that God is greater than man and the Church."[57]

Such a reading of Rahner's construction is consonant with recent, creative efforts to reread his theological enterprise in a postliberal manner so as to reassess his supposed "foundationalist" commitment, and to see his theological anthropology as growing out of his Catholic doctrinal commitments. Russell Reno, in his analysis of Rahner's treatment of the central concepts of nature and grace, lays out the dilemma that one must avoid: on the one hand imagining God's creation as so distinct and self-sufficient that grace arrives as a stranger (extrinsicism), and on the other hand conflating the two and so obliging God to be gracious (intrinsicism). Reno points out that the governing factor here is the distinctively Christian understanding of divine love, growing out of a distinctively Christian understanding of the triune God himself. "One can and should define the essence of supernatural grace on its own terms. . . . It is correct to say that its essence is God's self-communication in love."[58] He discerns the elements of the Christian

---

57. TI, V, p. 134.

58. Russell Reno, *The Ordinary Transformed: Karl Rahner and the Christian Vision of Transcendence* (Grand Rapids: Eerdmans, 1995), p. 111.

grammar that are steering Rahner's anthropological vision. The moment of resolution when nature is graced so as to avoid the extrinsic and intrinsic pitfalls, the moment when "God's self-communication in love" is fully revealed, is the incarnation itself; Rahner's treatment of nature and grace in its own way moves back from the "final primacy" of the Christian doctrine of God.[59]

In this light, one can see that Rahner's proposal for an "anonymous Christianity" is consistent with the grammar of final primacy. Just the same, it has serious weaknesses that render it prone to the sort of misunderstandings and misuses we have seen. Let us consider two examples. First of all, Rahner's understanding of Christ as the "final cause" of grace at work in human history proves problematic. This kind of causality may be neither consistent with nor sufficient for Rahner's larger claims. For example, in his case for the abiding importance of mission, Rahner argues that, because history "presses toward its sacramental incarnation . . . it is not impossible for this effective sacramental symbol of this same grace to be itself a cause of the grace and not merely its outward expression."[60] At this key point Rahner seeks to ward off just the kind of weaker reading of Christ as "final cause" that might distort his construction. But he does so by invoking, not just Christ's final, but his efficient causality for grace.

The point can be illustrated by a look back at Rahner's Christology. He first means to show how an evolutionary view of human history helps to make sense of the concept of "God becoming human." But conversely, he also asserts that the ground and condition for God coming into the whole of universal human history, of Spirit realizing itself in matter, is the "the greater, more comprehensive, and more radical possibility of God expressing himself in the *Logos*" in Jesus Christ.[61] In other words, the incarnation "proper" is a condition for the wider sense of "incarnation" in human history. The entry of God into human history, including religious history, depends on the "*Logos* empty[ing] himself."[62] Unless one reduces the *Logos* to a principle with

59. See Nicholas Healy's "Indirect Methods in Theology: Karl Rahner as an Ad Hoc Apologist," *The Thomist* 56, no. 4 (1994): 613-33.

60. TI, XII, p. 171.

61. *Foundations of the Christian Faith: An Introduction to the Idea of Christianity* (New York: Seabury, 1978), p. 223.

62. *Foundations of the Christian Faith*, p. 224.

only symbolic expression in Christ, then one must say that this universal religious history requires Christ to do something. So, to maintain the proper relationship between the central dogmatic claim and the subsequent affirmation about human history, a tacit assumption about Christ's agency, which is to say, his efficient causality, and not only final causality, is packed into Rahner's argument. But he is not consistent in asserting such efficient causality for Christ in order to accommodate his wider vision of human history.

On a second, quite different front, one might criticize Rahner's view for the low profile given to the doctrine of sin. If it is as *Ursakrament* of God's universal grace that the church exists in the world, then strictly speaking the church *qua* church is not sinful, but only members themselves are as they fail to live lives consonant with this symbolic reality.[63] Such a view helps in the task of conceiving, by "retrospective narrative," other human histories, and particular other religious traditions, as adjunct to the church's life. But at the same time one weakens the sense in which the church, as sinful, exists in solidarity with adherents of other traditions, aspects of whose traditions are (as Rahner never fails to insist) invariably sinful. To the extent that one's categories render the sinfulness of the church plausible, to this extent possible offense in the "presumption" of a Christian construction about the beliefs and practices of other traditions is lessened. By this means the final primacy of Christ, and never of the church per se, is reinforced.

A phrase has meaning only as it is used in a theological context, which in turn assumes an array of background assumptions. In Rahner's case this background includes, as he frequently reminds us, the dogmatic inheritance of the Roman Catholic Church.[64] Only

63. On the church as "Ur-sacrament" see, e.g., TI, "the theology of symbol," IV, 5.9, p. 241.

64. With respect to Catholic dogma, a question remains whether or not Rahner's idea of the "anonymous Christian" is in fact "within the bounds." Mikka Ruokanen argues convincingly that *Nostra Aetate* of Vatican II conceives of non-Christian religions as "entities of value," but not as "vehicles of supernatural divine revelation or salvation" per se. Ruokanen goes on to mention that Rahner himself realized that the statement had not gone as far as he had, since he complained that the document did not envision a positive salvific role for the social and material elements of the religions. (This is indeed a neuralgic point, one that has been raised about Rahner himself, his intentions notwithstanding, and one that others such as Schlette have raised about him.) Even if his con-

against this background can this construction be evaluated. A charitable reading requires that one recall the strong Christological affirmations of that background, in the foreground of which, one may readily and sympathetically understand the concept of the anonymous Christian as a grammatical Christian theology of other religions, with a subtlety and power derived from his careful weaving together of scholastic, biblical, and modern philosophical themes.

Pannenberg and the Religions

Consideration of the theology of the religions in the German Lutheran systematic theologian Wolfhart Pannenberg will follow the same procedure, first to sketch his proposal about the religions, and to identify criticisms of it and so expose its weaknesses. Secondly, having placed the proposal in Pannenberg's theological project as a whole, the argument will seek to show how it conforms to the grammar of final primacy, and so how his proposal, properly understood, can be defended.

As with Barth and Rahner, so with Pannenberg, his understanding of the religions exemplifies his vision of theology as a whole. At the center of that vision is Pannenberg's theology of human history. If one wishes to understand the phenomenon of the diverse religions of the world and our human religiosity spawning them, look first, says Pannenberg, not at the Scripture (as with Barth), or at any supposed essence of the human person (as with Rahner), but rather at the actual collision and conflict between religions, at their rival claims to truth, at their competing demonstrations of explanatory power.

---

struction is outside the bounds of *Nostra Aetate,* Rahner's awareness of the background of doctrine and his intention to be a Catholic theologian are patent.

We might, however, venture a word in defense of Rahner contra Ruokanen's judgment, a word made possible by the perspective of final primacy. At the risk of splitting hairs, one might suggest that Rahner is not finding salvific or revelatory status for the religions absolutely and in themselves (that is what we have perceived Schlette to be encroaching on). Rather, he has understood them to be revelatory and salvific insofar as they are prior to, tending toward, and preparing for the Christian gospel. Final primacy shows us that it is simply insufficient to ask if the religions in their concreteness do or do not have salvific power — one must go on to ask in what sort of argument, with what sort of larger intent is this question asked.

For Pannenberg there are distinct advantages in focusing on history. An awareness of historical change and relativity characterizes modernity, and it is to the modern "cultured despiser" of Christianity that the theologian must speak.[65] There is a close relationship between history and the Christian faith itself, which grew out of Israel's confession of Yahweh as the God who acts in history. Awareness of ongoing historical flux is also closely related to openness to the future. These same themes of history, futurity, and the roots of modernity will be crucial to Pannenberg's decision to start with the actual interactions of religions in history.

The classic, early essay in which Pannenberg's vision of the historical conflict of the religions is laid out is "Toward a Theology of the History of Religions."[66] There Pannenberg claims that such a theology will present itself objectively, as one considers the history itself (as opposed to needing the bulwark of confessional presuppositions). He begins by assuming that each religion is a system endeavoring to explain the world in its entirety. Within each religion is some fulcrum, some concept or principle possessing the power to draw all the other elements of the system into a whole. (Pannenberg calls this the religion's *"Integrationskraft."*) In most cases the concept of God or the gods serves this function, but other ideas could so serve as well.

Matters become truly interesting when these systems collide with one another. They then call one another into question: Which system can better explain reality as a whole? *Die Wahrheitsfrage,* "the question of truth," is raised, and over time the explanatory powers of the competing systems are tested. An important feature furnishing explanatory power to a particular religion is its power to assimilate elements of its competitors into its own view, and to this Pannenberg applies the term "syncretism," purged here of its frequent negative connotations.

Different competing religions exert themselves to assimilate new claims, and by so doing they seek to adjust to an open, changing religious scene. But many religions, especially archaic local traditions, are ill suited to this task. For typically they make sense of the world by re-

---

65. Ironically see Reinhard Hütter, review of *Systematic Theology,* in *Modern Theology* 9, no. 1 (January 1993).

66. The argument is also developed in the later *Theology and the Philosophy of Science* (Philadelphia: Westminster, 1976) and finally reappears in Volume I of Pannenberg's *Systematic Theology* (Grand Rapids: Eerdmans, 1991). Henceforth cited as ST.

ferring things back to archetypes in the past, and so imagine reality to be static. As a result, the future is precisely that which they are not conscious of, and historical change takes place "behind their backs."[67] Like King Canute they order back the tide of historical consciousness, since the ongoing history of religious contact, accelerated in our own time, works toward the "progressive religious integration of humankind."[68] Increasingly all the religions "play on the same field," and the one that best thrives in this atmosphere of contact and acts most dynamically as the element of "ferment" will prevail.

In such a competitive field, what would be the most potent virtue a religion could possess? Surely it would be a clear sense of its own historical provisionality. Such a religion would most decisively embrace the futurity of the revelation of God, and would most wholeheartedly open itself to questioning and change. Such a religion would find itself swimming with the tide, since the field of competition between the religions would become in a sense coterminous with its own pursuit of truth. It should come as no surprise that Pannenberg finds in Christianity, centered on the eschatological revelation of God guaranteed in the resurrection of Jesus, just such a religion of history and the future designed to thrive and prevail in the contest of religions.

One can better understand the subtlety of Pannenberg's argument if one considers the intellectual predecessors from whom he has borrowed, and the manner in which he has emended their ideas. Friedrich Schleiermacher understood the basis of religion to be the experience of the *Universum*, of the whole *(Ganzheit)* of reality. For Schleiermacher the apprehension of this totality is initially in feeling, and so is prior to our ability to express it in words.[69] The process of giving expression to feeling bears fruit in the plurality of religions, which Schleiermacher is, in pioneering fashion, able to view in a positive manner.[70] What Schleiermacher's account lacks is a positive role for the actual historical interaction of the religions, and specifically

67. "Toward a Theology of the History of Religions," in *Basic Questions in Theology,* vol. 2 (Philadelphia: Westminster, 1971), pp. 109, 115.

68. "Toward a Theology of the History of Religions," p. 95.

69. See Schleiermacher, *On Religion* (New York: Harper & Row, 1958), speech 2.

70. See Ernst Troeltsch, "The Absoluteness of Christianity and the History of Religions," in *Christian Thought: Its History and Application,* ed. Friedrich von Hülge (Westport, Conn.: Hyperion, 1979), p. 173.

their contention over differing claims to truth. Pannenberg is able to enrich Schleiermacher's insight into religion as *Ganzheit* with just these elements.

This leads naturally to the second major source for Pannenberg's case, the "absolute religion" tradition in nineteenth-century German theology referred to in our opening chapter. Here Pannenberg's primary conversation partner is Ernst Troeltsch, with whom his essay shares important features: the insistence on seeing Christianity as a "religion among the religions" and its consequent exposure to the challenge of historical relativism.[71] Troeltsch represents both the culmination and the foundering of the absolute-religion line of thought. For Troeltsch the absolute-religion argument proved faulty, since it artificially imposed a definition of religion on the profuse diversity of history, and then proceeded to find the perfect example of its own presupposition. In so doing it imposed a premature closure on history, since history remains open and "absolute truth belongs to the future." Still, Christianity deserves its due, since its consciousness of history has made possible this perception of a convergent field of conflicting claims of the religions in which humanity moves continually toward closer approximations of truth. In all this Pannenberg's kinship to Troeltsch should be clear.

Remarkably, Pannenberg at once affirms Troeltsch's rejection of the argument for absolute religion, and offers an emended "absolute" argument himself. How is this possible? Pannenberg redefines the religious essence as those very features that call the positing of a religious a priori into doubt: questionability, historicity, futurity. Far from representing a premature closure, Pannenberg's "absolute religion" is the very one that takes the open process between the religions into itself, so that its very lack of a moment of final resolution summarizes its perfection. In such a religion the final revelation of God himself would have to reside in the open process of testing. Thus Pannenberg, turning the usual critiques of absoluteness on their head, has proceeded to refashion them into a new absoluteness argument.

This brings us to the third intellectual derivation for Pannenberg's theology of the history of religions, the philosophical science of Karl Popper. Here we must focus on the crucial theme of conflict so promi-

---

71. See "The Absoluteness of Christianity," p. 115.

nent in Pannenberg's proposal. The divergent truth claims of the religions are tested in an ongoing process as religions contest with one another. Pannenberg applies to the field of religions and their claims the central principle of science, the testing of rival hypotheses. Among the religions, as with scientific theories, verification may be impossible, but ongoing falsification is attainable.[72]

There is another reason for the prominence of the theme of conflict. Conflict as testing takes place in light of the denial of religious truth presented by atheism. The real claim to truth, in the modern era, is connected to the rediscovery of the necessary link between the emergence of the historical struggle for a single religious truth and the emergence of monotheism itself. Breakthrough-alienation-rediscovery: the Hegelian overtones are unmistakable. This fourth influence is only confirmed when the testing of truth takes place against a horizon of the totality of meaning possible only at the end of time.[73] While the Hegelian claim to final knowledge is overturned by this futurist note, the idea of a final state, in relation to totality, confirms the Hegelian pattern of thought.

Though the essay "Toward a Theology of the History of Religions" was an early work, the repetition of this argument in essentially the same form, at the outset of his magisterial *Systematic Theology*, establishes its enduring importance for Pannenberg. The problems with the argument are, however, not hard to identify. The first concerns the meaning of the word "power" *(Macht)*. To assume that a religion prevails because of superior explanatory power is to make some considerable assumptions. Is it not possible that a religion might thrive because it offers encouraging lies to its followers? Or that true claims might fall victim to sheer military force? While Pannenberg is surely right that an unabashed reductionism in terms of power will not do, its opposite seems equally implausible, and lends itself to a dubious kind of intellectual Darwinism.

This leads to a second criticism, that Pannenberg's examples are too selective, coming as they do mostly from the history of Israel and her neighbors (the evolution of Egyptian religion, the struggle with Baal, the aftermath of the Babylonian Exile). Could it not be that this

---

72. *Theology and the Philosophy of Science* (Philadelphia: Westminster, 1996), pp. 62ff.
73. Pannenberg's teacher, Karl Löwith, is an example of this influence.

narrow band of examples skews the results in favor of the victory of the Christian claim? Isn't the result predetermined, so that the line of thought moves inevitably toward a focus on the power of explanation not between religions, but rather within the religion of Israel itself, i.e., in its assimilation of its own prophetic witness?

Pannenberg would again respond that this selectivity is justified, since this is not any swatch of history, but rather that part of history in which history itself came to consciousness. Its emergence took place, not coincidentally, together with the emergence of monotheism. But the critic might respond that Pannenberg falls prey to the genetic fallacy, since the condition of an idea's birth dictates neither its interpretation nor its truth. Many who have traced the progress of historical consciousness have admitted no such advantage for the cause of monotheism, as Pannenberg well knows.[74]

Finally, one might offer the counterargument that even a cursory survey of the history of religions offers little evidence of progressive convergence into a single field of contestation. On the contrary history attests a fissiparous process. Otherwise why would the variety of sects within each religion be so hostilely set against one another, with no evidence of rapprochement among the major religions on the horizon? Once again one suspects that the convergence Pannenberg speaks of takes place where certain Christian assumptions about philosophy and historical research are found.

At this point a doubt of a different sort suggests itself: Even if this argument were valid, would this be good news for the cause of Christian theology, or would it represent a Pyrrhic victory? Consider more closely that religion which Pannenberg claims would be in ready position to prevail in the unified field of interreligious contestation in the present. The most evolved of religions is the one open to the future, aware of its own historicity, able to transform itself in the light of challenges, identifying revelation with the provisional resolutions of ongoing historical conflicts over truth. Now think back to the preceding chapter, and its description of pluralism as traditional Christianity's *Döppelgänger*. Might not pluralism make a strong claim to be this victorious religion? Doesn't John Cobb argue for just such an open and provisional process for Christianity, and Gordon Kaufman for just such an

74. See ST, I, p. 168.

awareness of history, and John Hick for just such a unified field of adjudication, and Wilfred Cantwell Smith for this weaker sense of the particular revelations of the particular religions? In other words, pluralistically revisionist Christianity, for which Pannenberg has no use due to its abandonment of traditional doctrinal claims, itself has a strong stake in futurity and historicity. Pannenberg would retort that pluralism has abandoned the conflict over truth. And the pluralists would reply in turn that they are perfectly happy with a contest over truth, so long as it is conducted on a single, level, interreligious field of dialogue. The profound ambiguity of the criteria of Pannenberg's argument comes clear.

How then might one read Pannenberg so as to redeem his view of the religions, and, along the way, affirm the coherence of his theological project? Since the argument for a theology of the history of the religions was transposed into the opening section of his *Systematic Theology*, one finds there the clue. Arguments take on new significance in new theological niches: What does this seemingly identical argument come to mean in its new home in the larger systematic work?

To answer this question, one needs to back up and make a more general observation about the overarching structure of Pannenberg's project. His great concern is apologetic, namely that when Christianity emphasizes its own confessional underpinnings, it plays into the hands of those who see it only as illusion or wish, and even some Christians who would base their faith only in subjective value-choice. Christianity's credibility, says Pannenberg, depends on more solid underpinnings in the understanding of the world at large (hence the major emphasis on theology as science). A result of this starting-point is that Pannenberg's own accounts of his method tend to overplay the strictly rational, historical, scientific nature of the enterprise. One may observe this tendency in his insistence on a "Christology from below," on the demonstrability of the resurrection, on a foundation for theological argument in anthropology,[75] etc.

But the manner in which Pannenberg actually works (behind his own back, as it were) is more complex and dialectical. For Pannenberg's method actually involves a twofold movement, simultaneously

---

75. A particularly clear example may be found in *Anthropology in Theological Perspective* (Philadelphia: Westminster, 1985), p. 15, on anthropology as a "foundation."

from below and from above, which converges in a tension-laden unity around the particular term or issue at hand. One might compare his method to a drawing of Escher, a single pattern that may be seen at once from two angles, rendering two different patterns.

Take for instance the crucial concept "the future" — what does Pannenberg actually mean by it? Beginning on the anthropological side, Pannenberg shows, with the help of the discipline of hermeneutics,[76] how all thought drives toward future understanding, against an implied horizon of eventual, total comprehension. But at the same time he uses the term, with respect to God, "from above," in a different way. In this second movement, the triune God, standing at the end of history, emerges from the future into history. For God "the future" is that reign God already has which need not squelch real human freedom in history.

God's ability at the same time to rule the future and to submit himself to history obviously distinguishes him from human beings. This difference constitutes the central analogy by which talk about God is distinguished from talk about us humans (along the lines of Aquinas's *analogia entis*, for example). The human use of "future" reaches up, as it were, toward the divine, so that humans can gain an inkling of what talk about God means, and the triune God reaches down in self-emptying condescension so as to open himself to the human experience of futurity, abandonment, and risk in the incarnation. In other words, in Pannenberg's *analogia futuri*, these two distinct senses meet and illumine one another, though a tension remains between them.

This same convergent, tension-filled, twofold pattern characterizes virtually every area of Pannenberg's endeavor. As a result, Pannenberg's claims for his apologetic project are valid, for the anthropological movement of his theology has its own discreet integrity. The insistence on the priority of scientific investigation amounts to a formal privileging of the movement from the human side. At the same time the "doxological"[77] movement "from above" is materially prior. The credibility of the project as a whole depends (though Pannenberg

76. See, e.g., *Theology and the Philosophy of Science* (Philadelphia: Westminster, 1976).
77. See *Basic Questions in Theology,* vol. 1, on "Analogy and Doxology," ch. 3, "Hermeneutic: A Methodology for Understanding Meaning."

might not admit it) on the sense of coherence rendered by the movements striking against one another's flint.

What does this dialectical subtlety of method mean for Pannenberg's theology of religions?[78] The argument for a theology of the history of the religions constitutes the anthropological movement in this twofold pattern. It suffices that it should suggest the strength of the Christian claim, however ambiguously, and that it point the reader in the direction of important terms like "history," "conflict," and "future," whose meaning will only be redeemed with the second movement.

At this point one needs to take note of another vein of discourse about the religions in *Systematic Theology*. The religions, after their initial part, never again occupy center stage in the work. Pannenberg makes it clear that individual adherents of the religions may be saved, though by the grace of Jesus Christ whom they do not know.[79] The problem of making sense of the religions themselves as systems of meaning remains. So Pannenberg moves to the perspective of the God who is coming into the world from the eschaton. Pannenberg proceeds to unwind his trinitarian vision backwards from the final consummation into the present in which those religions may be found in conflict and ambiguity

The place to begin is with the end.[80] At the consummation God will reign in such a way as not to obliterate the diversity of creation, but rather to embrace it. The God of Israel will there stand in no "mere opposition to the plurality of other gods"[81] but will raise ("sublate" in

---

78. Steffen Lössel's more recent "Wolfhart Pannenberg's Response to the Challenge of Religious Pluralism: The Anticipation of Divine Absoluteness?" *Journal of Ecumenical Studies* 34, no. 4 (Fall 1997): 499-519, confirms a number of the conclusions of my dissertation: the problem of the standard between the religions being Jesus' "love of neighbor" (rather than Jesus himself), his reliance on the ancient example of Israel and its neighbors, the assumption of a "religious Darwinism," and the failure to take into account nonrational factors. Thus Lössel's argument, as far as it goes, supports my own. However, he limits himself to what this essay has called the "anthropological movement," and fails to take into account the second, "doxological" movement, which offers another meaning to terms like "End" and "future."

79. *An Introduction to Systematic Theology* (Grand Rapids: Eerdmans, 1991), p. 54.

80. Cf. Robert Jenson's advice in "Jesus in the Trinity: Wolfhart Pannenberg's Christology and Doctrine of the Trinity," in *The Theology of Wolfhart Pannenberg: Twelve American Critiques*, ed. Carl Braaten and Philip Clayton (Minneapolis: Augsburg, 1988), p. 188.

81. ST, I, p. 445.

Hegelian terms) that opposition into a higher unity of reconciled creation. For the church this will be the fulfillment *(Vollendung)* of their submission to the divine Lordship, while for the rest of humanity, including the religions, this rule will be new.[82] Both will also experience the *Reinungsfeuer* ("purifying fire") who is Christ himself as Judge.[83] Pannenberg's focus is not on speculation about how matters will be sorted out for adherents of the religions, but rather on Christ the coming One, from whose glorified, wounded, world-inclusive Body the consummating Spirit will stream.[84]

In the doxological movement of Pannenberg's thought, the religions can only be evaluated as one looks "back" into the present from this strongly Christocentric vision of the consummation of the world. The consummating goal of creation ought not to interfere with the necessity of proclaiming the gospel to the religions, nor to diminish their need to accept its news. Pannenberg puts the matter in typically Lutheran terms of certainty of salvation: "Communion with Jesus Christ through faith and baptism is the only way to present certainty of final salvation."[85] How is this claim consistent with the more expansive vision of the End we have sketched? The consistent element is Christ himself, who is at the center both of the future consummation and the present proclamation. A mode of salvation in the present other than Christ, e.g., the religions, would amount to works righteousness.[86] As the servant of the triune God coming "back" into history, the church must collide with and confront the religions and their claims, and so conflict and debate necessarily result.

---

82. Pannenberg has been critical of proposals about a prospective salvation (see, e g , his "Religious Pluralism and Conflicting Truth-Claims: The Problem of a Theology of World Religions," in *Christian Uniqueness Reconsidered: The Myth of a Pluralistic Theology of Religions*, ed. Gavin D'Costa (Maryknoll, N.Y.: Orbis, 1990), though it is helpful to bear in mind that for him all salvation is in a sense prospective.

83. ST, III, 15.4.a, also p. 665. Pannenberg makes use here of the tradition about purgatory though he is aware of its dangers, especially as it attributes the purification to an "intermediate state."

84. ST, III, p. 677.

85. "Religion und religionen. Theologische Erwagungen zu den Principien eines Dialogs mit den Weltreligionen," in Andreas Bsteh, ed., *Dialog aus der Mitte christlicher Theologies* (Mödlig: St. Gabriel, 1987).

86. "The Religions from the Perspective of Christian Theology," *Modern Theology* 9, no. 3 (July 1993): 293-94.

Beginning with the purgative fulfillment of the End, and moving through the proclamatory collision of the present, Pannenberg's understanding of the religions comes finally to the question of the status of the religions themselves as "intimations" or "broken echoes" of God's revelation. The goal of the Creator is to be worshiped freely by his diversely united creation, and so the religions play a positive role as the first signs of that relationship, however broken and limited may be their representation of it. Their very plurality is an anticipation of the reconciled diversity of creation as an image of the triune God.[87]

Pannenberg's account of the religions bears similarities to the *Logos*-type, where one also finds the idea of vestiges, traces, or seeds of the full truth. But the crucial element for Pannenberg is the order of the accounts, the way in which the imperative of the present follows from the vision of the future. The background for this ordering is the view of salvation history in eschatological perspective central to his entire project.

For present purposes Pannenberg's construction represents a classic example of the rule of final primacy. Even in the present the religions are "before" the full truth of the consummation, and so "before" its acceptance in the moment of proclamation and response. Their value presumes the temporally structured backbone to his thought. Pannenberg's claims about the religions in his "doxological" mode are all highly traditional, their eschatological framework more peculiar to him, but its deeper structure conforms to Christian theology's traditional grammar.

The lingering question is how to evaluate the "theology of the history of religions" with which this section began. Here one finds the same dialectical relationship between the perspectives of the consummation and the present as throughout all of Pannenberg's work. Arguments "from history alone" or arguments "founded in science" point one's attention to key themes like "history" and "the future" which are treated, a second time, in a more distinctly Christian fashion. Thus the argument for a "theology of the history of religions" cannot stand alone, and does not amount to basing a theology of religions on objective and generally available data. It assumes a rich background of theological assumptions derived from Pannenberg's project as a

---

87. This argument will be considered in greater detail in the next chapter.

whole, and so a more modest claim for the history-of-religions argument proper is required.

Such a reevaluation becomes more urgent when one realizes that, in one crucial respect, the theology of the history of religions and the theology of the consummation come into actual conflict. Not surprisingly (in light of final primacy), the pressure point is the uniquely decisive importance of the particular person, Jesus Christ, in the two respective moments in Pannenberg's theology. It has already been shown how pluralism could make a claim to be the religion that would prevail in the conflict of religions. But how does this inconsistency relate to the specific person of Jesus Christ?

Much like the "Protestant principle" of Paul Tillich,[88] Jesus is, in Pannenberg's theology of the history of religions, "the revealer of the infinite God only because he in his person points the way to the coming reign of God."[89] But this takes the proper form of "breaking up existing religious forms of life," and may be contrasted to "dogmatic finitizations" to which Christianity has fallen victim.[90] So Jesus, as he is accessible to the scholar of the history of religions, against the horizon of the concept of the future, initiates a new way to conceive of God. Remembering him becomes the occasion for opening oneself further to the future. Jesus spurs a breakthrough in religious consciousness, and remains significant as his memory may be associated with the continuous exercise of that consciousness.[91] In short, what is decisively new and distinctive about this breakthrough can be described in terms of religious consciousness and so without necessary reference to the person of Jesus himself. He serves as a means to describe the origin of the insight.

While in the theology of the history of religions, the specific person of Jesus is incidental to an account of salvation, in the theology of the consummation, his person is central, since the crucified and glori-

---

88. Tillich in fact is the theologian whose later writings on the religions offered a starting-point for Pannenberg's theology of the history of the religions. See *Basic Questions in Theology,* vol. 2, pp. 65ff.

89. *Basic Questions in Theology,* vol. 2, p. 117.

90. *Basic Questions in Theology,* vol. 2, p. 114.

91. In this regard Pannenberg is careful to disassociate this stage of consciousness from any relationship to Christian theology, and thereby its dogmatic commitments to the person of Jesus Christ. See *Basic Questions in Theology,* vol. 2, p. 117.

fied Jesus Christ is identified with the End itself.[92] On this point the difference could hardly be sharper — can Pannenberg have it both ways? Once more the key distinction offered by Bruce Marshall on Christology, already cited in the analysis of Rahner, can do service.[93] Marshall emphasizes the incompatibility of accounts based on general philosophical categories (e.g., Plato on the nature of Being) with accounts that make a particular individual central (e.g., a novel). Particular description can be neither "logically necessary" nor "materially decisive" for the former; such an exclusion is entailed in the very notion of a general philosophical account. And furthermore, if this is so, then one cannot import such a particular account after the fact and render it necessary or decisive. In other words, one could offer a particular person Sue or John as an example, but one could not make the details of this Sue necessary or decisive to the category in question.

If we bring this distinction about particular identity to bear, a gulf is fixed between the two Pannenbergian arguments in question. His enduring commitment to the ultimate theological significance of the person of Jesus Christ (like Rahner's)[94] thus comes into conflict with his claims for his theology of the history of religions. The very coherence of his method as a whole, the feasibility of its balancing act between "anthropological" and "doxological" movements, hinges on this question of the unique importance of Jesus.

How then can one so read Pannenberg as to preserve coherence between these movements? How can one order these two arguments about the religions, and thus maintain the proper validity of each? The rule for a Christian grammar of the claims of the religions offers just such a way to "save the appearances." First of all take the two argu-

92. Origen speaks of Christ for example as *autobasileia*. See Karl Ratzinger's *Eschatology: Death and Eternal Life*, vol. 9 of *Dogmatic Theology* (Washington, D.C.: Catholic University Press, 1988).

93. See *Christology in Conflict: The Identity of a Saviour in Rahner and Barth* (Oxford: Blackwell, 1987). He appeals particularly to the work of Strawson.

94. Pannenberg would argue that the comparison with Rahner is unfair, since his method differs from Rahner's. While this is true, the difference in question does not affect the criticism at issue here. Pannenberg changes the material content from which he commences in his apologetic move from human subjectivity to the field of human history as a whole. But the logical distinction between accounts for which particular description is decisive and those for which it is not remains unaffected. On the question at hand Pannenberg and Rahner are close relatives.

ments together, and start with the argument from the consummation. Understand it as an assertion of the final primacy of Jesus Christ. Then understand the theology of the history of the religions as a construction dealing with historical phenomena that are prior chronologically (in some cases), but subsequent in theological and logical senses. The argument from the history of religions serves to assimilate and affirm much of the data of alien traditions in accordance with final primacy. As an apologetic argument it shows how the narrative moves from the conflictual interreligious "before" to the changed situation after Christ. Thus one can read the theology of the history of the religions in a manner subordinated to the later, systematic construction. The weighting of the latter argument, and a reading of the former, apologetic proposal in the latter's light, preserves coherence.

Such a "grammatical" reading does not erase the distinctive contribution of Pannenberg's argument, namely that he focuses not on this religion or that, but rather on the whole field of the religions throughout history, a field full of provisionality and contestation. The field is thus seen as a single "alien tradition," but without flattening its real differences and disagreements. This strength of his proposal is in no way endangered by a ruled attempt to bring it into consistent relation to the rest of Pannenberg's theological vision.

Conclusion

No authors in twentieth-century systematic theology have had a more prominent approach to the religions than Karl Barth, Karl Rahner, and Wolfhart Pannenberg. Yet the theory of each has come in for strong criticism. Each theory can be understood as coherent. But the "condition for the possibility" of overcoming those criticisms and finding coherence is the rule of final primacy.

Two of the authors considered in this chapter, Karl Barth and Wolfhart Pannenberg, both self-consciously identified with the Reformation tradition, present in many ways a picture of contrasts. Barth rejects the very nineteenth-century predecessors, Schleiermacher and Troeltsch, whom Pannenberg employs in order to transcend them. In rejecting what he calls "immunization strategies" that seek to avoid the obligation to intelligibility in the university and society at large,

Pannenberg specifically distances himself from Barth. To Pannenberg, Barth has not faced the "crisis of the Scriptural principle," while for Barth, Pannenberg represents just the sort of grandiose, world-historical constructions that led modern European theology to no good.

As one might expect, Barth and Pannenberg begin their consideration in diametrically opposite places, on the one hand in the "a priori" dogmatic contrast between religion and revelation, and on the other in the general consideration of the historical data of the encounters of religions. Yet, when the day is done, what they want to say about the religions bear strong similarities. At the center both want to assert the irreplaceable importance of the proclamation of the gospel, and the decisive role of Jesus' person in that proclamation. Both then want to offer an embracing vision of salvation at the End, and both acknowledge how the religions may anticipate that consummation in a fragmentary way, either as "lights" (Barth) or as "traces" (Pannenberg). For all their initial differences, this convergence may be traced back to their common adherence, in the deeper grammar of their respective theologies, to final primacy. In the light of this rule, tensions or seeming points of incoherence engendered by the question of the religions in the systematic project of each can be resolved.

Karl Rahner shares that same modern German theological tradition, though his reflection is obviously also built on the Catholic dogmatic tradition. From the store of the latter he reaches for concepts unavailable to his Protestant colleagues, in particular the concept of implicit faith. But he shares with Pannenberg a commitment to "fundamental" theology. Though his proposal about anonymous Christianity is uniquely his own, its effect is similar to Barth's and Pannenberg's views, especially as it is considered by the gauge of final primacy. For Rahner too the religions' truths are prior and partial, whose validity can only be understood "until" and even "in spite of," whose adherents have a lesser chance of being saved. Each expresses, in his own way, the ruled logic of "before" and "after."

From the perspective of these common commitments, one can in turn see that each theologian brings a particular aspect of the tradition into relief. Barth, by placing the question of the decisiveness of Jesus so early in his system, and by expressing the contrast with human religious experience so starkly as *Unglaube*, trumpets the "discontinuous"

Christocentrism of the rule. Both Pannenberg's and Rahner's work highlights the narrative continuity of the rule, the way that the truths and practices of the religions may be shown to move toward Christ. Each identifies a different aspect of human religiosity that makes the retrospective and inclusive narrative possible. Rahner, a theologian of the *imago Dei,* emphasizes our innermost orientation toward God. Pannenberg, for his part, offers a complementary emphasis on the "restlessness" of hearts that would rest in God. By the very collision of religious claims, humans are driven on toward the gospel. Both emphases offer warrants for the hope that underlies the activity of forming retrospective narratives of charity and inclusion itself, at the same time that they preserve the primacy of Christ.

4 Final Primacy and the Religions in the Economy of Salvation

Testing Final Primacy among Contemporary Trinitarian Theologies of the Religions

The preceding chapter considered several of the greatest systematic theologians of the twentieth century, with special reference to their theologies of other religions, and it suggested that seeming tensions in their constructions could be resolved when they were considered in light of the grammar of final primacy. This chapter aims, once more, to consider the contemporary systematic theological scene with the question of the religions in mind. But the approach in this chapter will be different, for now it will consider a single strategy, a single tack, which a variety of theologians have pursued to make Christian sense of the religions. More specifically, it will analyze attempts to bring modern construals of the doctrine of the Trinity to bear on the interpretation of the diversity of religious traditions.

As it turns out, the theologians already considered, Barth, Rahner, and Pannenberg,[1] are themselves key figures in the renaissance of interest and creativity in reflection on the locus of the Trinity. The reason

1. For Barth, see *Church Dogmatics* I/1; for Rahner, see *The Trinity* (New York: Seabury, 1974); for Pannenberg, see *Systematic Theology* (Grand Rapids: Eerdmans, 1991), vol. 1, *passim*.

for their interest in the Trinity, and for its rippling effect among numerous others, is not hard to find. Common to the variety of new proposals in contemporary trinitarian theology is what one might call a "logic of retrieval," that is, a desire to meet external challenges from within, by a return to the resources of the tradition itself. In the case of the Trinity and the religions, recent theologians who follow in the footsteps of the generation of Rahner and Barth are turning their attention to a locus once thought quintessentially unproductive. The Athanasian Creed declares stringently of the Trinity that "this is the catholic faith, unless which a person believe, he cannot be saved. . . ." To make this doctrine the very basis of an expanded appreciation of other traditions seems at the outset daring, to say the least.

Yet one may at the same time observe how prima facie well-suited to this task the doctrine of the Trinity might also appear to be. If at the heart of all projects of retrieval lies the need to balance preservation of the integrity of Christian identity with greater breadth of intellectual engagement, then the doctrine of the Trinity seems uniquely apt. If one would maintain a concentration on unique Christian claims while expansively finding truths in new and unexpected places, the doctrine of the one God who is Father, Son, and Spirit seems promising.

But matters may not be as simple as they seem, for one must be ready to see how the same claim, made in different contexts, actually says different things. For example, David Kelsey has pointed out how, behind varied modern systematic theologies lie differing central visions that serve to arrange and control the assorted claims that are made. Thus, when Paul Tillich says "the authority of Scripture" he means something different than does Karl Barth or Benjamin Warfield.[2] In the same way, one may reasonably suspect that appeals to the doctrine of the Trinity in contemporary theological arguments, for example as they involve assessment of the place of the religions, subserve different central visions in different systematic projects. How then is one to determine what an appeal to "Trinity" really means?

The question can be put this way: What counts as an appropriate understanding of the Trinity? It will not do simply to use the formulae of the post-Nicene era as a ruler for the expressions of contemporary theologians. One must take account, conversely, of the possibility of

---

2. *The Uses of Scripture in Recent Theology* (Philadelphia: Fortress, 1975).

saying the same thing in new conceptual terms. Is a particular theologian's construction saying the same thing in a new way, or saying something essentially different? Only then can one turn to the question of how the doctrine is applied to the question of the status of other traditions.

Addressing these prolegomenal questions requires the following premises. It will be assumed, first, that the orthodox, Nicene understanding of the Trinity is authoritative with respect to what it says, though not necessarily with respect to how the Creed says it, i.e., one could use different words with the same orthodox intent. By what standard then will one gauge that a new expression has wandered out of bounds of the normative Christian doctrinal identity? Here the conclusion of Claude Welch's classic analysis of modern trinitarianism is useful. Welch asserts that the doctrine of the Trinity is indeed the "supreme doctrine" in that it follows "directly and [as] an immediate explication of the confession that God has revealed himself to us in Jesus Christ"[3] (given classic voice in the *homoousion* of the Nicene formula). To affirm the *homoousion* is in short to say that God truly is as he there reveals himself, and this bears directly on the doctrine of the Trinity's intent.

The implication here is that the affirmations about the Trinity and Christology stand in the closest relation one to another; they imply one another, and guard the same mystery of "God in Christ" in answer to different challenges. This insight in turn determines what Christians mean by referring to God as creator, redeemer, sanctifier, etc. If these conjoined doctrines are at the heart of the Christian faith, then metaphysical claims may follow on theological trinitarianism, but only as implications and extensions of the doctrine of the Trinity, i.e., in such a way that they do not replace the doctrine itself.

The force of Welch's point, and its importance for the present enterprise, can be illustrated by means of an example, namely the proposal for a trinitarian theology of the religions by Ninian Smart and Steven Konstantine.[4] They affirm the unique revelatory status of Christ,[5] and endeavor continually to reconceptualize traditional doc-

---

3. *In This Name: The Doctrine of the Trinity in Contemporary Theology* (New York: Scribner's, 1952), p. 238.

4. *Christian Systematic Theology in a World Context* (Minneapolis: Fortress, 1991).

5. *Christian Systematic Theology in a World Context*, pp. 271ff., "On Avatar and Atonement."

trinal affirmations in the terminology of diverse religious traditions. This eclectic effort amounts to a series of implied piecemeal retrospective narratives quite in keeping with final primacy. But the larger epistemological framework of the argument undercuts all these doctrinal affirmations. It affirms a broadly Kantian view of transcendence that can and must be given thematic content in globally diverse ways, in order, in keeping with the requirements of practical reason, to foster understanding and curb conflict, i.e., "to serve the world." But the limits transcendence imposes on a particular religious enclave like Christianity are severe: "The root of the Christian faith has to do with Israel and Christ: but it functions for the Christian much as the highlands and the lochs do for the Scot."[6] Smart and Konstantine's proposal amounts to a kind of epistemic Arianism, according to which robust claims can be made about Christ within the Christian worldview, but these are strictly separated from the transcendent, "the Beyond," about which nothing more can be said. So if one considers not just the formulation of the Trinity but its purpose, namely that talk about Christ not be severed from talk about God the Creator, then one can see that Smart and Konstantine talk a great deal about the Trinity in the service of a profoundly anti-trinitarian project.

Following from this assessment of the basic function of the doctrine of the Trinity, one can privilege the ecumenical creeds themselves as the paradigmatic expressions of the doctrine, models of fulfillment of the rule comprised therein, not least because, in the struggle culminating in their promulgation, the very identity of normative Christian faith came to be forged. To reiterate, this does not mean that a novel means of expressing the trinitarian truth could not be offered. But it does mean that such a novel expression would need to accomplish this same doctrinal "task" in order to be considered orthodox. Likewise it would follow that those novel expressions that represent, in their own theological environments, close analogies to alternatives rejected in the early debates of the church as heretical will most likely prove to fail the test offered above. So, in this indirect sense, one can legitimately accuse a particular contemporary trinitarian theological construction of being "modalist," "tritheist," "subordinationist," etc.

Note the close connection between this theological protocol and

6. *Christian Systematic Theology in a World Context*, p. 99.

the rule of final primacy. First of all, in orthodox versions of the doctrine, the incarnation of Jesus Christ is materially decisive[7] for the meaning of all other terms applied to God, and this same decisiveness drives the rule of final primacy. Secondly, this distinction allows the theologian to distinguish between proposals in which philosophical tools are employed to give expression to the doctrine of the Trinity, and others in which the Trinity is conformed to pre-existing philosophical norms. This contrast follows closely what is in this essay called "nuanced internalism" and "nuanced externalism." In other words, to wield such a trinitarian criterion in the field of the religions entails application of the test of final primacy.

With these prolegomena in mind, one can state the foremost issues to be addressed quite simply: First, what is specifically "trinitarian" about a particular theology of the religions? and second, is the deployment of the doctrine of the Trinity in question consistent or compatible with that which the classical doctrine sought to express?

Of course the idea that there exists some relationship between the Trinity and the beliefs of other religious traditions is not a new idea. As was made clear in the typology of approaches to other religions, from the time of the Fathers one can find the idea of *semina* or *vestigia Trinitatis,* seeds or traces serving as anticipations of the Trinity, in the religions of the pagans. On the basis of such a notion the Fathers could point out various triads of gods or powers in the classical world. Likewise the early missionaries, for example to Hindu India, could find similar threesomes in the religions of their host cultures. Such suggestions are examples of the *Logos*-type of argument. The idea does indeed allow some breadth of appreciation of other traditions, though of course on Christian terms.

Why then doesn't the pattern of *vestigia* suffice to accomplish the ends intended by contemporary trinitarian theologies of the religions? This pattern fails to offer an account of how the plurality of religions itself is expressive of a "providential diversity."[8] It offers no reason to see the existence of a diversity of religions itself as contributing or ac-

7. So again Bruce Marshall, *Christology in Conflict: The Identity of the Savior in Rahner and Barth* (Oxford: Blackwell, 1987).

8. Joseph DiNoia makes a case for this in *The Diversity of Religions: A Christian Perspective* (Washington, D.C.: Catholic University Press, 1992).

complishing anything, as in itself furthering our knowledge of religious truth. For, according to the idea of *vestigia*, all that one could know of God is found in the Christian revelation, and only hints of those same truths may be found scattered elsewhere. Once the full truth has come, the existence of the plurality of other faiths adds nothing new.

Another way of stating the difference between Patristic appeals to the idea of *vestigia* and contemporary references to threesomes in other religious traditions pertains to the strength of the respective claims. Here one can profitably heed the warning that resounds throughout St. Augustine's magisterial *On the Trinity*, that the creaturely vestiges to which he pointed (which happened in Augustine's argument to be located in the human soul rather than in the doctrines and practices of other religions), should be understood as merely suggestive. The orthodox doctrine itself is assumed throughout, and Augustine bows before its surpassing mystery. Since the soul as the image of God is triadic, then one can, according to Augustine, espy a glimpse of the truth of the Trinity, but the argument closes by dissolving itself in humility and adoration. It suffices here simply to note subtitles serving to summarize the closing sections of the work: "ch. 22, 'how great the unlikeness is between the image of the Trinity which we have found in ourselves and the Trinity itself,' ch. 23, 'Augustine dwells further on the disparity . . . ,' ch. 24, 'the infirmity of the human mind,' ch. 28, 'the conclusion of this book with a prayer and an apology. . . .'"[9]

The Long Shadow of the Hegelian Begriff

So with an Augustinian lightness of touch one might discern suggestive similarities between triads in other religions and the doctrine of the Trinity, while assuming the latter as doctrine. Such a position would be consistent with words like "vestiges" or "seeds." This must be distinguished from stronger claims, for instance to find beneath both Christian doctrine and the beliefs of other traditions an undergirding triadic truth, of which even the orthodox Trinity would be but

9. Trans. Arthur Hadden (Grand Rapids: Eerdmans, 1966), pp. 221, 222, 223, 227.

a symbolic representation. For the classic expression of this latter type of claim, in contrast to the *Logos* type, one must turn to the reinterpretation of the doctrine of the Trinity that lay at the very center of the philosophy of religion of Georg Wilhelm Friedrich Hegel.

Many contemporary trinitarian theologies of the religions, it turns out, are not so much retrievals of the doctrine of the Trinity in Christian theology's "grand tradition" as emendations or expansions of Hegel's trinitarian philosophy. The thought of the long-winded Teutonic idealist is not easily given to short summary. Even so, the following may suffice: behind all religious representations, in the very nature of reality, lies a threefold movement with moments of abstraction, subsequent alienation, and consummation. To put it another way, thought first gives expression to reality in such a way as to lead naturally to its opposite, its negation, which in turns opens the door for a concept that synthesizes and surpasses both preceding moments of thought.

Since for Hegel truth itself is always historical and dynamic, these stages play themselves out in the very history of the concept of God. Human beings first worshiped immediate forces of nature in their religions of paganism. By considerable effort humans came to a high concept of the divine, the One, historically through Judaism and Greek rational religion. But this concept of God was defined over against finitude and was, as a result, tacitly limited. So the second term in this progression of thought is the alienation from the world implied by an abstract or transcendent Godhead. Only then can human beings achieve a concept of God or Spirit *(Geist)* that both inhabits and surpasses concrete representation. In other words, shorthand for the history of religions is the movement from idolatry to "the God of the philosophers" to incarnate religion.

But it would be a mistake to suppose that for Hegel all religious history finds its culmination in the Christian doctrine of the Trinity. The latter is itself still "picture thinking," a symbolic representation of the truth that has not yet become self-conscious in thought. In other words, the Trinity is a symbol awaiting its elucidation in philosophy (especially of course Hegel's). So Hegel discerns behind the Trinity a deeper logic inherent in all of reality. He puts the relationship between the symbol of the Trinity and its truth this way: "In religion the truth has been revealed as far as its content is concerned; but it is another matter for this content to be present in the form of the concept, of thinking, of the concept in speculative thought."[10]

One can now consider the specific way Hegel uses the persons of the Trinity in his dialectic. The Father is the first element, "the Idea of God In and For Itself," while the second element (i.e., the Son) is "Representation," which comprises "the differentiation . . . play of love, separation and rupture" to be found in the creation of a world that is free, independent, and other than God.[11] The third element is termed alternately "Spirit" and "Community." One should note how dramatically this diverges from a traditional understanding of the Trinity. For the immanent Trinity involves a claim about the nature of God precisely before and distinct from the work of the triune God economically in creation. Hegel has conflated the topics of the nature of the triune God and that of the relationship between God and the world. In so doing Hegel becomes the sire of most subsequent efforts to think about the latter relationship in a panentheistic manner. To be sure, in classical theology the triunity of God has implications for how one understands God's relationship to the world, but the doctrine itself serves precisely to guard against efforts to make God's relationship to the world determinative of the nature of the Godhead itself. The original doctrine of the immanent Trinity functions in this safeguarding way, and Hegel's reconstruction undoes just this restraint.

One may therefore attribute to Hegel three ideas that have been decisive for many subsequent trinitarian theologies of religions. First, the doctrine of the Trinity itself expresses a deeper logical and ontological truth. Second, the moments or elements of that deeper logic have worked themselves out in the history of religions itself. Third, the Trinity bespeaks a relationship between God and creation, namely one of self-emptying and consummation. It is in respect to these three features that many contemporary trinitarian theologies of the religions may be seen as grandchildren of Hegel.

The first type of recent trinitarian theology of the religions stands altogether in the Hegelian shadow just described. Consider as a paradigmatic case the work of the German theologian and Hindologist, Michael

---

10. *Lectures on the Philosophy of Religion* (Berkeley: University of California Press, 1988), p. 425.

11. *Lectures on the Philosophy of Religion*, p. 434.

von Brück, *The Unity of Reality: God, God-Experience, and Meditation in the Hindu-Christian Dialogue*.[12] Von Brück's proposal builds on the perceived similarity between the Hindu concept of the non-duality, *advaita*, in the relationship between ultimate reality, Brahman, and the world on the one hand, and the relations of the persons within the Trinity, distinct yet one, on the other. Is this not just the sort of suggestive analogy for which one would hope in a trinitarian theology of the religions?

A different comparison, however, lies at the heart of von Brück's thought, one bearing the features of the Hegelian lineage. For what von Brück means by the Trinity is the transcendence of God, historical particularity as found in the life of Jesus Christ, and the true universality of a "non-dual" God identifiable with the Holy Spirit. Here the persons of the Trinity in fact stand for the God-world relationship, since (as with Hegel) the first and second persons may be equated with abstract transcendence and the finitude of the world. Furthermore, one should note that, in this conceptual translation, the term "particularity" has to do not with the particularities of Jesus' identity and life, but rather with the category "particularity" (which is not in itself particular at all). The saving specifics of Jesus the Christ are lost in the shuffle.

For von Brück, then, a trinitarian theology of the religions amounts to the perception of a structure, expressible philosophically, behind the symbol of the Trinity. This deeper structure is a substratum of reality for whose expression the religious traditions offer differing symbols. So von Brück must alter not only the classical Christian understanding of the Trinity to fit this structure, but the classical Hindu concept of *advaita* as well, since its utter monism allowed for none of the relationality, or the Hegelian movement and sublation, that von Brück interjects into non-duality. In other words, for Hinduism, no less than for Christianity, the underlying structure threatens to force terms on the traditional symbol. We find here a signal-case of the danger that pluralism, in the name of dialogical listening and inclusivity, comes to undermine the specificity of the other tradition under consideration.

In this first category of proposals, the *Begriff*-approach, the concept of an underlying triadic structure to reality is central. Von Brück's pro-

---

12. Trans. James V. Zeitz (New York: Paulist, 1991). The work was reviewed appreciatively in Ted Peters's *God as Trinity: Relationality and Temporality in the Divine Life* (Louisville: Westminster/John Knox, 1993).

posal is in no way unique. The more renowned theologian in this camp is Raimundo Panikkar, though his later thought is also more florid and elusive to analysis. In his *The Trinity and the Religious Experience of Man: Icon-Person-Mystery,* Panikkar offers an analysis of mystical experience in which, in good Hegelian fashion, the stages of consciousness (divine as absolute, as personal, as indwelling) correspond to and are worked out in the stages of world religious history (Old Testament/ New Testament/"breakthrough to new self-awareness"[13] and "mutual fecundation" between the religions).[14] In this final stage one sees that the stages of the whole history "coinhere." Here too the pattern of "non-duality," worked out historically, is the structure of reality to which the symbol of the Trinity gives expression.

To be sure, many of the observations made by von Brück or Panikkar would be (in the latter's term) "fecundative" if one started with background assumptions of the *Logos* sort, accompanied by the Augustinian lightness of touch. But these authors are making a stronger claim than that. And if one recalls the close connection between the Trinity and Christology,[15] then any trinitarian proposal that cuts the cord with specific claims about Jesus Christ ipso facto cannot be in continuity with that doctrine. On both scores the strategy of finding an underlying structure is suspect.

Panikkar's "Joachite" idea of the working out of the Trinity in history, and in particular the age of the Holy Spirit, blurs into our second category of trinitarian theologies of the religions. One can call this the

13. Raimundo Panikkar, *The Trinity and the Religious Experience of Man: Icon-Person-Mystery* (Maryknoll, N.Y.: Orbis, 1993), p. 76.

14. Panikkar, *The Trinity and the Religious Experience of Man,* p. 53.

15. Another way of stating Welch's point is in terms of "governing doctrines," to use William Christian's term. One might say that the classical doctrines of the Trinity and of Christology make up in fact a dual set of "core" or central doctrines, in the sense that they require one another for correction or protection against misunderstanding. In fact they came about in roughly the same, formative period of Christian history, and each explicates the mystery of Jesus Christ in relation to the God of Israel, Trinity by means of a "wider" lens, and Christology by focusing more narrowly in Jesus himself. But the Trinity without Christology will, as Welch reminds us, fall into philosophical speculation, in which "the Spirit" will break loose of the Godhead. Christology without the Trinity will end up in either in a narrow Jesus-olatry or in a liberal exemplarism. The doctrines are better understood as a single "set" of doctrinal safeguards for a Christian doctrine of God.

"division of labor" strategy. While in the church one sees the primary work of the second person of the Trinity, the Son, in other religions one witnesses the primary work of the third person, the Holy Spirit. The Spirit's is a related but distinct dispensation, so that the umbrella of the economic Trinity is wider than the province of Christianity alone. The general idea is summed up, in this case from the perspective of an Orthodox theologian, in the following sentence from Bishop Anastasios of Androussa: "in addition to the 'economy of the Logos' the Christian east, full of hope and humble expectation, gazes at the 'economy of the Spirit.'"[16]

The bishop's statement in fact is problematic from his own doctrinal tradition. The Augustinian adage in classical trinitarian theology is *"opera Dei triuni non divisa sunt."* To be sure, Eastern Christianity has typically had its complaints with the West over the relation of Son and Spirit, but these differences concerned the nature of the immanent Trinity.[17] Both East and West have classically been in agreement that in the economy of salvation the persons of the Trinity work in concert, the outward form of their intra-trinitarian circumincession. In classical trinitarianism, one could only speak of the atonement as the work of the Son, for example, by the doctrine of appropriation, according to which, in the economy, the work of one person may be more prominent. Still it remains a work of that person in concert with the other two.

The reason for this insistence is not hard to find. Where the economy of salvation has separate subdivisions for the persons, quickly the world is balkanized into separate realms for the persons, and one arrives at a virtually tritheistic situation in which the persons preside over distinct bailiwicks (one of the key signs of the transgression of final primacy). The only way to avoid this unsatisfactory result is to re-

16. Bishop Anastasios of Androussa, "Emerging Perspectives on the Relationships of Christians to People of Other Faith: An Eastern Orthodox Contribution," *International Review of Mission* 78 (July 1988): 338. This sentence is part of an article whose main argument is a more defensible presentation of the traditional, Patristic idea of the *logos spermatikos.* A purer example of the economic "division of labor" approach would be Darrol Bryant's "Interfaith Encounter and Dialogue in a Trinitarian Perspective," in Peter Phan, ed., *Christianity and the Wider Ecumenism* (New York: Paragon, 1990), pp. 3-20.

17. A helpful treatment of "Augustine's rule," *omnia opera Dei ad extra indivisa sunt,* may be found in Philip Cary's "Classical Trinitarianism: Rahner on Trinity," *The Thomist* 56, no. 3 (July 1992): 368ff.

treat into some form of subordinationism or monarchianism, in which the Son and Spirit are but modes of working of the one, essentially undifferentiated God. One could speak of economies of the Son and Spirit, but to do so one would have to say more in order to ensure that these economies relate to one another in such a way as to preserve a single, overarching economy of salvation, presided over finally by the single triune God. More would need to be said, and that "more" would consist in some way of making explicit the relationship of reciprocity and unity between Son and Spirit in the economy of salvation. Otherwise one could not in the end speak of the God involved as triune.

Grammatical Constructions: Visions of Eschatological Plentitude

Having in a sense marked the boundaries of an appropriate trinitarian theology of the religions by criticism of these two types of proposals, one can consider a subtler group of constructions in closer continuity with the classical tradition, though it does contribute new dimensions as well. One needs to ask of these proposals the following question: What are the conditions and features that serve to render these proposals more satisfactory attempts to balance integrity and expansiveness?

In his study of the relationship between the aim of Christianity and those of other religious traditions, *Salvations*, Mark Heim aptly entitles the section directly presenting a trinitarian theology of religions "Plenitude and Trinity."[18] For the idea of plenitude lies at the heart of the var-

---

18. We have chosen to cite the final chapter of *Salvations*, though he has recently offered a more ambitious trinitarian theology in *The Depth of the Riches: A Trinitarian Theology of Religious Ends* (Grand Rapids: Eerdmans, 2001). The concluding chapter of the latter, also dealing with plentitude and the afterlife, again beholden to Dante and DiNoia, is essentially compatible with the earlier treatment. However, from the perspective of final primacy, *The Depth of the Riches* limps between two opinions. In the end his emphasis on the sheer difference of the other ends, and his desire to validate those ends as partial realizations of dimensions of the triune life (impersonal transcendence, personal relation, and being-in-communion), works at cross-purposes. The latter view is implicitly "grammatical" in the sense that the ends are subordinated to the triune life. At the same time, however, Heim has quietly introduced a Christological assumption that opens his proposal to just the problems one finds in the authors to whom he is indebted, Panikkar on the one hand and Smart and Konstantine on the other. "The scope of divine activity

ied presentations of this third type of approach. The argument proceeds in this way: human persons and communities, in the image of the tri-une God, reflect the Father (by contrast) in their creatureliness, reflect the Son in their distinct particularity, and reflect the Spirit in their capacity to be drawn together in an enriching unity. One can discern these same threefold marks in the religions of the world. Next, one argues that the revelation in Jesus Christ is the normative revelation of God, the goal toward which all else tends, so that one may discern in the other religions of the world an entelechy toward this revelatory consummation. An important aspect of the finality of the Christian revelation is again, in good Hegelian trinitarian fashion, its concrete particularity, into which the Spirit can, in the process of history, gather other, prior or lesser, revelations. Seen from the perspective of salvation-history and against the backdrop of the consummation of God's kingdom, the other religions conduce to a fuller plenitude in God's creation.

But a fuller plenitude of what? Here various authors offer different answers. Heim, in the book cited above, builds on the work of Joseph DiNoia as he suggests that the diverse religions will be means to

---

in all of religious history widens in proportion to the decisiveness of God's self-revelation in Christ, not the reverse. Christ is normative, not absolute, and so is the ground by which we can be open to other faiths" (p. 134). At this crucial moment of his argument Heim construes Christ's decisiveness as merely genetic ("the doctrine [of the Trinity] . . . arose historically from faith in Jesus Christ") and as the Christian example of divine particularity. From this point on, Heim's Trinity floats as a philosophical construct à la Hegel. In spite of this move, Heim also has a more Christocentric instinct, for example when he stresses that Christ must function not only as means but also as end (p. 51), or when he asserts that even other final ends are realized, though unknowingly by Christ's work (p. 286). In connection with the latter passage one can see the other persistent problem in the proposal, a doctrine of the human person that combines a very high view of the image of God (both we and God are beings-in-communion) and the very low profile that sin keeps throughout (for example, in the absence of any sense that sin cripples our freedom), so that communion with the divine seems at times to become a resource for the believer's fulfillment rather than a needed gift of redemption.

In spite of these problems, there is much to commend the book. Without calling it such, Heim uses his trinitarian construal as a rule by which he imagines how new ideas from other traditions might challenge and enrich Christian theology with respect to a certain "dimension" of the doctrine of God. This amounts in our terminology to the construction of a retrospective narrative. As for the project as a whole, at its best it reminds us of Nicholas of Cusa's De Pace Fidei in both protection of diversity and its appeal to the Trinity, though he is never mentioned by Heim.

fuller revelation of that human flourishing which God brings about, though understood in diverse ways. So the Buddhist will allow one to see the good of the renunciation of the will more clearly, the Muslim the imperative of submission to God's will, etc. Gavin D'Costa[19] imagines a plenitude of insight into history, neither focused exclusively on Christ nor eschewing him as the norm for religious truth in history. Daniel Sheridan[20] conceives, in good Catholic fashion, of a plenitude of religions rooted in different cultures, striving and pointing toward that catholicity of the church, which is itself an anticipation of the consummation in the Kingdom. And as has already been treated, Pannenberg, with his eschatologically recast *Logos* theology, offers a classic example of just the same kind of argument, according to which the Kingdom, decisively revealed and initiated in Jesus' resurrection, is anticipated in hints in the religions on the way toward its ultimate, and richer, fulfillment.

These examples of the "plenitude of creation as trinitarian anticipation" type have certain features in common. Each points to aspects of creatureliness or particularity, which tend toward unity as, in effect, *vestigia*. But these proposals differ from those of the Hegelian *Begriff*-type, for each, whether it acknowledges the fact or not, employs some conceptual device by which the other religions are subordinated to the Christian revelation, even if only eschatologically. These devices ensure, in fact, that one can speak of the plenitude only in the wake of the Christian revelation. Sheridan for example uses the Aristotelian-Thomist notion of an entelechy, while Heim (remarkably for a Protestant) uses the Dantean idea of circles of purgatory and heaven allowing lesser religious aims to maintain some value. These mechanisms are fully in keeping with the grammar of final primacy and its emphasis on narrative sequence. They find a valuable place for the religions precisely in relation to Christ, who retains eschatological priority.

Pannenberg, with his emphasis on the resurrection, most forcefully illustrates a third feature, namely that each combines this subordination with an appeal to some sort of eschatological resolution of the

19. "Toward a Trinitarian Theology of Religions," in Catherine Cornille and Valeer Neckebrouck, *A Universal Faith? Peoples, Cultures, Religions, and the Christ* (Louvain: Peeters, 1992).

20. "Grounded in the Trinity: Suggestions for a Theology of Relationship to Other Religions," *The Thomist* 50, no. 2 (April 1986): 260-78.

perplexities of many religions and one revelation in Christ. This allows some breathing room in the interim for provisional value and for the affirmation that the diversity itself is providential.

To return to the question asked at the outset, one can now say that what makes this third type of proposal trinitarian is its discernment in the religions of both distinctiveness and a tendency toward unity befitting creation in the image of the triune God. In other words, these proposals are not "trinitarian" in the proper sense, for they do not have to do with the doctrine of God, but rather the term "trinitarian" describes certain features of the created order reflecting its triune Creator. These features are the result of the working out of the triune relations in the economy of salvation, and in the consummation. It is in this sense that this type of argument can affirm a providential diversity of religions.

Other features in this type, often latent, also make these accomplishments possible. First, all these constructions assume, in keeping with our rule, the finality of the revelation in Jesus Christ and of a Christian salvation-historical schema. The assertion of a providential diversity is subsidiary to, and dependent on, these dogmatic premises. Second, one must admit that, pinned as they are on these premises, such "trinitarian theologies of the religions" break less new ground than they sometimes suggest. Earlier applications of the rule, most notably the *Logos*-theology of the early church and the scholastic idea of implicit faith, depend on precisely the same dogmatic underpinnings, and achieve just the same sort of subsidiary affirmation. Trinitarian theologies amount to variations of such theological antecedents distinguished mostly by an expanded application to the religions and a specifically eschatological recasting.

The very balance of integrity and comprehensiveness sought after depends on this tacit backdrop of concomitant dogmatic assumptions. This compels a note of caution at the conclusion of this analysis. Where these assumptions are lacking, the very same propositions about Christianity and the religions can have a drastically different meaning and can, in some cases, cause serious havoc. Bishop Anastasios, Raimundo Panikkar, and Wolfhart Pannenberg can make many of the same claims, but to dramatically different effect. This is an example of the implied nexus of belief and practice so decisive in interpreting seemingly identical claims discussed in Chapter 2. Within the same field of trinitarian theologies of religions may be found both thinkers of traditional commitments meaning to expand the church's vision, and others for whom the Trinity is a means to scuttle the finality of Jesus Christ and so the distinctiveness of the Christian doctrine of God. Here too, under an ambiguous banner, as if in one army, forces clash in the dusk. Distinguishing the promise from the risk in such constructions is a legitimate task of final primacy.

The Trinity and the "Providential Diversity" of the Religions

Some Scholastic Distinctions

Analysis of trinitarian proposals for a Christian theology of the religions has revealed that other doctrines and goals strongly influence the shape of such a project. There is no single genus called "trinitarian theology of religions." One cannot help but wonder, as a result, to what extent this whole avenue of trinitarianism is helpful. Along the way the question of the status of the plurality of the religions itself was engaged. The motivating force for such constructions is the need to make sense of that plurality per se. For some authors, implicit in the development of a trinitarian proposal is the assertion that this "providential diversity" is willed by God himself. What are the implications of making such an affirmation? The preceding section offered analysis of the views of others by means of the application of the rule of final primacy. But the burden remains to offer a constructive answer to the question about the meaning of the plurality of religions in history and so their place in the economy of salvation.

Questions about salvation or revelation do lead naturally to this question about diversity itself in the providence of God.[21] If final primacy is adequate to guide and clarify Christian answers to the question of the religions in a diversity of contexts, it should also guide this essay's own answer. Along the way, it will be incumbent on us to show in what sense this answer is "trinitarian."

At the outset, one may ask in relation to what practices is the ques-

---

21. Jacques Dupuis, *Toward a Christian Theology of Religious Pluralism* (Maryknoll, N.Y.: Orbis, 1997), Introduction.

tion being asked. Is the church asking as it is confronted by questions in the midst of proclamation, or conversely, is it seeking to avoid such proclamation where it is culturally uncomfortable? And in reply to such questions, final primacy, employed in tandem with our distinctively Christian, threefold practice of witness, retrospective inclusion, and neighborliness, emphasizes the inextricable two-sidedness of Christian construals of the religions, whereby value and significance are found in the religions in the very theological act in which they are brought into encounter with Christ as their telos. At the same time, these answers will be contestable, one with another. If one adds these observations up, one may safely distrust any simple, undialectical answer to a question such as "are the religions providentially willed by God?" Any answer will depend on the prior answers to these questions.

It is not being suggested that the question be dropped. On the contrary, it proves a most enlightening case for the argument of this essay. But one must begin, like a good scholastic, with some careful distinctions. In order to demonstrate the need for breaking the question down into a series of questions, consider the following, admittedly severe biblical example. Isaiah 10:24 tells the reader that Yahweh is using the Assyrians, coming to decimate Jerusalem and Judah, as his "rod" of judgment. In a subsequent chapter the prophet tells us that the Assyrians in turn will be punished for their insolence. Sennacherib is acting in accordance with the providence of Yahweh, but this in no way obviates the coming judgment on him. The "providential" Assyrians play several roles simultaneously in the complex plot which is Yahweh's relationship to Israel and the world on the way to salvation.

Consider a second, equally extreme example. When Thomas Aquinas considers the status of the damned in hell, he points out that one must think of their status in two ways. Even in hell the damned *are*; since being is a good gift from God, one may say that, *qua* existents, even those in eternal torment have a "positive" place in God's final order.[22] Of course, *qua* rebels, they have a decidedly negative place as well. Now one would not want to suggest that either insolence or damnable rebellion adequately characterizes the religions. On the contrary one may argue that if even these extreme cases require twofold answers to the question about their "positive role" in God's economy,

22. See, e.g., Thomas Aquinas, *ST*, I.104.4.

how much more do the religions require a complex answer, presenting as each religion does a variety of true claims and good practices?

This brings us to the needed distinctions. First, *qua creatures* of God existing in the world, the religious traditions, both as human communities and as phenomena of human history, may be seen to have a "positive place" in God's economy of creation. But what of them *qua traditions*, as webs of claims and practices in ongoing traditions, i.e., in the sense in which they have been treated throughout this essay? Here a second basic distinction suggests itself. Is one asking whether God intended them to be as they are, or is one asking whether they, in God's wisdom, play a positive role in his economy? The former question is an intensely difficult and mysterious one for which we may not be able to provide a single answer. For surely aspects of the religions are responses to the promptings of grace, and other aspects are manifestations of human rebellion. Could not the same be said of the church? And if some aspects of a certain religion were manifestations of human rebellion, even this does not preclude God's using them for good, for, as in the days of Joseph, God can turn what humans intend for ill to good.

Even here one cannot let matters rest, for thirdly, the motive of the asker remains at issue. Is the question part of a theological project, for example, that aims to create a "separate but equal" space for Christianity and its neighbor religions in such a way that evangelistic efforts are discouraged? "Providential diversity" cannot be divorced from such other questions lying in its shadow. At the heart of the rule of final primacy is the assertion that Christian theology cannot accept any balkanizing comities of separatism, or any cordoning off of the relevance of Christ for truth or salvation. God may be doing something else, itself valuable, in the religions, but it cannot be a "something else" segregated from the finality of Jesus Christ. Likewise if "providential diversity" is in any way a code for the secession of evangelistic activity, this motive must be brought out into the open.

Does this leave any possibility of "something else," of a way in which the plurality of religions might have a positive role aside from anticipating the arrival of the gospel? The question is by now in danger of being hopelessly lost in a thicket of distinctions. But a way out of the maze may be found by a fourth and final distinction, this one native to Christian theology itself. Recall that final primacy refers to the relationship of Christ to the religions, but not to the relationship between the church and the religions. The church may be the necessary means of the encounter of the religions with Christ, but it must not thereby be identified with him. To be sure, the realm of creation inhabited by the Buddhist or animist is none other than the realm of redemption. There is no room, in the wake of Christ's victory, for an answer that somehow leaves his rule to the side. Still, based on the distinction between Christ and church, more needs to be said. For even where the religions do not respond to the proclamation about Christ, they may have a providential role vis-à-vis the church.

One may highlight three roles they can play in relation to the church. They correspond roughly to the practices this essay has offered for the church. First of all, the church is called to proclaim, but it does so fitfully, guiltily, confusedly, inaudibly. When the religions refuse the message, they may also do so because someone has not adequately proclaimed the message. Thus the religions may serve a purpose in the divine providence as they do not believe, for they could be a witness of judgment against the church's faulty proclamation. They witness thereby to the church's own resistance to Christ's Lordship. For example, remnants of Aztec religion, unconverted in the wake of mission in the era of the conquistadores, were surely such a witness.

The church also is called to hopeful imagination, as it constructs retrospective narratives that include and transform the beliefs of religions the church encounters. So conceived, the religions are, to be sure, subordinate to the truth of Christ. But in fact many of those adherents will not convert, and these different traditions will endure. As the unconverted but imaginatively included, the religions serve, in themselves and in the meantime, as worldly signs of eschatological hope. As such they are living reminders that the kingdom of God, brought in by the returning Christ, will be wider than the church, and that his grace and truth will be shown to have been at work in yet unimagined ways. The recalcitrant difference of the religions in no way relieves the church of the need to form such inclusive narratives, but it serves in the providence of God as a guard against the prideful notion that such narratives adequately describe the whole of the triune God's gracious work, or that Christ's kingdom may be extrapolated simply from the church as it now presents itself.

The third practice of the church among the religions was neighborliness, and, engaging in this activity, the church may most clearly see the providential diversity of other religious traditions. For the church must acknowledge that many true claims and good practices, quite different from anything claimed in Scripture or enacted in the Christian life, may be found in the religions. What the Zen Buddhist knows of the rigors of silence, or the Sufi knows of the profundity of bodily movement, do not fit into pre-existing Christian categories, nor need they. It is only on this premise that retrospective narratives are necessary or possible.[23] So, as the teachers of all of these truths and exemplars of all of these practices, the religions are indeed providentially ordained by God, though one cannot predict or systematize how and where these will appear.

Here it may be helpful to recall that within the canon itself is found the corpus of Wisdom literature, wherein Israel benefits from the insights into human life of non-Israelite neighbors and understands these ideas as guidance from Yahweh himself. Such wisdom reminds us that the triune God is the creator of all things, and that the religions are fellow members of the creaturely world, whose order and beauty testify to the goodness of God. So every example of the true, good, and beautiful found in the diversity of the religions bespeaks *eo ipso* their place in God's providential order.

In Praise of the Piecemeal

Such an answer may fail to satisfy because of its piecemeal and tentative quality.[24] Instead of affirming the providential diversity of the reli-

23. A compelling case for such an attitude toward "alien" truths may be found in Paul Griffiths' "open inclusivism" with respect to truth in his *The Problem of Religious Diversity* (Malden, Mass.: Blackwell, 2001), pp. 60ff. This view is compatible with final primacy, which provides the template by which these other truths are brought into relation to Christian truth.

24. A critic might object that we have not found a place for religions as wholes or per se within the providence of God, but only for parts that come into providential view only as they interact historically or intellectually with the church, and that this is all the more problematic given our coherentist view of the epistemology of traditions. A helpful comparison on this point is the Catholic teaching at Vatican II on salvific possibilities in other religions. It judged that there could be saving grace at work, through such grace at work in the religions *qua* religions. In both cases, to say otherwise is to make major claims on behalf of other traditions that will turn out to be strong cases of inversion.

gions in a single, grand, world-historical gesture, it affirms a diverse number of particular times, examples, aspects, and groups as providentially intended, and in a diversity of ways. But upon reflection one realizes that such an answer has a prima facie credibility given the pied, particular, complex nature of God's created order itself. Why would one expect there to be a single, decisive answer to such a question? Is it not more credible to say that, to the extent that the religions, in a myriad of particular ways, exhibit such elements of the true, good, and beautiful, one can say, as a generalization, that they do indeed have a place in God's providential order?

Lest this account seem overly abstract, one can consider an example of a particular religious community, the contemporary Native American church on the plains of the United States. One might object that the N.A.C. is an unrepresentative case, since their beliefs are already influenced by, and in part react against, Christian beliefs and practices. But this may also be seen as an advantage, since it belies any tacit assumptions about "untainted" examples. In this case the rejection of Christian sacramentalism represented by N.A.C. views toward peyote, i.e., that Christian holy communion is a pallid source of mystical insight, constitutes a critique of the spiritual and sacramental teaching as proffered by the missionaries (as well as their accompanying lack of charity). The vivid sense of expectation of the Spirit's restitution of the land, fusing as it does Plains vision traditions and Christian eschatology, is a potent sign to the Christian observer of the hope that God's final consummation will usher in justice for oppressed native peoples. The N.A.C. could offer insights into the mystical communion of humans and animals, or concerning prayer as it relates to the times of day, month, and year, which in themselves need not contradict or confirm Christian beliefs, but certainly merit reflection. Of course one would need in this last case a full-blown theological construction, after the pattern of final primacy, to sift the net between elements congenial to and detrimental to Christian truth. Still, there is every reason to think that particular truths and practices could be signs of God's wisdom "deep down things" in ways simply different from the extant Christian claims.

The answer here offered is complex and piecemeal through and through. The answer has been crumbled into bits because the practices of the church are many, the beliefs of the other tradition many, and the specific questions one might ask of those traditions many as well. Is one left with a hodge-podge of judgments? With respect to the religions themselves, the answer is "yes."

There is indeed a coherence to be found here, but it is lodged, not in the religions themselves, but rather in those who ask and answer the question about "providential diversity," namely in the church. The religions' positive roles "in their own right" come clear, ironically, only as the church engages in its own distinctive triad of practices. The same church must be proclamatory, hopefully reflective, and neighborly, and the church engages in each and all these practices in obedience to the same triune God.

With this variegated answer in hand, one can turn back now to the question with which this chapter began, that of the possibility of a "trinitarian theology of the religions." Most simply, theological consideration of other religions is "trinitarian" because it takes place as a faithful response to the triune God. But in this sense everything the church does is "trinitarian," and one has not designated any sense in which this particular field of theology should fit this description. Is there any further sense in which one may designate this theological effort as "trinitarian"?

If God is triune, one may assume that his image too will reflect in some way that triunity. Now the image of God in humankind may best be observed, amidst the wreckage of the Fall, as human beings in community respond in faith, by divine grace, to the gift of the gospel of Jesus Christ. To the extent that they do respond, we see a pledge of the image eschatologically restored (though of course to the extent that they remain sinful, they never reflect here the full reality of that image). Thus one may safely expect that the life of the church *qua* community of faithful response will show most clearly, here under the conditions of fallen creation, the image of the triune God, though even here the observer is still gazing "in a glass darkly."

Think now of the triad of practices offered in this essay: proclaiming the incarnation of God's Son, expressing imaginative hope in the Spirit for the consummation of creation, and observing the rich diversity of the work of the creator God. Of course each of these works — incarnation, consummation, and creation — is accomplished, indivisibly, by the one God in three persons. But think now of the principle of "appropriation," whereby, in the divine economy, a particular work

may be attributed to a certain person of the Trinity due to the prominent, "high-profile" role that person plays. According to the principle
of appropriation one may attribute the incarnation to the Son, or the
consummation of all creation to the Spirit. It represents a kind of theological shorthand, for one bears in mind that, in truth, all three persons
were coinherently active in that work. By analogy with this use of appropriation in the doctrine of God, one may think of the triad of practices — proclaiming, imagining, and serving in neighborliness — as
"appropriated" to the persons of Son, Spirit, and Father.

If one thinks of these practices of the church toward other religions, ingredient as they are in its faithful response to God and so reflecting the image of God, in what consists their "trinitarianness"? It
cannot lie merely in their threeness, for with more thought one could
doubtless find others. Here one may borrow, by analogy, another term
from the theology of the divine Trinity — coinherence. Each person is
itself in relation to the others, and all work in concert *ad extra*. By analogy one may say that each practice of the church suggests and supports the others: the church proclaims, and in so encountering other
traditions finds it must make sense of them, and at the same time is
compelled to distinguish itself from its Lord, to discover its humble affinity to its neighbor, to learn new things from them, etc. "Trinitarianness" is found in the way in which the practices of proclaiming, imagining, and being neighborly coinhere in the light of the one God who
alone is properly triune.

Is there a providential diversity of religions in the economy of the
creating and redeeming triune God? Of course, and in a myriad of
cases, each of which one may profitably observe and debate. Can one
then discern a trinitarian pattern? Not in that diversity per se, but
rather, tentatively and fragmentarily, in the practices of the church doing the discerning, insofar as it is responding in faith to the one, triune
God. The pattern is best seen in the manner in which those practices
coinhere as they refer back to that God.

It is appropriate to close this section with the distinction with
which it began, that between the church and Christ, to whom it must
witness. This section has considered the religions, with one eye on the
church, for it is in itself another creature of God, a neighbor religious
community to them. But if one considers the religions as if standing directly before the throne of Christ himself, then one may see more

starkly what is at stake in such a question. There can be no place for a "providential diversity," if there lies hidden in that notion any sense in which the imperative of the practice of proclamation is blunted, and so as a result any sense in which a boundary between the realm of Christ, and some other, neutral zone is envisioned. The God who foresees all creation and all history is none other than the God of Jesus Christ, and all diversities come from, are guided by, and will return to stand before that divine unity. But so long as answers to this question show themselves innocent of such a hidden intent, there is no reason Christian theology cannot accommodate many expansive and creative answers in the affirmative.

5 Testing Final Primacy in the Theology of Mission

"Continuity" and "Discontinuity" at Tambaram: A Historical Moment Lays Bare the Issue

The International Mission Council's conference in Tambaram, Madras, India, in 1938 is commonly taken to be a watershed event in the history of Christian missions.[1] It marked an end to the optimism of the great Edinburgh conference of 1910, and to the liberalism of common religious values between the traditions in the face of secularism evinced at Jerusalem in 1928. The meeting was also the first time a substantial number of third-world church leaders attended such a gathering. But Tambaram is best remembered as the moment of confrontation between the theology of Hendrik Kraemer, the Dutch missiologist commissioned to write the background text for the conference,[2] and his opponents, most notably the well-known Indian missionary and recently retired principal of Madras, A. G. Hogg. The conflict came to be captured in the antinomy of terms found in the opening volume of the report of the conference, namely "continuity"

1. For a good narrative summary of the events and ideas leading to and emerging from Tambaram, see Timothy Yates's *Christian Mission in the Twentieth Century* (Cambridge: Cambridge University Press, 1994), I.4, esp. pp. 102ff.

2. Hendrik Kraemer, *The Christian Message in a Non-Christian World* (London: Edinburgh House, 1938).

(represented by his opponents) vs. "discontinuity" (represented by Kraemer himself).[3] These terms came to epitomize alternatives in a Christian theology of mission.

Whatever their allegiance, participants remembered the occasion as a time of exhilarating theological clarity and challenge. Lesslie Newbigin recalled the moment in this way: "We had become accustomed to what Visser 't Hooft called 'Hyphenated Christianity.' We had been busy commending Christianity to our contemporaries because it was 'relevant' to their concerns . . . all our talk was Christianity and this, Christianity and that. . . . We were part of the great confusion, the great betrayal. It was against this European syncretism that Barth raised his powerful (not to say strident) voice. . . . Kraemer . . . carried this protest into the heart of the missionary movement through the debates that followed here at Tambaram."[4]

While one can applaud the clarion call, exactly what meaning should be assigned to these contrasting terms? To this analysis our essay now turns. How successful are these terms at laying bare what is really at stake in theological and evangelistic discourse? As a starting-point, one should note that in the pivotal section of Kraemer's work,[5] he uses a series of terms in an interrelated way, all toward the same purpose. Ranged with "continuity" are "natural theology," "general revelation," "fulfillment," and "point of contact," all infected with the same disease. A first perusal tells us that "continuity" describes a general attitude, "fulfillment" describes the hoped-for goal of the process, and "point of contact" the means by which this fulfillment may come to be accomplished. But the terms float vaguely, and need to be given clearer content.

In this nexus of terms Kraemer is conflating several preceding theological and missiological conflicts with his own struggle, and by so doing he is implicitly arguing that they all present, in the end, the same sharp alternatives. The reference to "fulfillment," for example, alludes to a debate sparked by the preparation for the Edinburgh Con-

3. *The Authority of Faith* (London: Oxford University Press for the International Missionary Council, 1939), vol. 1 of the Tambaram series.

4. "A Sermon Preached at the Thanksgiving Service for the Fiftieth Anniversary of the Tambaram Conference of the International Missionary Council," in "Tambaram Revisited," *International Review of Mission* 78, no. 307 (July 1988): 327-28.

5. Kraemer, *The Christian Message*, ch. 4, pp. 144ff.

ference of 1910, in which the cause of "fulfillment" was championed by J. N. Farquhar, whose *magnum opus* was appropriately entitled *The Crown of Hinduism*,[6] and opposed by the same A. G. Hogg. Kraemer has subsumed this debate into his own, and intends some of his critique for earlier, theologically liberal missionary opponents.

The *Sitz im Leben* of the term "point of contact" is more strictly theological, for it was a prime bone of contention in the debate between Karl Barth and Emil Brunner over the subjects of natural theology and the "orders of creation," and a partial cause of their falling out. To be sure, on the subject of "points of contact," Kraemer has missionary opponents in mind as well, but the figures of Barth and Brunner lurk just off the stage, and his ruminations amount to an effort to sort out his views vis-à-vis both figures.[7] In the deeper background one may discern Barth's antipathy for any form of natural theology, whether in its liberal Protestant or more venerable Thomist form. So the Tambaram debate can be better understood by first untangling these preceding polemical threads.

Farquhar vs. Hogg on Fulfillment

Considering these opponents in turn, one begins with the following question: What exactly did J. N. Farquhar mean when he advocated a relationship to Hinduism built on "fulfillment"? Farquhar, though writing a generation before Kraemer, begins in the very same place, the recognition of a dawning world civilization in which immediate communication between the great religious traditions should now be assumed.[8] But to this cultural observation he adds a second, namely that "whoever may be to blame, Hinduism is being disintegrated."[9] (In light of Gandhi and the resurgence of Hinduism as a nationalist force, this latter view seems in retrospect to be misguided.) Behind these as-

---

6. (London: H. Milford, 1913).

7. The relative influence of Barth and Brunner on Kraemer, given his affinity to neo-orthodox theology, is a significant theme of Carl F. Hallencreutz's *Kraemer toward Tambaram: A Study in Hendrik Kraemer's Missionary Approach* (Uppsala: Gleerup, 1966), especially "the Continental contribution," pp. 202ff.

8. Farquhar, *The Crown of Hinduism*, p. 26.

9. Farquhar, *The Crown of Hinduism*, p. 42.

sessments lies the liberal nineteenth-century assumption of an evolutionary framework of religious traditions and ideas. Each stage has its own good, but reaches its plateau, at which point it no longer satisfies: "What is the inevitable result? The religion through which he formerly received help is no longer of any use to him. He has seen truth and has refused to obey it. He is no longer a religious man."[10]

Farquhar saw signs of this stage of evolutionary shipwreck in the critiques of Hinduism offered by its own intelligentsia. Farquhar believed that in such a moment much of the dross of a religious tradition would be burned away.[11] But its highest values and themes could lead on naturally to a form of Christianity appropriate to India, in just the same way that "[Jesus] came to crown it [Judaism] by transforming it into the religion for all men." Thus in a way consistent with the "science of religion," Jesus proves to be the "consummation of religion."[12]

Farquhar's notion of fulfillment builds on two interrelated factors, first a scheme of religious evolution, and, second, a dissatisfied yearning characteristic of the people at the "seams" or plateaus of the scheme. In response and in critique of positions like Farquhar's, A. G. Hogg notes first that the diagnosis of Hindu disintegration is highly questionable. He also suggested that a wide variety of Hindu responses to Christianity could be observed, only one of which could be characterized by yearning. Furthermore, he pointed out that this yearning was borne not of internal weaknesses within Hinduism, but rather was induced by contact with Christianity: "Christianity is the solution of a religious problem which the typical Hindu does not feel, but which, under favorable circumstances, he can be made to feel."[13]

How may one assess Farquhar's position? Though his assumptions about evolution and a grand "science of religion" should be rejected, one may still transpose his claims into a more modest analysis of the relations between the claims and practices of different traditions. There Farquhar's second assumption, religious yearning, is intended as a description of their personal state of mind and heart. Even so Hogg, emphasizing the epistemological difference between tradi-

10. Farquhar, *The Crown of Hinduism*, p. 28.
11. Farquhar, *The Crown of Hinduism*, p. 54.
12. Cited by Eric Sharpe in his *The Theology of A. G. Hogg* (Bangalore: Christian Institute for the Study of Religion and Society, 1979), p. 49.
13. Sharpe, *The Theology of A. G. Hogg*, p. 52.

tions, observes that "in the areas of doctrine and ritual the term is virtually meaningless, and in the area of ethics and experience, since the
claim must be made from within one of the two religious traditions
concerned, it can neither be proved or disproved."[14] In this point about
"proving or disproving" Hogg is merely rejecting a position that
would assume some Archimedean point from which one could assess
one sort of "experience" against another.[15]

Barth vs. Brunner on Natural Revelation

The second major debate that contributes to the background of "continuity" and "discontinuity" at Tambaram was the theological debate in
1934 between the previously allied "neo-orthodox" theologians Emil
Brunner and Karl Barth around the term "point of contact," a debate to
which Kraemer makes direct and extended reference in *The Christian
Message in a Non-Christian World*.[16] In the manner of Chinese boxes, of
contexts within contexts, that argument itself had as its background
earlier conversations between the two. The place to start is with the
common perception of both Barth and Brunner that modern neo-
Protestantism had dethroned the revelatory knowledge of Christ, derived from Scripture, in favor of an Enlightenment-derived, anthropocentric, ultimately hubristic claim to a natural knowledge of God. Each
saw in this modern Protestant error a surprising kinship to the traditional view of Roman Catholic theology on the subject. The arguments

14. Sharpe, *The Theology of A. G. Hogg,* pp. 51-52.

15. Lest one present a caricature of Farquhar, certain qualifications to his argument
should be noted. First of all, he sought to avoid any identification of religious evolution
with a claim of Western cultural superiority. Secondly, he did not suppose any smooth
transition from the truths of one tradition to another. On the contrary he conceived of
the fulfillment of Hinduism in Christianity in the form of death and resurrection: "This
hard unyielding system must fall into the ground and die, before the aspirations and the
dreams of Hindu thinkers and ascetics can be set free to grow in health and strength so
as to bear fruit in the lives of Hindu villagers. Hinduism must die in order to live. It
must die into Christianity." Clearly "fulfillment" for him involved a triage of elements to
be salvaged and discarded, elements of continuity and discontinuity. One can in sum see
Farquhar's system as an example of the self-consciousness model of final primacy, albeit
with all the accompanying problems.

16. Especially pp. 115ff.

that follow involve accusations on either side of unfaithfulness to this initially shared theological commitment.

Such a common initial commitment did not mean that no constructive use could be made of the category of natural theology, at least for Brunner. In his earlier work he could propose "eristics" as a substitute for apologetics. While Barth did not himself employ such a negative account of the natural knowledge of God, opting instead simply for affirming the need of divine action for true knowledge, he could give a grudging acknowledgment to the position, even at the height of their mutual acrimony.[17] In this earlier position of Brunner's, the only "points of contact" between natural human reason and experience and divine revelation were negative in character. Humans can indeed come into contact with the divine, but only in the forms of bad conscience, despair, and uncertainty (in other words, in terms of a classically Reformation view of Law).[18] About this ironic view of the "point of contact," Barth himself acknowledges the affinity of Brunner's earlier position to his own: "[It was] a continuity which at the same time was discontinuity. . . . [T]he continuity was subordinate to the disconti nuity, and the contact to the contrast. . . ."[19]

Barth and Brunner are both Reformed theologians, and Kraemer stands in this tradition as well, and so all three contend one with another as they construe their common forebear John Calvin on the question of natural theology. As noted above, in Book I of the *Institutes of the Christian Religion,* Calvin affirms, in the spirit of Romans 1:18ff., that there is indeed an innate religiosity, a *sensus divinitatis,* that renders humans "without excuse." Talk of natural knowledge and innate religiosity is then possible, but the intent of that speech must be consis-

17. Karl Barth and Emil Brunner, *Natural Theology,* trans. Peter Fraenkel (London: Geoffery Bles, 1946), pp. 113ff.

18. On this point Kraemer's position is simply an adherence to a Brunnerian eristic position: "The main conclusion that follows from them and from the reasoning that preceded these illustrations is that, in the light of the dialectical situation of all religious life and of all religions, and in the light of the dialectical view of this religious life in Biblical realism, points of contact in the real, deep sense of the world can only be found in antithesis." *The Christian Message in a Non-Christian World,* p. 139.

19. *The Christian Message in a Non-Christian World,* p. 139. These same terms of "continuity" and "discontinuity" will dominate the Tambaram debates we are about to consider.

tent with Calvin's point, utterly to deny independent human religious possibilities and so to affirm the "utter depravity" of the human. It is within these parameters that the contention between Barth and Brunner (and Kraemer over against the other two) takes place. Thus, Brunner's earlier view of "contact" as eristics expresses this negative sense of the *sensus divinitatis*.

This common witness of Barth and Brunner to the primacy of the revelation of Jesus Christ, as well as their ensuing dispute over natural theology, provides for Kraemer the deeper doctrinal framework for his missiological views. But the fierce conflict that arose between the two, expressed acerbically in Brunner's "Nature and Grace" and Barth's responding "No,"[20] provided Kraemer with theological orientation as well. Positioning himself systematically with, and also between, Barth and Brunner, is the means by which Kraemer provided theological undergirding for his missiological proposal.

Given the Calvinist inheritance as well as the Christological commitments shared with Kraemer, a closer look at the neuralgic issue between Barth and Brunner is important. The heart of the matter was the question of the existence of "points of contact," *Anknüpfungspunkten*. The term hearkened back to the theological approach of liberal neo-Protestantism, and denoted first of all capacities or faculties of the human person, identifiable with the *imago Dei* and salvaged from the Fall, by which the creature could gain knowledge of the Creator. Candidates for such "points" have included such categories as reason, conscience, "the feeling of utter dependence," etc. As we have indicated above, Barth and Brunner rejected the straightforward assertion of any such capacity.

Brunner however went on to offer a distinction between a formal and a material definition of the *imago Dei*. The formal image, identifiable with human being as such, has been retained, e.g., in the capacity to hear. But humans lack the *imago* in the latter, material sense, which is to say any active capacity at our disposal by which to know God.[21] Barth does in fact acknowledge that such a distinction could

20. The debate is found in *Natural Theology*.
21. Barth points out correctly that, in spite of his anti-Catholic emphasis, Brunner here approaches the position of an "obediential image," passive in nature, which one finds in Thomas. See *Natural Theology*, p. 82.

be possible; he quips famously that "even as sinner man is man and not a tortoise."[22]

Barth however saves his most trenchant critique for the *intent* of Brunner's argument, to assert that humans have, "somehow," a "capacity for revelation" (albeit not savingly),[23] for in Barth's eyes, this compromises the very commitment to the sole necessity of revelation in Jesus Christ with which they both begin, however technically acceptable Brunner's formulations may be. Uneasy about this theological temptation, Barth asserts that "'natural theology' does not exist as an entity capable of becoming a separate subject within what I consider to be real theology — not even for the sake of being rejected."[24] "Natural theology" connotes for Barth not only this ultimately hubristic claim, slight though it may initially seem, but also any and every methodological accomplishment of such an intent: "Every *formulation of a system* . . . whose subject . . . differs fundamentally from the revelation of Jesus Christ and whose method . . . differs equally from the exposition of Holy Scripture." For Barth, then, the issue of "natural theology" is in the end an issue about how theology is conducted. Its symptom is any method distracted from its single-minded Christological basis.

By considering the Barth-Brunner controversy, not only with respect to specific positions but also at the level of larger theological intent and method, one can make better sense of Kraemer's position vis-à-vis that debate. In short, he formally assumes the Brunnerian position, since an affirmation of the errant, but nonetheless real, *sensus divinitatis* afoot in the religions is required of a serious account of the religions. But he does so with a thoroughly Barthian intent, namely to ensure that talk of "natural theology" or "points of contact" not take on a weight of its own independent of those central Christological affirmations. The hands were Brunner's, but the voice out into the missiological world was Barth's.

22. *Natural Theology*, p. 79.
23. *Natural Theology*, p. 79.
24. *Natural Theology*, p. 75.

Barth vs. Gutmann on "Points of Contact"

Anknüpfungspunkten has a second use in addition to that of theological anthropology and the *imago*. In the more concrete realm of church missionary practice, "points of contact" referred to the practices and the traditions of local peoples that might be borrowed in a particular area missionaries might go. Here Barth's treatment is a pointed polemic against the *Volkskirchliche*, "people's churchly" school of German missiology, led by figures like Bruno Gutmann and Christian Keysser, which played so prominent a role in the discipline in the 1920s. In the service of a theory of conversion of a whole people rather than isolated individuals, missiologists like Gutmann offered a romanticist vision of "primal ties" to clan and land.[25] Barth was well aware of this school of thought and its direct implications for the larger theological question of "points of contact," and weighed in on the question of their efforts directly.[26]

Whether or not this attack was fair to Gutmann, whose position entailed more nuance than described here, is not the issue here. Terms like *Blut* and *Volk* must have had a disturbing echo in Germany in the period leading up to the Nazi ascendancy. This helps to explain the strong reaction that the *Volkskirchliche* school evoked in Barth, and proves relevant to the subsequent debate with Brunner as well. For Brunner applied his concept of natural theology to the question of the *Ordnungen*, "ordinances" or "orders of creation," which included such institutions as family, the state, and the *Volk*. Barth was convinced that any concession in the more theoretical realm would result in aid and comfort to the cause of the German Christians with their fascist sympathies. So, while the debate took place in unusually severe circumstances, one could as easily argue that those very circumstances serve to show dramatically how much can be at stake.

With all of these preceding debates in mind, one can better under-

25. The classic study of this school of missiology, as well as its darker implications, is J. C. Hoekendijk's *Kirche und Volk in her deutschen Missionswissenschaft* (Munich: Kaiser, 1967).

26. "[D]oes not the truly prolific Gutmann literature sound all the way through like a single variation of the seductive song of the serpent: *gratia non tollit sed supponit et perficit naturam?*" Cited by Timothy Yates, *Christian Mission in the Twentieth Century*, p. 51.

stand Kraemer's main argument. For all these foes, near and far, missionary and theological, converge for Kraemer into a single phalanx under the banner of "continuity." Farquhar's fulfillment, Brunner's *theologia naturalis*, Gutmann's "points of contact" — all grow out of a more ancient error of alliance with philosophy reaching back through Aquinas to Origen, with the background set by the encroaching shadows of tyranny.

Kraemer's theological objection to "continuity" can best be understood in light of two concepts central to his project: religions as comprehensive, coherent, "totalitarian" worldviews, and "biblical realism" as the distinctive perspective of Christianity in particular. In the former case he emphasizes the manner in which the elements of a religion, its ethical, doctrinal, liturgical features, etc., "embracing a system of culture and civilization and a definite structure of society,"[27] constitute a single vision, move toward a single goal, and so conspire to make a total claim on the concrete person of the adherent. From an external point of view Christianity would seem to be one such comprehensive worldview; but Kraemer resists such a conclusion, tending as it does to account for Christianity in "immanent" terms as a philosophy, ethic, etc.

Kraemer insists, assuming an "internalist" perspective, that Christianity coheres, not around the Christian *idea* of God, but rather around the commanding and pervading reality of that God, expressed in admittedly varied Christian theological views of him. "Biblical realism" is then "theocentric" in the sense that the utterly dominant reality of God requires the transformation of all our worldly thinking.[28] The coherence of Christianity as a system or worldview bespeaks "a coherence and rationality of quite a different order,"[29] derived from the reality of God himself. Likewise, while one might use the term "revelation" for the unveiling of a concept of God in a religious tradition, for Kraemer the term is only used properly in Christianity, where it is employed in its properly "radical and absolute manner,"[30] connected to the open offense of the divine acts at Bethlehem and Golgotha. Building on these concepts, Kraemer in fact uses the expression "inherent

27. Kraemer, *The Christian Message*, p. 102.
28. Kraemer, *The Christian Message*, p. 63.
29. Kraemer, *The Christian Message*, p. 64.
30. Kraemer, *The Christian Message*, p. 69.

incommensurableness," anticipating a major direction of philosophical reflection on the subject, to describe the possibility of comparison between other, "totalitarian" religions and "biblical realism."[31]

At the same time, in the tradition of *sensus divinitatis*, Kraemer maintains dialectical senses in which, in light of biblical realism, one can still speak of "natural theology," "point of contact," "continuity," and "fulfillment." In each case, looking backward, as it were, one can only grasp the proper uses of these terms in the light of the final revelation in Jesus Christ: "This 'general revelation' can only be effectually discovered in the light of the 'special revelation.'"[32] And while the only "point of contact" is Jesus Christ himself, Kraemer offers additional, alternative senses. It can refer to seeming points of similarity that, in light of the two systems as wholes, turn out to be "dissimilarities,"[33] or it can refer to the missionary or local Christian struggling to address a concrete situation.[34]

In such cases, as long as the radical nature of the "rupture" between another religion and Christianity is preserved, one may even speak of a "continuity," so long as it moves from biblical realism to assimilate such elements as may be helpful in the sole task of expressing the Christian truth: ". . . it is very important to ask in the light of biblical realism how they [religious themes in theology, worship, art, organization, etc.] can function so as to foster a pure and vigorous Christian life."[35] Likewise one can use the term "fulfillment,"[36] but only in a paradoxical and subversive sense, as the realization of hope in a form utterly unexpected, as, in the phrase of Nietzsche, the *"Umwertung aller Werte,"* "the transvaluation of values."[37]

---

31. Kraemer, *The Christian Message*, p. 83. For a capable study of Kraemer as a thinker anticipating postliberal trends, see Tim Perry's *Radical Difference: A Defense of Hendrik Kraemer's Theology of Religions* (Waterloo, Ont.: Wilfred Laurier Press, 2001).

32. Kraemer, *The Christian Message*, p. 125.

33. Kraemer, *The Christian Message*, p. 136.

34. See especially ch. 8: "The Missionary Approach."

35. Kraemer, *The Christian Message*, p. 325.

36. It is worth noting that we have by now accumulated the following meanings of "fulfillment": as cultural superiority, as evolution in religious concepts, as Christ's realization of Old Testament promise, as assimilation of foreign elements in the Christian grammar, and as consequent subversion of original meanings. We can see how difficult it is to answer the question of "fulfillment," since it covers so wide a semantic range.

37. Kraemer, *The Christian Message*, pp. 124-25.

Kraemer's position conforms precisely to the conditions of final primacy. His stress on the distinctiveness and normativity of biblical realism amounts to an affirmation of Christ as the *prima veritas* in the order of truth over against the plethora of possible truths and claims of other traditions. From this first principle are derived all his objections to the various terms he associates with "continuity." Thus when he says that "there are no bridges from human religious consciousness to the reality of Christ,"[38] he is affirming that one cannot move directly from alien religious accounts to the truth of Christ: one cannot argue directly from "before" to "after." Kraemer's theology of "discontinuity" amounts to a strong emphasis on this one side of the grammar. Kraemer then attempts to give the other side its due, namely the possibility and necessity of constructing narratives that move from Christ to the alien claims as they form narratives. For the sake of the argument in the next chapter, it is worth underlining that the very same theological criteria, and so the same underlying conformity to the grammar of final primacy, may be found in Kraemer's treatment of indigenization.[39]

Kraemer vs. Hogg in the Wake of Tambaram

The contention between Kraemer and his opponents provoked at Tambaram and its aftermath, around the flashpoint of "continuity" and "discontinuity," may now be considered. As one reads Kraemer's response, and as one bears final primacy in mind, a misunderstanding at a fundamental level comes clear.[40] For Kraemer offers Clement of Alexandria and Karl Barth as exemplars of continuity and discontinuity respectively. But about the former he admits that "Clement held strongly that true revelation is only to be found in Christ." Furthermore he admits that, when Clement comes to describe in more detail the relationship between Greek philosophy and the gospel, he finds as

38. Kraemer, *The Christian Message*, p. 132.

39. Kraemer, *The Christian Message*, p. 324: "In the problem of adaptation, therefore, as it emerges in the stress of concrete life, the crucial point is the same as in the case of the point of contact. No catalogue or vademecum can be made, but the great pathfinder is the apostolic urge to pave the way for Christ. . . ."

40. "Continuity and Discontinuity" in *The Authority of Faith*.

many weaknesses, "mixed up with idolatry and polytheism,"[41] as he does elements of preparation in which philosophy serves as the *paidagogos Christou*.

Kraemer's preference for Barth corresponds to Kraemer's strong insistence that the Christian must have a firm and clear place to stand, Archimedes' *pou sto*, in the unique revelation in Jesus Christ. Why then does he not see in the "Clementine" position the accompanying need to acknowledge the "mysterious workings of God's spirit" in the religions? Why can he not see that, in the "true, good, and beautiful in the non-Christian religions . . . God 'does not abandon the works of His hands' "?[42] Kraemer's worry is that such an affirmation will, by a general tendency of human thought, lapse into a larger or more systematic claim to "general revelation" that will come to challenge the primacy of the Christian revelation. He wants, therefore, to hedge such affirmations about the "mysterious workings" in a cloak of unsystematized uncertainty. Such workings doubtless exist, but the when, where, and how must remain undeterminable. Kraemer's point conforms closely to what this essay has called "inversion": "This indisputable and important fact [that human possibilities and realities in religion may resemble divine possibilities and realities in revelation] requires . . . that religion in its human manifestation never can be in any sense the source from which we derive our standard of reference for the revelation."[43] Given these concessions in Kraemer's account of Clement, one may conclude that, where the *pou sto* is firmly in place, and where sufficient notice of human sin is given, there Kraemer could acknowledge the possibility of an exploration of Greek antecedents such as Clement's. Such a possible exploration of how God might have worked in a non-Christian religion would amount to a Brunnerian "adjustment" to a generally Barthian perspective.

As for Kraemer's opponents, final primacy poses then the most basic question: Are they divided from Kraemer in the most fundamental way, as between "grammatical" and "ungrammatical" constructions? Or is one dealing here with different emphases on different aspects of the same rule, and hence with complementary views? If the

41. "Continuity and Discontinuity," p. 18.
42. "Continuity and Discontinuity," pp. 4, 22.
43. "Continuity and Discontinuity," p. 19

latter is the case, has conflict between different families of constructions (e.g., *Logos* vs. law/gospel) been mistaken for a conflict between "Christian" and "non-Christian"? In short, exactly what sort of controversy is this debate between "continuity" and "discontinuity"?

A. G. Hogg insists, *contra* Kraemer, that both Christianity and non-Christian religions have a dimension of purely human consciousness, so one must be willing to say that revelation may be found in them all: "In non-Christian faith may we meet with something that is not merely a seeking but in real measure a finding...."[44] Hogg thinks that Kraemer's talk of "the faiths" must be complemented by talk of "faith" in which God is active in revealing himself to them.[45] Hogg seems to affirm just the sort of "general revelation" that Kraemer would consider outside the ken of appropriate Christian theology.

Matters become more complicated, however, when one takes into account the careful qualifications with which Hogg also nuances his position. First of all, he agrees with Kraemer that the religions must be considered as wholes, and as such they are so different that "points of contact" can then "only be found in antithesis." On this point Hogg, the expert on Hinduism, goes so far as to say ". . . this dye [of monistic mysticism] has become so 'fixed' as to render it doubtful whether any strands of Hindu conceptual thought can be safely woven into the web of an Indian formulation of Christian doctrine."[46] This is a judgment more stringent than either Kraemer, or this present essay, could accept!

Given such a strong qualification, what then is one to make of Hogg's talk of non-Christian "faith" as opposed to talk only of "faiths"? By the most plausible interpretation Hogg is affirming in a general way that it is possible that God is at work in the spiritual lives of others ("finding"), though the Christian may only perceive it through the revelation in Christ (with reference to Colossians 3:3, Hogg says that their spiritual lives are "hid with Christ in God"). He is speaking of a possibility the identification of whose instances he makes no effort to provide. "Faith" then means for Hogg the human response to a real action of God, though where and when this might be

44. A. G. Hogg, "The Christian Attitude to Non-Christian Religions," in *The Authority of Faith,* p. 103.

45. Eric Sharpe, *The Theology of A. G. Hogg,* pp. 79-80, has noted that on this point Hogg anticipates the later, well-known claim of Wilfred Cantwell Smith.

46. Hogg, "The Christian Attitude to Non-Christian Religions," p. 109.

taking place he makes no attempt to systematize. In fact, he makes it clear that for the Christian, the saving act of God is "inextricably bound up with Christ in its every feature."[47] We are in the same precinct in which Kraemer is willing to acknowledge the possibility of such work of God.

This same conclusion is borne out as one considers the other missionary scholars arrayed with Hogg in friendly opposition to Kraemer. H. H. Farmer, the British philosophical theologian, claims from the outset of his essay that "[I]f I rightly apprehend what Dr. Kraemer means by 'biblical realism' . . . namely that . . . God's activity as Holy Will directly operative amidst the concrete situations of history . . . then we were, and are, all 'biblical realists.'"[48] As for "fulfillment," whose meanings he analyzes in detail,[49] Farmer affirms only that someone's aspirations, when met in an utterly new and unexpected way, could be said to be "fulfilled" in a way not offensive to Kraemer.

When he turns to the crucial question of validity of non-Christian religious faith, Farmer wishes to affirm this possibility. His first argument in its defense is that some Christian theologies emphasize the divine Will, while others imagine God to be primarily educative, the latter option being a friendlier framework for his contention. This option amounts, in terms of final primacy, to an appeal to the *Logos*-type of argument. Farmer's second argument is that converts sometimes see their conversions as fulfillments, sometimes as revolutions, and that both perceptions can change with time.[50] In either case the example tacitly presumes precisely the context of faith in the form of the convert's retrospective gaze. Again Farmer's argument amounts, for our purposes, to an appeal to the breadth of final primacy with its different families of arguments, and its need to form retrospective narratives.

In the aftermath of Tambaram, Farmer returned to the debate, and here too he opened with an emphasis on the incommensurability of the religions as total systems of thought and action: "Considered as

47. Hogg, "The Christian Attitude to Non-Christian Religions," p. 113.

48. Hogg, "The Christian Attitude to Non-Christian Religions," p. 164.

49. Farmer distinguishes between fulfillment as ideas needing completion, aspirations realized in an utterly surprising form, and biblical promises realized. The third is so restrictive as to be tautological, and the first is clearly false if one considers the religions in their reality. Farmer focuses on the second.

50. "The Authority of the Faith," in *The Authority of the Faith*, pp. 176, 180.

systems or organisms, they are all in a real sense wrong . . . despite incidental and solitary rightnesses . . . the reason [being] that they leave (and must leave, being without Christ) the basic problem of man's existence unsolved — the problem being his alienation from God. . . ."[51] Ready to affirm this Kraemerian premise at the outset, as a defense against the "human tendency" to turn toward our own religiosity, Farmer then states the nub of the difference over the question of God's activity in other religions in this way: "Revelation seemed [to one side] to be almost equated with the incarnation. . . . [On the other hand there] were those who feel impelled by what they regard as given in the incarnation, namely God's love as active love going out to meet his children." But from the perspective of the rule, so long as the foundation is in place, these two affirmations ought to condition, rather than inhibit, one another.[52]

Has it simply been a mistake, then, to suppose, as so many historians of missiology have, that two roads truly did part at Tambaram, that its sharp debate did serve to isolate a real and basic distinction in approaches to other traditions? Such a conclusion would be too strong. First of all, the whole conference took place against the background of earlier, more extreme voices, pushing as they had the earlier conclusions of Jerusalem, voices advocating a relativist or pluralist alternative. Hocking's *Layman's Report* was after all a significant part of the background of Tambaram, for it shocked many into seeing the need of a work like Kraemer's.[53] And while others may not have agreed with Hocking's case for the end of missionary evangelism, they may have lacked the clarity or stamina to withstand the "tendency" in that direction. On this point the opponents are a united chorus of praise: Kraemer performed a service in what must be sought first, so that all else could be given in turn.

So there was in the air at Tambaram a struggle between views that were, in the terms of this essay, orthodox and pluralist. At the same time, however, the debate between Kraemer and Hogg *et al.* was clearly not such a conflict, but rather one better understood within the terms of

---

51. *International Review of Mission* 38 (1939): 176

52. The very same sort of distinction within the terms of the grammar may be found in D. S. Cairns's (a friend of Hogg's) response in the same edition of *IRM*.

53. See Yates, *Christian Mission in the Twentieth Century*, pp. 72ff.

final primacy. Likewise "continuity" and "discontinuity" may be better understood to refer to the two moments within the construction of retrospective narratives, and to differing families of arguments granting greater weight to one moment or the other within final primacy.

What difference then does a reconsideration of the debate at Tambaram make for the practice of contemporary missiology? That aspect of the Kraemerian case which won bilateral applause was the emphasis on the unique, Christocentric nature of revelation as a starting-point, and that aspect of the case of his opponents which Kraemer on second thought could have approved was the possibility and necessity of seeking, in a tentative mode, specific moments in which God has been active in the religions, their beliefs and practices. But the Tambaram debate was *not* helpful insofar as it leaves the impression that a divide is to be found here where in fact one has only competing expressions of the grammar.

What if one were to capture the lessons of Tambaram, so as to imagine the method by which Christian theologies should relate themselves to other claims and practices? Kraemer has stressed the holistic nature of traditions: What kind of method does this allow for the relating of one tradition to another? Tambaram makes one chary of "points of contact," and yet there is a constrained sense in which they are possible: How might one find and use them? How can one assess the "continuous" and "discontinuous" aspects of retrospective narratives? Finally, one must recall that Tambaram was the first international conference at which leaders from the "front-line" third-world churches themselves were present. How then should one relate one Christian proposal about alien claims to another, in particular to a construction by Christians in immediate contact with that alien environment to other constructions at a further remove? The articulation of such a method is this essay's next agendum.

Anatomy of the Body Catholic

If the thesis of final primacy is correct, then it ought to apply to all the theological occasions that call forth such assessments. So far the essay has considered mainly "in-house" examples, either from the history of Christian theology or from modern systematics, that illustrate the deployment of this rule. At this point, however, one may fairly require that the thesis be tested over against those "alien claims" themselves. The rule ought to show itself of use closer to the actual line of engagement, whether evangelistic or dialogical. After a bit more methodological throat-clearing, alien claims will come under consideration, first of the Hindu tradition (in Chapter 6), and then of local traditions in African Christian theology (in Chapter 7).

Before one addresses this mandate, however, several possible confusions should be removed. First of all, what of the scholars who labor diligently simply to give an accurate account of what adherents of other traditions believe and do? What about Buddhologists analyzing Tibetan ritual, phenomenologists who analyze diverse forms of sacrifice, anthropologists who study the structure of the societies in which such practices arose, or of philosophers of religion who analyze logical arguments about language that may have come from the same Buddhists? To be sure, each of these disciplines has its own assumptions, its own internal disputes. The Christian theologian is both in their debt and at their mercy, and the varied and contestable nature of these other disciplines, mediating as they do knowledge of the other traditions to the Christian theologian, is yet another reason why the theologian's constructions will in turn be contestable.

The consideration of alien claims according to final primacy, self-consciously Christian and theological though it be, need not be hostile to such specialized and "non-confessional" disciplines. They consider the same beliefs and rites, though under a different formal object, according to the norms of their own method. The Christian theologian, precisely as he or she is clear about the distinctive nature of their own enterprise, is free to learn about the other traditions with the help of these other disciplines, and to borrow philosophical or sociological tools for the testing and assimilation of selected beliefs and practices. Christian theologians are free to understand these other studies as disciplines in their own right, at the same time that they may consider them as "subaltern" disciplines in relation to theology, since this judgment itself is built on a properly Christian theological basis.[54]

Secondly, within the Christian field itself, one finds estimations of

54. Thomas Aquinas, *ST,* I.1.5.ad.2.

other traditions and their claims in a variety of different disciplines, each distinct both intellectually and sociologically. One scholar is a Tamil Christian writing a theology for the South Indian church, another is a sympathetic Westerner writing a history of Dalit Christian theology, another treats Tamil Christianity in a chapter of a global theology, and yet another is engaged in a dialogue with Hindus themselves. Each is a Christian theologian engaged in a distinct subdiscipline as he or she assesses Hindu claims and practices.

The same rule of final primacy comes, then, to be used (or neglected, for that matter) by Christian theologians in a variety of different disciplines. Before considering its employment, one needs some kind of classification, some "anatomy," to use a term more suited to the body catholic, the church. How ought one to think of the relationship of the different disciplines where finally primary discourse might be found? Such an anatomy in fact shows how the disciplines themselves, for example the protean discipline of missiology, ought to be related one to another.

Christian communities seek to make sense of the claims and practices of other traditions in a variety of ways. Churches form retrospective narratives as they appropriate vocabulary, at an unself-conscious level, as they preach, teach, and make moral decisions. Communities make decisions again as they engage in the business of second-order, formal theology. So the preaching of a third-century church cannot help but appropriate, and also emend, the Platonic concept of eternity as it tells its listeners about the Christian God. Along comes Origen who articulates this implicit retrospective narrative, at once continuous and discontinuous, in his *On First Principles,* especially as he articulates a cosmology whose center is Christ but whose main activity is contemplation. At yet a third level of remove is an ecclesial account more distant from the actual context of the other community's beliefs and practices. So Aquinas in the thirteenth century, or Zwingli in the sixteenth, or Maritain in the twentieth, might also have an account of the relation of Platonic to Christian claims. A vastly variegated picture emerges, though the same grammar of final primacy is at work throughout.

What conclusions can be drawn from this crazy quilt of challenges and responses? Missiology, contextual theology, theology of religions, global theology, and studies in interreligious dialogue: What do all these have to do with one another? In each case, the basis for reflection is contact between the church and an alien community, be it direct or indirect. In each case the rule for the resulting reflection is that of final primacy, though the disciplines differ with respect to object and audience.

Imagine Christian theology as a single organism,[55] in the dimensions of time (in which a construction has relations to earlier views) and in space (where constructions have differing degrees of proximity to the alien traditions themselves). A third dimension of "depth" is provided by the relation of one construction to another, of a work of systematic theology to a piece of homiletics, of one Christian confession or tradition to another. One could then attempt a kind of anatomy of constructions. In the case of Platonism, one would locate Origen near the point of actual contact with the external neighbor, Hellenism in this case, and yet separated by an element of "depth" from an Alexandrian street preacher. He is separated by space from a Syrian deployment of Platonic ideas, and by time from a work like Daniélou's.

Another example is helpful to illustrate the way that constructions may be "anatomically" located and related one to another. Evangelical Christians preaching in the villages of India engaged in the formation of retrospective narratives, "on the fly," as they sought examples that would speak to a village sweeper. This might stand in continuity, but also in contrast, to the more philosophically articulated, and more Catholic, attempt to build an Indian theology on the ground of Advaita philosophy found in Bramabandav Upadhyaya. Both would stand in continuity and contrast to the more idiosyncratic spiritual reflections of the wandering Christian mystic Sadhu Sindar Singh. Still, all of these constructions are attempts to articulate Christian truth, and all are planted in Indian soil. To this list one might add an author like Bede Griffiths with his long experience of the subcontinent. Each viewpoint grows out of direct and personal contact with Hinduism itself. At another remove would be the treatment of Hinduism in a Western theologian of dialogue, in Harold Netland or Heinrich Vroom, or of a systematic theologian proper such as Karl Barth. In each case

---

55. There is a long history of thinking about tradition in light of organicist metaphors (Newman comes to mind), and there are attendant dangers, e.g., overemphasis of continuity. But in this case we intend the metaphor of the body to point only to the interrelatedness of the different construals.

one finds the same basis and rule, but one can determine differentials of object and audience, of location and distance, between these different Christian constructions themselves.

What then is the relationship between these different Christian constructions? What is their relationship to their object, the Hindu community, its theologians and their claims and practices? To answer the former question, one should recall MacIntyre's concept of tradition as a "running argument." The relationship of Christian claims and practices to those of alien communities amounts to an "essentially contested concept,"[56] a question that generates in its myriad particular forms unending disagreement, since of the finding of continuity and discontinuity, and the forming of suitable retrospective narratives, there is no end. At the same time the "essentially contested concept" implies as its condition a background of common assumptions against which, like a boundary demarcating a playing field, the disagreement can take place. For example, the question of how the Buddhist concept of *sunyata*, emptiness, might inform, transform, or be fruitfully emended by, the Christian concept of mystical union or the virtue of humility, cannot be finally resolved, but the ensuing endless debate enriches the Christian self-understanding.

In light of this quality of a "running argument," one can discern a crucial corollary of the rule of final primacy, which can be called "resonance." This indicates the way in which different Christian constructions answering the claims and practices of the same alien community serve to check, challenge, and inform one another. No construal is an island, but rather each must give an account of itself before its peers. This has missiologically profound implications. Consider another example from the Indian context. The Christian dialogician in the Western academy finds various veins of continuity with the high philosophical tradition of Brahmanical Hinduism (one is reminded of the earlier example of Michael von Brück). At the same time Christian peoples' movements from the nineteenth century on have been strongest among Dalits ("untouchables") and have entailed therefore a critique of Hinduism and the caste system it supports. One would not

---

56. For an insightful application of this concept of the philosopher W. B. Gallie to theology, see Stephen Sykes's *The Identity of Christianity: Theologians and the Essence of Christianity from Schleiermacher to Barth* (Philadelphia: Fortress, 1984).

wish to claim that the more generous account, based in the Western academy, is invalidated, for it too could be a construal of alien claims according to the rule. At the same time the blithe offering of such generous accounts at a distance must confront and be accountable to other interpretations of those same Hindu claims and practices, at closer range such as one would find in the Christian Dalit movement. There ought to be a resonance, a reverberation between these Christian accounts of the same set of alien data, each located in a different place in the one body missionary. It is this very process of listening for the resonance between (which will often mean the dissonance between) different accounts that can serve to connect all constructions, no matter how second-order, or how embedded in Western academia, to the originating context of the church proclamatory.[57]

We are dealing here with an occluded context, an "excluded middle."[58] The tacit dimension so easily lost sight of in the assessment of alien claims and practices,[59] especially by a Western Christian scholar imagining himself or herself to confront another religion, is the church, and more specifically the local church that interacts with adherents of that religious tradition daily. Our goal here is simply to bring this occlusion into the conscious theological field of vision. Dialogue with Hinduism is fine, but one must not forget that Indian Christians, and especially those of the early generations, embody in themselves and recapitulate in their personal narratives the final primacy of which theologians ought to speak.[60]

---

57. It is at this point that much of the philosophical discussion about dialogue can better be understood as descriptive of the intra-Christian relationship between construals. The single, shared horizon against which all interpretation takes place is in fact the ruled boundary of Christian doctrine. This common horizon makes shared *Verstehen*, in the midst of the conflict of interpretations, possible.

58. Paul Hiebert, "The Flaw of the Excluded Middle," *Missiology: An International Review* 10 (1983): 35-47.

59. Here one can compare the "rediscovery" of native agency in the process of conversion in younger churches, to be found in church historians such as Richard Gray, Andrew Walls, Lamin Sanneh, and John Karanja.

60. One may compare the way that Bengt Sundkler speaks of the native pastor as the real "middle man" in his classic *Christian Ministry in Africa* (London: SCM, 1960), ch. 6.

Receptor Sites

How then do theologians of the Christian tradition, as they encounter an alien tradition, actually go about forming retrospective narratives? At this point one needs to switch the metaphor from anatomy to virology. Imagine two microscopic organisms coming into contact with one another. Each has, on its outer coating, where its identity lies encoded, distinct points where contact with the other organism is possible. Such points of readier access are called "receptor sites." While nothing logically rules out a myriad of possible points of conflict or convergence, in fact any two traditions tend to encounter one another around a limited number of issues, similar enough to attract comparison, but capable at the same time of crystallizing the telling differences between the traditions.

What is the relationship of the "receptor site" to the *Anknüpfungspunkt* mentioned earlier? The site has nothing to do with a human capacity, describable in general terms, but is rather a point of doctrinal comparison, grounded in and specific to traditions understood as coherent wholes. In keeping with the conclusions of the previous section, the sites are apt occasions for debate, because they involve both continuity and discontinuity rendered articulate by final primacy.[61]

Consider the example of Kenneth Cragg's *The Christ and the Faiths*, where he proposes a method of conversation between traditions called "cross-reference theology." Cragg intends to avoid any suggestion of a common fund of agreement between religions, for he respects the particular doctrinal and moral commitments of each tradition. As a result he imagines one tradition "interrogating"[62] another concerning key issues around which the interlocutors share an interest, though the resulting discussion more often than not serves to expose a key point of contention. In the case of allowing Christianity to be interrogated by Islam about Christology, Cragg zeroes in on the cluster of issues having to do with embodiment and the sacramentality of creation, with a vector toward the centrally contested claim of incarnation in his chap-

61. Here our point has similarities to the Brunnerian concept of "eristics" discussed below.
62. Kenneth Cragg, *The Christ and the Faiths* (Philadelphia: Westminster, 1986), p. 15.

ter entitled "Theologies of Magnificat."[63] The question of agency human and divine leads in turn to the question of the relation of revealed and Revealer, and so the relation between Holy Scripture's authority and the need for its interpretation, its "Capacities for Revelation."[64] According to Cragg, the "negotiation" around these points of "cross-reference," these points of convergent and salient disagreement, amounts to engagement at what this essay is calling "receptor sites." His work, in sum, offers a sterling example of generous but distinctively Christian reflection based on the identification of such sites.

The main features of the grand tradition of Christian proposals about other claims, consistent with final primacy, are the *anatomy* of the Body, *resonance* within that Body, and *receptor sites* at its periphery. How would such features work themselves out in practice? To the task of showing this by means of an example — that of Indian Christian theology coming to terms with Hinduism — this essay now turns.

63. Cragg, *The Christ and the Faiths*, ch. 2.
64. Cragg, *The Christ and the Faiths*, ch. 3.

6 *Testing Final Primacy —*
   Indian Christian Theology

Similar Dissimilarities

It has been cogently argued in recent years that the very reference to
"Hinduism" is an error of the Western mind, it being at most a cluster
of religions geographically defined by the Indus Valley.[1] It is worth observing, in the context of this essay, that some historians of religion
have contended that "Hinduism" became a religious entity precisely
with the onslaught of Westerners, scholars as well as colonialists, in
the Indian subcontinent in the nineteenth century. In other words, it
came to be a single "religion" in the same period, and in the wake of
the same forces, in relation to which Christianity's traditional claims
became problematic.

Hindologists argue over the heart of "Hinduism," for it displays
so much diversity as to defy easy characterization, including at once
polytheists, theists, pantheists, atheists, espousing as well as criticiz-
ing caste, practicing austere ritual purity in some of its sects and the
flouting of those very norms in others. It has been contended, for example, in the face of this bewildering diversity, that only the Vedas as
sruti, as authoritative revelation, may be offered a ubiquitous "sacred

---

1. Gavin Flood, *An Introduction to Hinduism* (Cambridge: Cambridge University
Press, 1966), pp. 5ff., mentions such views.

thread" running through all forms, though the writings are ancient and cryptic enough to provide minimal constraint.[2]

Even if this be granted, certain features tend to recur. Even in the case of disagreements, they tend to emerge from shared assumptions and to deal with shared problems. Furthermore it is safe to say that each and every one of those frequently (if not universally) shared features is in stark contrast to orthodox Christianity. While all forms may not share the pantheism of Advaita Vedanta, at the very least they offer neither clear distinction of Creator and creature nor a clear affirmation of the latter's reality. The pervasive allegiance to caste involves a view of human nature contrary to the "image of God," as well as a contrary view of human destiny, not to mention justice. Both religious end and means could not be more different. The purifications of the Brahmin, the austerities of the sannyasin, and even the ecstasies of the bhakti devotee speak to the Christian works righteousness. Understood on its own terms, Hinduism's traditions do imagine themselves to offer the devotee merit, power, and progress. Likewise, at the more popular level, the ubiquitous practice of *puja*, of personal sacrificial offering offered to a designated deity, cannot but look like idolatry to the Christian. Finally, the tradition of the avatar, as expressed for example in the *Baghavadgita*, even in its seeming similarities,[3] stands, in its denial of Christ's finality, in the starkest contrast to what Christians mean by "incarnation."

Things of course look different if one takes the pluralistic detour; and gymnastics, exegetical or metaphysical, are always available. But the truth is that if one holds up the most basic doctrinal norms of Christianity, the variegated reality called "Hinduism" cannot help but meet, in its most fundamental elements, a series of straightforwardly negative assessments. If one is looking for Christian doctrinal grounds to reject what Hindus believe, one can readily find them, and nothing that follows in this chapter can or should accomplish this judgment's reversal. The polemicists of both the Hindu and Christian persuasions in the early encounter were not wrong when they saw "irreconcilable differ-

2. So J. L. Brockington in his *Sacred Thread: Hinduism in Its Continuity and Diversity* (Edinburgh: Edinburgh University Press, 1981).

3. For these see esp. E. Geoffery Parrinder, *Avatar and Incarnation* (London: Faber, 1970).

ences" on every front that mattered. Brahmabandhav Upadhyaya, an eloquent advocate of a daring Upanishadic Christian theology (and so a deeply sympathetic interlocutor with Hinduism, one who insisted that he was a "Hindu Christian"),[4] himself summarized these "erroneous and mischievous" doctrines of Hinduism in general: "(1) God is all, all is God; (2) God, man, and matter, all three are eternal; (3) the doctrine of transmigration. These three doctrines are eating into the victuals of the Hindu race."[5] Standard evaluations such as this one stand, but surely there is more to say. The trick is to find those more generous and constructive judgments in such a way as not to pretend that these blunt initial judgments are somehow undone.

Vast as the Himalayas is the literature about Hinduism, and far beyond the reach of this author's expertise. More modest, but tall enough still, is the literature of the relations of Christianity and Hinduism, and a thorough review would far exceed the available space. More pertinent is the task of showing what light the preceding conclusions about interreligious method in a traditionary mode and "points of contact" can bring to the customary points of comparison between the two traditions. For it is key to notice that in each judgment listed above, acerbic though it be, a comparison was involved (e.g., that *puja* was a practice to be evaluated under the rubric of "works righteousness"). And each comparison in turn involves a cluster of decisions, and each such decision has collateral implications.

In what follows the methodological light of "final primacy" will shine on the task of analysis of these comparative judgments, and in particular the more positive or promising evaluations that accompany these initial negative judgments. For in each case something in Hinduism was, after all, similar enough to attract a comparison whose outcome was a verdict of "dissimilar." But if each "site" of the sort discussed in the preceding chapter is a point of convergent divergence, then one can fairly expect that arising from the very litany of rejections may be more positive implications as well. The Christian theologian must also ponder which *locus* on the Christian side will be most promising for comparison. For example, while the rejection of non-duality is

---

4. See Upadhyaya in Kaj Baago, *Pioneers of Indigenous Christianity* (Bangalore: Christian Institute for the Study of Religion and Society, 1969).

5. Upadhyaya in Baago, *Pioneers of Indigenous Christianity,* p. 118.

convincing when the comparative term is the doctrine of creation, there may be more promising possible mates.

Two more preliminary observations, growing out of this essay's methodological assumptions, are in order. First, religions encounter one another as traditions, and they seek to make sense of their interlocutor within a tradition of reflection. This is as true of Hinduism as Christianity, for it too tends to interpret other religions, and especially Christianity, according to its own "doctrine of alien claims" (to borrow William Christian's phrase). In this way neo-Hinduism, strongly determined by Advaitic philosophy, has tended to see all religious roads as equally serviceable insofar as the object of devotion is *saguna Brahman* (with attributes), though it alone is able to lead on to *nirguna Brahman* (the Absolute without attributes). In other words, what appeals to Western pluralists as a kindred doctrine is in fact a deeply Hindu way to construe other traditions, an approach itself embedded in a Hindu tradition of reflection.

So Hinduism not only interprets other traditions in its own light, all the time maintaining its pluralistic appearances, but also imagines an influence on those other traditions, at once consistent with its rejection of evangelism but all the same analogous to Christianity's basic practice of witness. Swami Vivekananda imagined for world Hinduism not proselytism but rather "the peaceful penetration and absorption of other religions."[6] By this gradual influence the hard edges of exclusivist particularities so offensive to the Hindu outlook would be smoothed, and other traditions come more to resemble the congenial model of alternate *darshanas*, "visions." Tradition is the medium in which such assessments work, no less in Hinduism than in Christianity.

Likewise Christians offer construals of Hindu claims in keeping with their own "doctrines about doctrines," construals themselves embedded in streams of tradition. Christian assessment of Hindu claims is an intra-Christian conversation about what to make of those other claims. In the present case this involves not only the "great tradition," but also the substream of Indian Christian reflection on the Hindu claims of their neighbors. Assessing Hinduism means conversing with Shankara and Ramanuja mediated proximately through the likes of

6. Paul Devanandan, *Preparation for Dialogue*, ed. Nalini Devanandan and M. M. Thomas (Bangalore: Christian Institute for the Study of Religion and Society, 1964), p. 90.

Sundar Singh and Upadhyaya, and more distantly Paul, Augustine, Luther, etc. In a manner consonant with the argument of this essay, this exercise requires making the location and interrelation of Christian conclusions within this tradition conscious and explicit.

Secondly, one need not imagine that Christian theology must come to terms with the five-thousand-eyed apparition called "Hinduism," nor that it need settle the question of Hinduism's essence before the reflection can begin. This essay has argued that one tradition cannot possibly come to terms, as if in a single gulp, with a rival tradition, itself full-orbed, with its own internal logic, its own mythological and doctrinal backing, its own concomitant practices, etc. It can at best strive to assimilate claims, practices, or clusters thereof, into its own contestable retrospective narratives. In other words, the process of comparison inevitably means dealing with the other tradition in parts and by degrees, which is to say insufficiently. Thus Christianity will, by the very nature of the enterprise, seek to come to terms with monism on the one hand and dualism on the other, the doctrine of avatar in one exertion and *hatha* yoga in another. The question of Hinduism's unity becomes moot, insofar as Christianity could not come to terms with such an entity, even if it could somehow be divined.

Encounters at the Level of Practice

The foregoing account of the encounter between traditions placed its emphasis on the receptor sites or nodes especially susceptible to comparison, *loci* of continuous discontinuity that aptly focus attention on key issues and bring light to bear on crucial differences between the traditions. This is particularly true of the Christian encounter with Hinduism, which has centered on a handful of doctrines. But it is worth noting at the outset several kinds of comparisons, and hence several kinds of assimilations of a proto- or extra-doctrinal sort. One may here cite the recent tradition of Christian ashrams, harkening back as they do to the more distant precedent of Roberto de Nobili's vision of the community of Christian sannyasins. Here one can mention Bede Griffiths' Kurisumala Ashram in Kerala, living out the Christian ascetic tradition in an Indian mode. The life they live is surely a more eloquent encounter than the account Griffiths gives of its life. For the latter is based as it is on a romanticist account of the medieval synthesis of sacred and secular, prior to its corruption by modernity, in this case applied to an idealized caste system.[7]

One may also think of the practice of composing devotional literature, in particular poetry. While one must deal with the relation to *bhakti* in a more formal, doctrinal vein in relation to the Christian concept of grace (see below), the greater impact of this movement may be found in hymnody. For example, the renowned Narayan Vaman Tilak was a converted Brahman who was himself instrumental in the revival of Maranthi literature. In the following hymn lines there is implied an assimilation of a style and images native to Hindu *bhakti*, but turned to the service of Jesus Christ: "Tenderest mother-Guru mine,/Saviour, where is love like thine?/I would snare Thee and hold Thee ever/In loving, wifely ways;/I give Thee a daughter's welcome/I give thee a sister's praise."[8] In the same vein the hymns of the Telugu church were thoroughly influenced by the *bhakti* style of poetry, though the authors would be careful to avoid religious themes (e.g., union with the divine) that they considered inappropriate.[9] Such borrowing of form or mode implies a continuity, a comparison with *bhakti* spirituality, though the content of the hymns themselves remains utterly orthodox.[10] In both the case of the ashram and of hymnody one is reminded that the judgments made as one tradition meets another are made by adherents with the whole of their lives. This serves as a corrective to the temptation to think that such work is the sole province of theologians.

This emphasis on encounter in the realm of practice can be considered from the Hindu side as well. In his introduction to Hinduism enti-

7. See Bede Griffiths, *Christ in India: Essays towards a Hindu Christian Dialogue* (New York: Scribner's, 1966), introduction.

8. Robin H. S. Boyd, *India and the Latin Captivity of the Church: The Cultural Context of the Gospel* (London: Cambridge University Press, 1974), pp. 115, 117.

9. R. S. Sundara Rao, *Bhakti Theology in the Telugu Hymnal* (Bangalore: Christian Institute for the Study of Religion and Society, 1983), ch. 5.

10. Another example of this sort of "formal" appropriation would be the devotional and spiritual writing of Dhanjibhai Fakirbhai, the clearest example being *Shree Krist Gita: The Song of the Lord Christ* (Delhi: ISPCK, 1969). The work consists exclusively of quotations from the New Testament, though the format is meant to imitate that of a discourse between yogic guru and devotee. Here the act of theological judgment of assimilation and discrimination consists solely in the choice of a framework or ordering of the Scripture itself.

tled *The Sacred Thread*, Brockington, concerned that most of his work has been an extended treatment of schools of Hindu thought, suggests that the truly shared ground for most Hindus is the everyday experience of devotional practice among individuals, families, and communities.[11] At this level the differences between non-dualists and qualified non-dualists would induce a look of incomprehension. Brockington suggests that one can identify certain central themes that express themselves in this common round of observance.

There is first of all the pervasive concern for purity and the avoidance of defilement. This contributes to the enduring power of caste distinctions. But Mary Douglas has explained in depth how these rules go beyond social norms to a view of a full-blown cosmology, which in turn is correlated to the understanding of one's own body as microcosm.[12] So the maintenance of purity and its accompanying ritual requirements go beyond individual welfare to pertain to the maintenance of a right ordering of reality as a whole.

This idea reaches back to the very roots of Hindu religion, and leads naturally to the second common theme, that of sacrifice. Here the roots reach all the way down to the sacrifices offered by the Brahminical priests themselves in the earliest period of Hinduism to preserve the right ordering of things: "By the period of the *Brahmanas*, these fundamental laws of the universe came increasingly to be identified with the laws of sacrifice. *Dharma*, which replaces the older term *rta*, is then supremely the sacrificial act that in effect conditions and maintains the cosmic order."[13] Sacrifice, though no longer in the original Vedic form, and in many cases bloodless, has also run consistently through Hindu tradition, as has this function of orienting and righting the world. Brockington again makes the point: "The cell set on its plinth was equivalent to the Vedic flame and its pile of firewood from which the flame leapt up or was identified with Mt. Meru, the *axis mundi*, while the carefully delimited area of the sacrifice persists in the successive courtyards characteristic of South Indian temples."[14]

The third theme of everyday Hindu devotion is that of the real

11. Brockington, *Sacred Thread*, pp. 204ff.

12. See Mary Douglas, *Natural Symbols: Explorations in Cosmology* (New York: Pantheon, 1970).

13. Brockington, *Sacred Thread*, p. 34.

14. Brockington, *Sacred Thread*, p. 202.

presence of the deity, ritually rendered in the holy place. The family shrine or temple is the place where the deity resides. His or her story is mythically recalled, the deity's power is acknowledged with gifts, and the devotee is granted a glimpse of the deity in glorious light in the *darshana*, the vision or unveiling. Located in such holy places is a wide array of sacred activities important in ordinary Hindu piety: the pilgrimage, for instance to the Ganges, the seasonal festival, for instance Pongal, rites of passage such as birth, name-giving, and marriage. This whole life of observance in relation to serving and beholding the deity makes clear the Hindu emphasis on *anubhava*, "experience," even among those who do not take part in the ascetical life per se.

If one takes the everyday piety of the Hindu devotee, characterized by these features, as the common denominator of the tradition and if one focuses not on doctrine, but rather on worship as the arena of encounter between traditions, to what conclusion is one led? Where lies the most promising site of "mutual interrogation"? On this score one need only listen to the Old Testament accounts of the piety of the Temple to hear of these very themes. "In days to come the mountain of the Lord's house shall be set over all other mountains, lifted high above the hills" (Isa. 2:2, the *axis mundi*); "In the year of King Uzziah's death I saw the Lord seated on a throne, high and exalted, and the skirt of his robe filled the temple" (Isa. 6:1, vision of the Lord in his glory); "O Lord God of hosts, who is like thee? . . . Thou didst crush the monster Rahab with a mortal blow . . ." (Ps. 89:8-9, the mythic account of the deity at the world's foundation); "The Lord spoke to Moses and said, 'say this to the Israelites: "these are the rules for any man who inadvertently transgresses any of the commandments of the Lord and does anything prohibited by them."'" (Lev. 4:1-2). We hear of the holy place, sacrifice, and the maintenance of ritual purity. In sum, the most basic connection, the *Ur*-comparison, may not be directly between a Hindu doctrine and a Christian doctrine, but rather between the themes central to ordinary Hindu piety, taken together as a *Gestalt*, and a second set of themes identifiable from the Old Testament account of worship in the Temple.

Here too, the identification of this similarity only serves to shine a light on the most pertinent areas of dissimilarity. For concealed under the genre of myth is an enormous difference with respect to the historical grounding of the stories in question. Hindu practice is blithely unconcerned about this question, and the import of the mythic references in the comparable Old Testament material is precisely the "de-mythologized" and historicized nature of the action of Yahweh on be-half of Israel.[15] Likewise the ritual purity of Leviticus is meant to be in the service of Yahweh's election of and sanctifying of Israel, and if Isra-elite purity and Temple devotion have any relation to the righting of the world, they do so only in obedience to his sovereign agency. (So at any rate do the scriptures attest, though Israel obviously did try to use their holiness for the sake of power and manipulation.) Finally this whole cluster of themes in the Old Testament undergoes "trans-valuation" in the New Testament, for all these themes are now read through the work of Jesus Christ. So this practically derived site of contention requires a two-step interpretation, first to highlight the dif-ference in meaning from the ritual life of the Old Testament, and then to effect the further distancing involved in comparison with the whole Christian canon. This is in keeping with the narrative sequence under-lying the template of the Scripture, as discussed in Chapter 1 of this es-say. Still, for all these differences, no matter how the instincts to purity, sacrifice, and cosmic order are sublimated, a similar cluster of themes has been found within the authoritative scriptures of the Christian church, and so an arena for understanding and debate found.[16]

15. Gerhard von Rad, *Old Testament Theology I,* II.i.i, "The Place in Theology of the Witness concerning Creation."

16. The above reflection on practice has turned eventually to the doctrinal commit-ments of each community, and so shown how such a line of demarcation cannot be main-tained. This is after all entailed in the assertion that religious traditions make their claim on the whole life of the believing community, as well as the claim that the doctrines help de-termine what one experiences. It is at this point that Ninian Smart's argument for a "point of contact" between Christianity and Hinduism in the realm of experience falls down (in *The Yogi and the Devotee: The Interplay between the Upanishads and Catholic Theology* [London: Allen & Unwin, 1968]). Smart begins by appealing to the six dimensions of any religious tradition (mythological, doctrinal, ethical, ritual, religious experience, and social life). He contends that forays into natural theology have limited themselves to the realm of doc-trine, while a yet more promising field would be that of experience. Turning to the Hindu tradition, he suggests that a focus on the contrasting experiential strains of *dyana* (yogic contemplation) and *bhakti* (devotion to a personal Lord), found in a variety of Indian schools, serve on the one hand to overcome an anthropomorphic view of the Absolute, and on the other to make worship as personal address possible. Thus this balance provides a better way to look at the conflicts between non-dualism *(Advaita)* with its monistic ten-dency, and dualistic options such as the school of Madhva, which separate the Lord from his creations, souls and world. Smart then goes on to suggest that traditions that lack this

The Classic Sites

Having laid the groundwork, and granting certain advantages in comparing apposite *Gestalten* of devotional practices, past and present, one still must acknowledge that a great deal of the literature in the tradition has been devoted to the consideration of certain key receptor sites, the *loci classici* of comparison. These require careful analysis of their own. The first such frequent comparison, for the more speculatively minded, is between the Hindu school of *Advaita* (non-dualist) Vedanta and the Christian doctrine of the Trinity. A good place to begin is with an amateur summary of the teaching of *Advaita*'s greatest proponent, Shankara, who worked in the early ninth century A.D. First of all, it refers to the non-dual relationship between *atman*, the real, inner self, and *Brahman*, the indescribable source and reality of all that is.[17] Shankara refers

---

balance of emphases are inferior, and one such tradition coming in for particular criticism is evangelical Protestantism. The argument shipwrecks on a number of points: 1) the orthodox grammar of the Christian tradition does not try to balance grace with some works (pp. 166ff. on the "Two Sided Anthropology of 'Religious Experience'"), and Aquinas would certainly not own such a view. 2) The Christian view of God and the world, whether Catholic or Protestant, could never accept Ramanuja's assumption that God needs a world as a soul needs embodiment (pp. 122ff.). So the Lord's full instrumental control of the world is not a sufficient rendering of the Christian meaning of transcendence. This leads to several endemic problems in Smart's argument: (1) while there may be dimensions to any religion, they cannot be strained out and analyzed in isolation one from another, for a tradition is precisely the unified interaction of these elements. Hence one cannot isolate doctrinal from experiential, or an "experiential" source of revelation somehow independent of the "mythological." This is precisely what the concept of the revealed authority of Scripture means to exclude (on this point one would imagine that the pious Hindu, devoted to *sruti*, would sympathize). (2) Tradition as such a unified interplay has its own internal and unique logic. The concept of grace that allows the cooperative as well as the operative in Thomas is an example of just such an internal logic.

Does this then mean that Smart's argument is null and void? Hardly, but it has a value other than what he has proposed. What he has shown is that the debate in Hinduism over the Absolute and the world, rooted as Smart points out in the strains of practice of *dyana* and *bhakti*, raises the key issue in the problematic of God and world. It marks the field, but cannot find the treasure. For a God who is free of the world but in lovingly creating the world is intimate to the world as well as transcendent over it, is just the answer the Christian tradition offers to the problem. But, as will be shown, this answer requires the full range of doctrines, including Christology and the Trinity.

17. This account is dependent on the following sources: A. D. Herman's *A Brief Introduction to Hinduism: Religion, Philosophy, and Ways of Liberation* (Boulder, Colo.: Westview,

to the classic passage in the *Chandogya Upanishad* that expresses this deep, underlying unity: "This invisible and subtle essence is the spirit of the whole universe. That is Reality. That is Truth. Thou art That."[18] To be sure, in everyday life there are innumerable particular, finite beings, which do have a lesser kind of reality. But from a higher point of view one comes to see them as involved in the veil of illusion *(maya)*. Shankara uses the example of a person who thinks he sees a snake in the dark, though in fact he sees a piece of coiled rope. He did indeed see "something," but one would have to admit that the "snake" had no re- ality.[19] It should be noted that all religious devotion to a personal God, to the Lord, *Isvara*, takes place at this lesser level, beyond which one must aspire to move.

The realization of this non-duality comes not in discursive thought, which still partakes of the distinctions characteristic of *maya*. Rather, such enlightenment about the true nature of reality comes in contemplative experience *(moksa, atmavidya)*, for which the enlight- ened one *(jivamukti)* is prepared by yogic discipline. While the school of *Advaita* saw a place for the other "ways," the other *margas* of sacrifi- cial duty and personal devotion *(karma* and *bhakti)*, these are of lesser importance than *jnanamarga*, the way of contemplative insight. The former can bring only knowledge of *saguna Brahman*, Brahman con- ceived to have definable attributes, while the adept in the latter can come to know *nirguna Brahman*, the unknowable, attribute-less Brah- man. Only with this insight can the adept come to that *moksa* which overcomes *karma* altogether.

The two central elements of classical *Advaita*, non-duality and the primacy of contemplative experience, are employed in innovative ways by contemporary Christian theologians who appeal to this school. Here our central distinction between orthodox and pluralist approaches comes into play. For those employing the latter,[20] the strategy is to un-

---

1991), and P. J. Raju's *The Philosophical Traditions of India* (Woking, U.K.: Allen & Unwin, 1971).

18. *Upanishads*, trans. Juan Mascaro (London: Penguin, 1965), p. 118.

19. Gavin Flood, *An Introduction to Hinduism*, p. 241.

20. Here one may cite Stanley Samartha's *One Christ — Many Religions: Toward a Re- vised Christology* (Maryknoll, N.Y.: Orbis, 1991) and especially the section titled "The Unitive Vision of *Advaita*" in the chapter called "Toward a Revised Christology." On the Catholic side one could point to Michael Amaladoss's recent *Making All Things New: Dia-*

derstand the noumenal Mystery behind all the phenomenal representations of the particular religions as Brahman. They privilege a common
mystical experience found in each religion as *jnana,* contemplative religious insight. These appeals to *Advaita* tradition become warrants, first,
for finding a parity of religious traditions whose rites and beliefs are all
helpful in a limited way, but are all ultimately unreal, enmeshed in
maya, insofar as they suppose that their particularities correspond to
the Absolute itself. They produce, secondly, a warrant for the kind of
pluralist knowledge that allows one to remain in the particular tradition precisely because by this deeper *jnana* one's faith may be identified
non-dualistically with the Mystery itself. One can pray to the triune
God so long as one is, in doing so, seeing past that symbol. There results
an argument that would make Vivekananda or Lessing equally proud,
one in which the Hindu doctrine is deployed as a warrant for what this
essay has called "departicularization."

If one were to reject this sort of pluralist appeal to *Advaita,* how
might the comparison at this receptor site work? Recall that at receptor
sites traditions converge so as to illumine salient disagreements.
Advaita then serves to make clear what the Trinity is not saying. Put
another way, the issues whose debate produced pluralist *Advaita* bring
into focus a series of conundra, in relation to which the Trinity may be
seen as a radically different sort of answer.

An eloquent account of this first sense in which *Advaita* can be
"fructifying" for a Christian doctrine of the Trinity may be found in an
earlier (and thoroughly orthodox) work of Panikkar, his classic *The
Unknown Christ of Hinduism.*[21] There he focuses on the verse at the beginning of the *Brahmasutra:* "Brahman is that whence the origination,
sustenance, and transformation of this world comes." Panikkar considers the verse, with the help of the commentary of Shankara, and
connects it with the natural theological tradition of cosmological arguments for the existence of God. But he also underlines the *atman* aspect
of the verse by pointing out that the human being who wonders

---

logue, Pluralism, and Evangelization in Asia (Maryknoll, N.Y.: Orbis, 1991), where a similar
argument is made but with more emphasis on the commonality of all religions when
considered in terms of the social-functional role of their systems and the phenomenology of symbol. Amaladoss stresses that the latter stand in a relationship of *advaita* (p. 82).

21 (London: Darton, Longman & Todd, 1964), esp. ch. 3, "God and the World according to *Brahmasutra* I,1,2."

whence he or she has come is among those very things so originated. Such knowledge does not depend on the human intellect (for by Hindu tradition it is granted by revelation). Humans are capable of this knowing, and yet it cannot be *Brahman* who is known. So far the argument tracks closely the theme of unknowability such as one might find at the opening of the *Summa Theologiae*.

But it is precisely in the conundrum of the particular human knower and the transcendent Known, *Brahman*, what Panikkar calls the problem of the "bridge to the transcendent," that one reaches the limits of the concepts involved. At this very point yawns open the problem of *atman* and *Brahman*, but also the problem of the relationship between *Brahman* and *Isvara*, a personal Lord, since both *atman* and *Isvara* are subsumed under the question of the relationship of *Brahman* to the world of persons and things. At this point the cosmological argument in its Hindu form hits a predictable snag, since the Cause, divine power, the Lord, the Creator, or the Prime Mover are "all expressions for the principle of the world, but not for the Absolute as such."[22] At the point of this conundrum, the relation of the Absolute to the world, all the famous debates of the Hindu philosophical schools over dualism and monism erupt. On each side of the divide there is the search for an adequate means of mediation between Absolute and world so that the two both maintain their integrity while achieving an intimate connection. Rather than seeing this as a failure, the Christian theologian must see this quandary as a success. Here is the appropriate limit of such an argument. Furthermore, the irresolvable battle between monism and dualism serves eloquently to testify that the resolution of the question of personhood and utter transcendence cannot be found in a consideration of the God-world relationship. These are the very points on which Christianity would interrogate Hinduism.

At just this point the classical doctrine of the Trinity suggests a radically different point of comparison, one that Hinduism could never have imagined. *Brahman* points to the One who is utterly transcendent origination, the unknowable *Arche*. *Advaita* thinks of *Isvara* as the divine person "responsible for the creation of the world."[23] But what if one were to retain the concept of personhood, derived from

22. Panikkar, *The Unknown Christ of Hinduism*, p. 115.
23. Panikkar, *The Unknown Christ of Hinduism*, p. 123.

Isvara but quite foreign to *Brahman,* who in the Hindu tradition is *apurusha?* What if one applied that concept to the whole of the God-head? What if one retained transcendence and unknowability, as well as the need for revelation, for *sruti,* and then applied personhood to the Godhead itself, and not to the God-world relation, albeit in a suit-ably divine manner? What if one preserved the utter unity of *Brahman* by a "non-duality" within the Godhead itself, but one in which the personhood is as real as the unity? In classical Christian theology the Persons of the Godhead reside in just such a relation to one another, so that the comparison of *Advaita* and Trinity proves fruitful as it sug-gests, with Hinduism's own terms, a kind of relation utterly unique, challenging, and surprising for Hinduism's philosophy.

The key question is this: To what Christian doctrine is the other claim, in this case having to do with the concept of *Advaita,* to be com-pared? In the example at hand, the other doctrine became fruitful when the comparison was *transposed* to another object, from the God-world relation to that of the intra-trinitarian relations of the Persons. This transposition makes it clear that the most appropriate analogy is not the most obvious one. The analogy between *Advaita* and the persons of the Trinity does shed light on the original question, that of Absolute and world but indirectly, "around the barn," as it were. For while the doctrine of the Trinity is not, in the first place, about the God-world re-lation, it brings in its wake new possibilities for seeing that relationship. The comparison of *Advaita* and the Trinity produces just such a wake.

It is at this point that the contribution of the great twentieth-century Indian theologian Brahmabandhav Upadhyaya is particularly helpful. His trinitarian reflection, in both prose and hymnody, on the famous expression for *Brahman, Saccitananda* (Being-Truth-Bliss), fol-lows in the footsteps of the pioneering but heterodox Keshub Chandra Sen. But of more interest for present purposes is his reinterpretation of *maya,* classically understood by advaitins as the illusory nature of cre-ation as *asat,* non-being, in contrast to *Brahman.* Upadhyaya borrowed from the school of Ramanuja the affirmation of creation as real and contingent, though he preserved the advaitin emphasis on the unreal-ity of creation in and of itself. By means of this mix-and-match borrow-ing, and in keeping with his method, by which he sought to deploy Shankara's non-dualism in a manner analogous to Thomas Aquinas's use of Aristotle, Upadhyaya reinterpreted *maya* as *creatio passiva,* a derivative reality grounded only in God. In other words, insofar as creation presumes its own status, it is non-being, but seen in relation to God, it bespeaks reality and power *(Sakti)*. Here he appeals to sacred support: "The word *Maya*, in its significance of 'abundance' (see *Vedanta Sutra adh. 1 pada 1,13,14* . . .) is beautifully appropriate . . . for creation is . . . the overflow of the divine being, knowledge, and bliss . . . it [also] meant 'art, wisdom, . . . and supernatural power.'"[24]

Upadhyaya's interpretation has been criticized as unfaithful to the original Vedantic meaning of *maya*, but this is in fact the strength of his position. For in the same way that Aquinas transformed Aristotle's Unmoved Mover so as to instill it with the pure vitality and actuality of the Christian God, so Upadhyaya has transformed the God-world relationship that the Hindu sources assumed. He has suffused *maya* with qualities derived from God without tying its being necessarily to God, which is to say he has assimilated the terms to a Christian doctrine of creation. Upadhyaya has, in a word, implicitly offered a retrospective narrative employing both similarities and dissimilarities in the concept of *maya* in order to show the relation between the abundant being that is the triune God alone, and the contingent being of creation. Hindu terms are deployed to a deeply Christian end.

The other major sites of conflictual convergence between Christianity and Hinduism both derive from the province of the personal and theistic traditions particularly, though not exclusively in Vaisnavism. Thus it makes sense to consider both *bhaktimarga* and the *avatar* together. *Bhaktimarga* can be defined as the spiritual path of loving devotion owed to the deity who comes to the believer's aid so that no sacrifice or other offering can be a sufficient return. The Anglican theologian Fakirbhai defines it as "dwell[ing] in God's love with full trust."[25] Though the word is used in the *Bhagavadgita* to refer to Arjuna's devotion to Krishna, *bhakti* as a movement emerges in southern India in the seventh century. The movement that began at that time spread out to include the north as well as the south, to worship of Siva

---

24. "The True Doctrine of Maya," in Kaj Baago's *Pioneers of Indigenous Christianity*, p. 147.

25. Dhanjibhai Fakirbhai, *Kristopanishad* (Bangalore: Christian Institute for the Study of Religion and Society, 1965), pp. 25-26.

as well as Vishnu, all sharing the "the rapturous response to a very personal deity in his immanence[,] . . . a deep sense of the worshipper's own inadequacy . . . [and] an appeal to the deity's forgiveness and grace, accompanied by a total surrender to him."[26]

The close parallel to the doctrine of grace in the Christian tradition is obvious. Even Western theologians chary of talk of parallels have acknowledged this convergence.[27] It would seem hard for a Christian to object to the following prayer of the great Sri Caitanya: "Chant his name of the Lord and His glory unceasingly/that the mirror of the heart may be wiped clean/and quenched that mighty forest fire/raging furiously within." It is only as we look deeper at the accompanying assumptions that the yet greater dissimilarities appear.

One Christian theologian who has pursued the more fundamental or pervasive differences between grace and *bhakti* is Sabapathy Kulandran.[28] According to his account, the real parting of the ways between the two traditions cannot be caught if one merely compares statements of need or hymns of praise. In the case of Hinduism, the way of grace, even the "cat" tradition of utter helplessness, remains a means of salvation, a state, albeit of surrender and gratitude, to be reached. "*Bhakti* is being asserted [as] a *marga* or *upaya* (method). The emphasis is on a method adopted by man."[29] Kulandran offers two pieces of evidence to support his point. First, even where *bhaktimarga* is preferred, *karmamarga* and *jnanamarga* are not disowned. When Ramanuja says that the other ways culminate in *bhakti*, his "additive" logic is far from a Christian grammar of grace. Secondly, *bhakti* devotion itself is imagined to carry power. The Saivite saint Thiru Navatk Arasu says in this vein: ". . . If a man, whose body is rotting . . . of the lowest caste . . . is a lover of god, he shall be the God whom I worship."[30]

Now a Christian must admit that Christian faith too can be praised

---

26. John Brockington, *Hinduism and Christianity* (New York: St. Martin's, 1992), p. 72.

27. On the admissions of Barth and Kraemer of such close similarities, see Wesley Ariarajah, *Hindus and Christians: A Century of Protestant Ecumenical Thought* (Grand Rapids: Eerdmans, 1991), pp. 63ff.

28. See his *Grace: A Comparative Study of the Doctrine in Christianity and Hinduism* (London: Lutterworth, 1964)

29. Kulandran, *Grace: A Comparative Study*, p. 243.

30. Kulandran, *Grace: A Comparative Study*, p. 243.

in the New Testament as if it were a powerful entity in itself: "If ye have faith as a mustard seed. . . ." Still, between the two yawns the wide gap between faith and works. That gap cannot adequately be shown without rendering a fuller account of a variety of corollary beliefs. So, for Kulandran, the utter difference in the Hindu concept of *bhakti* requires an account of the autonomous system of meting out justice cosmically that is *karma*. It requires a reminder that the Hindu concept of soul is distanced from the concept of personhood. One must also recall how central the idea of emanation is to the Hindu relation of the Absolute to the world, so that talk of grace bestowed by Someone distinct from self and world is problematic.

Kulandran's argument describes yet another kind of pattern of similar dissimilarity. *Bhakti* presents remarkably close analogies of thought and piety, but the requisite object of that devotion, who is also the agent of grace's bestowal, is absent. The form is similar, but the matter lacking: the wedding feast of praise beautiful, the Bridegroom absent. Even here, Hinduism proves a most able propaedeutic to a proper understanding of Christianity itself, for it now turns out that grace is only meaningful for Christians as it describes, under the rubric of the doctrine of soteriology, their relationship to Jesus Christ himself.

All discoveries of similar dissimilarities involve, from the perspective of this essay, a retrospective narrative of final primacy discriminating between elements that could never lead smoothly on to Christ, and others that can be seen as promising in his train. Kulandran offers such a narrative by means of an implied contrast of form and content. Other prominent Indian theologians engaged *bhakti* more directly with respect to its thematic content. One finds them, dislodging, juxtaposing, and rearranging, pulling up aspects of *bhakti* in order to replant them together with new Christian elements and themes, and in so doing they do demonstrate a similar dissimilarity.

The following example can illustrate such rearrangement. When Vengal Chakkarai employs *bhakti*, he does so in conjunction with the Hindu concept of *sakti*, or "power," which pertains to mystical and spiritual experience, sometimes in personified form. But Chakkarai redeploys the concepts to describe the resurrection and ascension of Jesus Christ: "The first Easter joined together energy and love, laying the foundation for the Christian view of the *Avatar* of God in Jesus

Christ."[31] Using this collage of terms in the service of a strong affirmation of the unique particularity of Christ, understood by means of the biblical narrative, Chakkarai emphasizes in the strongest way the discontinuity with the Hindu background.

So far the question has been *what* Hindu proponents say, in the present case about *bhukti*, but the tradition of *bhakti* itself raises the question about *who* these Hindu proponents are, and the Christian church of India has pursued this question with zeal. For one may find, throughout Indian church history, Catholic or Protestant, a consistent undercurrent in its reaction to its Hindu surrounding. While in the sixteenth century the great Jesuit sannyasin was mastering the *Upanishads*, the question of communion between his Brahminical circle and the simpler, lower-caste Parava Christians arose, and eventually laid low his plans. In the nineteenth century, as more liberal Protestant leaders began to accommodate themselves by means of the notion of "fulfillment," the small explosions called the "People's Movements" continued in the villages, where untouchables, the *Dalits*, received the message of gospel acceptance, and at the same time, rejected everything that had to do with caste and its privileged members. Put simply, points of contact were the last thing they sought with their Hindu upper-caste oppressors. In this light one can hear the following *Dalit* Christian critique of the line of Indian Christian authors from Upadhyaya through the "Re-Thinking" group, who have been frequently cited in this chapter: "The roots of Indian Christian theology lie in the experiences of mostly upper caste/class Christian converts of this century and the last. . . . These thinkers and their experiences and search were very different from an average Christian's in India. . . ."[32]

In the same way Hindu-Christian dialogues tend to be gatherings of upper-caste Hindus and liberal Christians, with the resulting predispositions to pluralist agreements and occlusions of the interests and perspectives of ordinary Indian Christians.[33] Even at this unlikely

31. P. T. Thomas, *Theology of Chakkarai with Selections from His Writings* (Bangalore: Christian Institute for the Study of Religion and Society, 1968), p. 63.

32. In James Massey's "Ingredients for a *Dalit* Theology," in R. S. Sugirtharajah and Cecil Hargreaves, *Readings in Indian Christian Theology*, vol. 1 (London: SPCK, 1993), p. 153.

33. See Mark Heim, "Choosing Roots: The Contexts for Christian Theology in India," *This World* 21 (Spring 1988).

point one may find a similar dissimilarity, for *bhakti* itself tended to protest caste distinctions and to invite a wider range of devotees.[34] One might say that *bhakti* is similar in its frequent agreement with Indian Christians over caste, but dissimilar in its unwillingness to break its solidarity with the actual social and religious system that caste supports.

The issue of caste and *bhakti* is a clear example of the need for locating theological proposals within the Body catholic offered in Chapter 5. The construction by upper-caste Christians has to hear the resonance of protests of *Dalit* Christians. Their rejection amounts to a tacit argument for the flaws hidden away in the concept of *bhakti* rendering it ill-suited for use in a Christian ecclesiology or moral theology. Theologians using concepts like *bhakti* and other classical Hindu terms must be vigilant against the Hindu-derived tendency to pass over the issue of *koinonia* in the church as a necessary condition of the right understanding of other doctrines. On this score the *Dalit* Christians' argument, and the resonance that confirms it, resemble other moral-ecclesiological protests offered by liberation theologies of the poor.

Indian Christian theological evaluations of Hinduism may sometimes have the unintended effect of underplaying or distorting other Christian doctrines, and this in turn reveals those features of Christian faith and practice largely hidden in a Hindu-Christian dialogue. It is no accident that a number of the prominent early Christian theologians or spiritual leaders (Upadhyaya, Chenchiah, Sundar Singh, etc.) were unable to fit the reality of the church into their theologies or their lives. To be people with a sacred calling Hindus can certainly understand, though the concepts of election in history and conversion, so central to a Christian understanding of church, are foreign to Hinduism.[35] Likewise, that tradition of theologians offered eloquent accounts of the "Abelardian,"[36] moral-influence theory of the atonement, but struggled to complement or move beyond this subjective account.[37]

34. See Herman, *A Brief Introduction to Hinduism*, pp. 64-65.

35. See especially ch. 3, "Come, Join My Church," in A. G. Hogg's *The Christian Message to the Hindu* (London: SCM, 1947).

36. See Gustav Aulén, *Christus Victor* (New York: Macmillan, 1969), pp. 95ff.

37. An exception would be Bishop A. J. Appasamy, who stressed the moral-influence theory in a manner consistent with his stress on "Christianity as *bhaktimarga*," but late in his career was able to articulate a more "substitutionary" view: "The suffering

That same tradition of theologians struggled to give a satisfying account of the relation of divine and human natures in Jesus Christ. For example, Chenchiah could on the one hand emphasize the "raw fact of Christ," more basic than any later dogmatic construction, as well as the spiritual experience, the *"anubhava* of the living Christ." It is as if he can give an account, by reflection on Hindu terms, of the human nature of Christ on the one hand, and the divine on the other, but is stymied when it comes to their real union. Here he resorts to an evolutionary concept, derived from the Yogic thought of Sri Aurobindo, of the advent of Supermind: "He is the *adi-purusha* of a new creation. . . . In Jesus, creation mounts a step higher."[38]

It is no accident that these three Christian doctrines — church, atonement, and Christology — are often inadequate in Indian Christian accounts of the Christian truth vis-à-vis Hinduism. All three form a *Gestalt* in Christian theology, for all three presume a Christian anthropology according to which embodiment is integral to human personhood. The logic of a really human, embodied Lord whose actual, bodily death saves, and who now inhabits the real, embodied community called "church," challenges any account of the Christian faith that might veer in a more abstract, gnostic direction. Such a challenge to prominent accounts of Indian Christianity, and so to the Hinduism with which they seek encounter, is necessary.

That real death of Christ atones for human sin, and the church comes into being by the blood and water from his side. So the tendency of theologies borne of close dialogue with Hinduism to underplay sin has also been observed: "The Biblical tradition [of human sinfulness], confirmed as it is by the insights of Sundar Singh . . . , must receive more emphasis than it has in the past."[39] While the concept of *karma* has proved a useful starting-point, the distinctiveness of

He has borne for us is beyond our reckoning. . . . After the Cross no one can say that God forgives men because it is easy for Him or because He does not care to uphold the law that righteousness should prevail in the world." See Appasamy, quoted in Robin Boyd, *An Introduction to Indian Christian Theology* (Madras: Christian Literature Society, 1969), p. 135. While one need not see a particular kind of penal or forensic account, the grammar of Christian theologies of the atonement would seem to require some acknowledgment of the *pro me,* "in our place" aspect of the event.

38. Chenchiah, quoted by Boyd, *Introduction*, p. 150.

39. Boyd, *Introduction*, p. 245.

sin as an offense against God must be conveyed. Here too, an underlying coherence of Christian anthropology, in contrast to Hinduism, accounts for the occlusion. Those embodied human persons own a moral agency, and a moral corruption, that cannot be transcended or bypassed, and they must give an account of a God whose personhood is equally irreducible. The Christian account of Hinduism must reckon not only with sites of convergence and contest, but also with subjects *not* often mentioned.

This nexus of Christian doctrines often undervalued by Hindus, and even underplayed by Indian Christians writing out of a Hindu context, helps in the evaluation of the third and last of the key receptor sites, the Hindu doctrine of the *avatar.* The Christian may ask how much of the Hindu tradition here could be consistent with faith in Christ. The same selectivity is required, to see which elements are or are not consonant with Christian faith. The pattern of similar dissimilarity in the case of *avatar* is, again, between the initial convergence of features, and the yet more profound differences that emerge from the wider nexus or constellation of beliefs. At the first, external level, one can note such features as miraculous birth, divine compassionate intervention on behalf of humans, etc. One could go on to observe, of some of the *avatars* spoken of in the classic list in the epic *Mahabharata*,[40] that they are real, historical figures who are also divine, subject to death, and whose coming to the world has serious moral purpose.[41]

But this is the very point at which direct comparisons between traditions can deceive unless one considers each claim's natural habitat. The *avatar* doctrine's classic expression is the following verse from the *Bhagavadgita:* "Whenever there appears a languishing of *dharma*, when *adharma* arises, then I send forth myself. For protection of the virtuous, for destruction of the wicked, for the establishment of right, age after age I come into being."[42] From this alone one learns that this descent is cyclical, "accomplished in a spirit of imperturbable indifference."[43] This cosmology of recurrence in turn is related to concepts of reincarnation and *karma.* These amount to the systematic reversal of Christ's

40. *Mahabharata* 3, 115; 5, 96.
41. Here I am dependent on Geoffrey Parrinder's *Avatar and Incarnation* (London: Faber, 1970), ch. 9, "Analysis of Avatar Doctrines."
42. *The Upanishads*, trans. Juan Mascaro (London: Penguin, 1962), pp. 62ff.
43. H. Zimmer, *Philosophies of India* (New York: Pantheon, 1951), p. 390.

finality. It is in this sense that one can understand the great "Yoga of the Vision," when in *Bhagavadgita* 11 Arjuna is shown the myriad, brilliant forms of Vishnu the transcendent.

Here, as with the doctrinal issues occluded in Indian Christian literature, the relationship of the *avatar* to the body, to historical agency, and to a full human nature is radically different than in the case of Christian incarnation. So, in spite of the extensive preliminary similarities a scholar like Joseph Neuner can find two logics that stand in the sharpest contrast: ". . . the basic thesis of all *avatar*-theories asserts that God, when he comes to earth, has nothing to do with nature, with *praktri* (the body)."[44] Such a conclusion is valid, but only in light of that web of presuppositions and implications in which the concept of *avatar* rests.

The *avatar* presents yet another example of similar dissimilarity. Only at this point does the theological task commence, for at such a "receptor site" the work of forming a retrospective narrative, of bringing both similarity and dissimilarity into relation to the *prima veritas* commences, though it may be accomplished by a considerable variety of arguments. But what of the most basic questions: Is truth taught in the Hindu concept of *avatar?* And can it be fruitfully employed by the Christian? To the first question comes a resounding "perhaps," for surely the longing for saving intervention in bodily form is an eloquent yearning. To the second question comes a decisive "it depends," especially on how clear the Christian author is that the term is employed to transform and overturn Hindu connotations and expectations. So one cannot answer such questions independently of the forming of retrospective narratives.

Another assumption underlying this entire essay is the correlation between claims and practices. In the case of the nexus of theological issues around embodiment, agency, and responsibility vis-à-vis the church, the atonement, and sin, the question of doctrine cannot be separated from the centrality of baptism, the public moment of response and commitment in which that atonement comes into relation with this sinner. It is at this point, for those seeking to be "Hindu Christians," as in the cases of Upadhyaya, that the moment of truth comes. One may consider in this context the suggestion that the gospel ought

44. In "Das Christus-Mysterien und die Indische Lehre von den Avatars," in Alois Grillmeier, ed., *Das Konzil von Chalkedon: Geschichte und Gegenwart*, vol. 3, p. 820.

to be, not a cause for the conversion of a few, but rather a leaven or catalyst for Indian culture as a whole.[45] Both kinds of talk can convey something true and helpful, so long as they are spoken on the Christian side of the baptismal line of public, lived, embodied commitment.

But must Hindu claims really pass through the criteria of Christian doctrinal norms? Other traditions can have other things to say, which may well be true in their own right, quite independently of Christian truth. Aren't there truths quite unique to Hinduism, from which the Christian can profit, without imposing the harsh superego of Christian norms of truth? The answer must be a qualified "yes." Surely a tradition as different as Hinduism has its own, quite alien points to make. Still, the mere recognition that a truth is "quite unrelated" itself implies a tacit "scan" of Christian claims. For example, there is a tradition of reflection on the human person in relation to nodes of energy, especially in Yoga, that are quite foreign to anything that has ever occurred to Christian theologians. These explorations in turn have implications for the relationship of matter to energy in the human body.[46] Such ideas might have something to contribute to Christian reflection quite unlike prior thinking, for example as Christians try to understand Paul's reflection on "spiritual bodies" in 1 Corinthians 15.

It is, however, inevitable that these alien concepts be brought into some relation to Christian truth. First of all, they themselves sit in relation to other claims a Hindu would wish to make. So the concept of *chakras* for a practitioner of *kundalini* yoga has mythological roots, as well as implications for one's idea of *moksa* through the "rising" of power into the head, which represents, microcosmically, the Godhead.[47] While a claim may seem, in itself, neutral to any Christian claim, it dwells amidst other Hindu beliefs that are bound to collide with Christian claims. Secondly, the Christian must assume that truths cohere, though he or she will only see that full coherence on the Last Day. Truths ultimately cohere around Jesus who is the *prima veritas*. This essay has emphasized epistemological difference between traditions, and hence the difficulty in seeing how that coherence pertains

45. The idea goes back to the Indian Renaissance, is echoed in liberal authors like Farquhar, and may also be found in a work like M. M. Thomas's *Risking Christ for Christ's Sake: Toward an Ecumenical Theology of Pluralism* (Geneva: WCC, 1987).

46. Jose Pereira, *Hinduism: A Reader* (Garden City, N.Y.: Image, 1976), introduction.

47. Gavin Flood, *An Introduction to Hinduism*, pp. 99-100.

between traditions until the Last Day. But the belief in that coherence, grounded ultimately in belief in Christ, enjoins us to strive to demonstrate it, to the extent possible, even now. While there doubtless are such alien truths, the Christian must strive to bring them into relation with Christian truths, by constructions with the shape of retrospective narratives. The tradition of Indian Christian theology in the twentieth century, cited frequently above, was just such an effort, faithfully, often creatively, sometimes defectively, to form just such retrospective narratives.

7 Testing Final Primacy among Theologies of Inculturation

Inculturation vs. Tradition

No question is more in vogue than that of "contextualization" (or "indigenization" or "inculturation," as the fashion has changed) of the gospel: How can the one gospel come to appropriate expression in each different cultural context? This question not only has dominated missiology, but has mushroomed at the very center of systematic theology itself. The reasons for this are not hard to spy: awareness of cultural diversity, and guilt about the West's behavior in an earlier era, with the impetus of liberation theology. But lying at the heart of this debate is a more basic philosophical question, that of the continuity of identity through historical change, with the accompanying fear of a dissolution into sheer relativity.

The exacerbation of this question is characteristic of the modern period, and so the question itself simply restates the challenge to traditional Christianity with which this essay began. What "historical consciousness" posed diachronically, the debate over contextualization has posed synchronically and geographically. As such, the debate simply recapitulates this essay's basic issue, occasioned externally by the challenge of the claims and practices of other traditions and internally by diverse claims and practices within the church catholic itself. If this is true, then the missiological field of diverse contextualizations should also prove a congenial place to test final primacy.

On this deeper question provoked by modernity, John Henry Newman was prescient. In his *An Essay on the Development of Christian Doctrine*,[1] he asserts that, lest one fall into the most "vexatious and preposterous scepticism, . . . [one must affirm that] the Christianity of the second, fourth, seventh, twelfth, sixteenth, and immediate centuries is in its substance the very religion which Christ and his Apostles taught in the first. . . ."[2] But how can one be sure, in the face of conflicts between Protestant and Catholic, both endangered by the acids of historical criticism? The argument Newman offers in response anticipates the debate over contextualization a century and a half later, and the major conceptual moves in that later debate are anticipated in his argument.

The options before Newman should not, by now, surprise the reader. Though he borrows the organicist imagery coming into popularity in his time, speaking as he does of the germination of the seed of an idea, Newman does not intend an external scheme of religious evolution, or laws to govern such a science. On the contrary, moving quite explicitly from his newfound commitment to the Roman magisterium, Newman deftly sketches the dynamics of a tradition in good working order. It is in this sense that his "tests of a true development" are best read. Such a tradition successfully "preserves the type or idea" (first test), which is to say that it rightly applies those deep structures or master images derived from Scripture. By so doing it preserves "continuity of principle" (second test), not in a static or reactionary way, but precisely by the "power of assimilation" (third test). The problematic features of such tests, especially for Protestant readers, are not hard to find: What about times when the tradition itself has become deformed or broken down? How is one to distinguish true growth from overgrowth requiring pruning? While these are valid indictments, they sting less if one realizes from the start that Newman's account assumes a rightly functioning tradition. The irony, as someone like MacIntyre

---

1. It is no accident that this work was an influence on those authors on whom this essay particularly leans, Alasdair MacIntyre in the philosophical realm and George Lindbeck in the theological. See, for example, Lindbeck's *The Nature of Doctrine: Religion and Theology in a Postliberal Age* (Louisville: Westminster/John Knox, 1984), p. 9.

2. John Henry Newman, *An Essay on the Development of Christian Doctrine* (Harmondsworth: Penguin, 1974), pp. 70-71.

might point out by his concept of the "epistemological crisis," is that second-order accounts of tradition such as Newman's are only necessary where tradition has broken down. This essay stands then as an epigone on Newman's shoulders, especially as it agrees that the crisis of relativism requires an account of the working of a tradition. The present chapter draws the necessary conclusion, namely that assessment of the contemporary debate over contextualization hinges on a right perception of the dynamics of tradition, though the literature seems unaware of this.

"Tradition" here ought not to be understood as an entity over against "Scripture" or "experience," and so ought not to be understood as the province of Catholic as opposed to Protestant arguments. Here popular accounts of "the three-legged stool" are particularly unhelpful and the language of the argument of this essay can be a useful corrective. The template is derived from Scripture. Particular families of interpretation flow from it throughout time and space. Other claims and practices, by means of which peoples "experience" life, can, in a working tradition, be assimilated creatively to the Christian life. "True development," which is to say appropriate "contextualization," involves a certain *Gestalt*, a particular historical process in which the "world is absorbed into the Scriptures."[3]

Contextualization then is a fitting arena for the application of final primacy, for it assumes tradition as a ruling formal concept. This claim is confirmed as one finds in the contemporary literature of contextualization implied concepts of tradition. Conversely it is strengthened as shortcomings in that literature can be traced to faulty or truncated assumptions about a working tradition. But if one reads these methodological treatments of contextualization, one often finds an abstract, even vague quality, sometimes making it hard to see how the theory will help in distinguishing true from false instances of contextualization. This should be no surprise, since such discernment requires a theory willing to set forth the common material shape of proper inculturation.

This reticence in theories of contextualization about acknowledging the parameters of the tradition will also prove familiar. For authors are reluctant to seem to foreclose from the start the creativity of new

3. Lindbeck, *Nature of Doctrine*, p. 117.

options, since the very point of such theories is that Christianity can take on a plethora of shapes and expressions in diverse cultural settings. Such reticence has not yet thought weightily enough about the risk of relativism. Our insistence that creativity and continuity not be conceived as contraries is equally true of theories of contextualization. Final primacy teaches that only as material shape and formal tradition are conceived together in such a way that the shape itself, definitive and distinct, is the condition for diverse and creative alternatives, can the root problem be addressed. As a result this section will seek to show that arguments about method in contextualization are adequate precisely as they assume and imply, however unknowingly, both the formal condition and the material shape of final primacy.

"We should be committed yet open"; "Christ is already present in the culture before the missionaries arrived"; "syncretistic Christianity": in the field of contextualization theory too one finds such ambiguous expressions, on whose pre-understandings hangs the theological tale. One sign of final primacy's helpfulness in assessing theories of contextualization will be its capacity to exegete what is really meant by such expressions in particular contexts. For such sentences are occasions either for what this essay has called "nuanced internalism," or else for "nuanced externalism." In other words, theories of contextualization place primary emphasis either on the explication of the surrounding culture, or on the grammar of the Christian tradition articulated in that culture. In the field of contextualization, as with interreligious dialogue, the tide of assimilation is moving in one direction or the other, though all arguments seek to compensate by the "nuance" by which they would display the contrasting virtue.

We can best consider the method at work in theories of contextualization as we analyze two classics: on the Protestant side, Charles Kraft's *Christianity in Culture,* and on the Catholic side, Robert Schreiter's influential *Constructing Local Theologies.* Kraft's main interlocutor is the conservative evangelical who worries that contextualization of the gospel will spell a fatal compromise of its absolute truth given inerrantly in Scripture. He seeks then to show how a "high" view of Scripture should make one, in Eugene Nida's phrase, a "Biblical cultural relativist," since it is the absolute norm that renders changing cultural mores relative. In a modified version of Richard Niebuhr's typology, Kraft identifies his view with "God Above-but-through-

Culture."[4] By this means Kraft would harness the forces of anthropology so important to missionary work, and effectively detach Christian truth from the cultural assumptions that missionaries themselves might too easily import. To this end Kraft borrows as well Kuhn's idea of the "paradigm shift" from the philosophy of science to describe both the coherence and distinctiveness of cultural worlds, and the dramatic shift that is conversion. Kraft might be termed a "Kuhnian realist," purchase on "the real" being acquired from biblical revelation.

At this point Robert Schreiter, in his typology of contextualization, characterizes Kraft as exemplifying the "translation model." For Schreiter this involves the view that biblical truth can be detached from culture as, in the classic metaphor, kernel from husk. Such a static and propositional view of biblical truth is for Schreiter inadequate. As a result this model places the weight on a truth outside the culture in question which contextualization must contrive to bring comprehensively to that culture. But is such an account of Kraft fair to his position?

To be sure, Kraft does not shy away from the dimension of revelation that conveys information, or from the aspect of biblical authority that rests on historical reference.[5] But throughout his work he complexifies this account, for instance in the insistence that revelation involves the stimulus to understand as well, a dimension that cannot overlook questions of cultural context. So the Bible becomes both a "yardstick" and an "inspired case-book."[6] For the former one must assume a Reformation understanding of the perspicuity of Scripture in "all things needful for salvation," but for the latter role one must know how to apply the cases, and this in turn requires doctrinal guidance and judgment on the part of the faithful reader. Furthermore, the truth found in the Bible must pertain to the whole person, understood within a total cultural context, where the will of the receptor is also involved.[7] While one may still describe Kraft's approach as "translational," to criticize it as a "husk and kernel" view overstates matters.

At the beginning of Robert Schreiter's work, he emphasizes the need to start with the communal expressions of implicit theology in

4. Charles Kraft, *Christianity in Culture: A Study of Dynamic Biblical Theologizing in Cross-Cultural Perspective* (Maryknoll, N.Y.: Orbis, 1979), pp. 113ff.

5. Kraft, *Christianity in Culture*, pp. 37, 41.

6. Kraft, *Christianity in Culture*, pp. 187ff., 198ff.

7. Kraft, *Christianity in Culture*, pp. 225ff.

the local church. When he goes on to describe tradition as a "series of local theologies,"[8] one wonders how this series will cohere and find adequate norms. But Schreiter allays this concern as the work progresses. He offers a semiotic account of culture itself, so that the contextualizing theologian must read one set of texts (Scripture, creeds, past masters) over against another local set (rites, works of art, etc.) so that each set challenges and informs the other. Another concern now arises: What if the second set comes to be an external norm for the Christian message? And how can this concern be answered without leaving the Christian theological community hermetically sealed?

It is at this point that Schreiter offers the linchpin of his argument, the concept of tradition. Borrowing the categories from Noam Chomsky, he speaks of tradition as the whole process of handing on a grammar and enacting new performances. For Christians the doctrines of the church are the grammar itself. Thus Schreiter completes the task of giving a cogent account of how the "series of local theologies" relate one to another. In his employment of the analogy of grammar and performance Schreiter's account is most thoroughly consistent with the approach offered in this essay. He also offers a sophisticated amplification of his account, showing how the normativity of a tradition is tied to its power comprehensively to address external questions, especially in times of dramatic or traumatic change. The compatibility of this account with MacIntyre's account of explanatory power and epistemological crisis is striking.[9]

In light of Schreiter's semiotic understanding of culture and the undergirding argument about theology as tradition, one may read more charitably some more problematic sentences. For example, he contrasts approaches like Kraft's, which impose a message, however carefully tailored, from without, with an approach that looks to find how Christ is already at work in the culture itself: "The development of local theologies depends as much on finding Christ already active in the culture as it does on bringing Christ to the culture." This notion, which he understands as "incarnational,"[10] is an example of the kind

---

8. See Robert Schreiter, *Constructing Local Theologies* (Maryknoll, N.Y.: Orbis, 1985), pp. 32ff.

9. Schreiter, *Constructing Local Theologies*, pp. 111-12.

10. Schreiter, *Constructing Local Theologies*, pp. 21, 29.

of ambiguous statement that final primacy can help to exegete. If one considers the whole argument of the book as the statement's tacit dimension, then one can find it valid. In other words, he brings an understanding derived from the tradition about who that Christ is who was already there, and he brings criteria from the tradition as well to discern when and how he might have been at work. Schreiter's quasi-methodological advice to look first for Christ in the culture really amounts to a counsel of sensitive listening. At the same time, seeing how these criteria of Schreiter's are "imposed" from the wider tradition should result in being less harsh about "translational" approaches, for the contrast no longer looks so stark.[11]

How may one compare the two approaches, and what common conclusions can one draw? First of all, the two works stand in closer relationship than one might initially suppose. Most obviously, both are influenced by anthropology as they seek to show how Christian boundaries of identity and worldview are preserved over time and geography. So both seek a kind of assimilation of the discipline of anthropology to the theological question about other claims and practices. In keeping with this common task is the common appeal to the discipline of linguistics and so the metaphor of language to the task of contextualization. While for one the root metaphor is translation and the key resource Nida's theory, for the other the root metaphor is understanding a text and guidance is sought from semiotic theory. But there is a family resemblance between them, and both metaphors are friendly to the perspective of final primacy.[12]

Secondly, both the translational and the semiotic approaches make an assumption about authority upon which contextualization is based. Each author assumes a process by which Scripture, the larger tradition of the church, and the culture of the local environment effect the expression of the faith, though they place the emphasis differently in keeping

11. In this regard one may point to the irony of Schreiter's use of *fides ex auditu* (p. 21). Schreiter is surely right that the gospel cannot be thought of in isolation from the church. But this phrase from Paul was used by Luther precisely to stress that the gospel must be heard, not only by the potential believer but also by the church itself, as a word from without.

12. For the importance of the practice of translation, see the following section on African theology. For the influence of semiotic anthropology on Lindbeck, see *Nature of Doctrine*, p. 20.

with their different theological backgrounds. For Kraft the emphasis is obviously more on the "data of Scripture," though his deployment of concepts such as "the inspired case-study book" and "dynamic equivalence" across cultures amounts to a tacit notion of a tradition of interpretation. Schreiter assumes the norm of magisterial teaching to ensure that tradition as a series of local theologies does not devolve atomistically, but can provide guidance. Behind that teaching he also assumes that Scripture provides normative shape to the doctrinal grammar of the tradition.[13] When one takes the spoken and the tacit together, the lineaments of a scripturally normed tradition of interpretation as the premise of contextualization are in both authors clear.

But each is reticent about drawing too much attention to this assumption, specifically because their espousal of contextualization seeks to overcome a naïve biblicism or narrow dogmatism. At the same time, each wishes to limit the extent to which the norms are submitted to critique as themselves mere instances of contextualization. From the perspective of final primacy, one can understand their desire to retain as much nuance as possible in their "nuanced internalism," as well as their desire to show the subtlety of the tradition's power to preserve identity in dealing with new and diverse claims and practices. At the same time one can see how each author clearly rejects both the relativism and the "externalism" that would disable the tradition from maintaining its identity in each new context.[14]

So, for both approaches, either implicitly or explicitly, a tradition in good working order is the foremost formal condition for contextualization. Kraft, like a good Protestant, gives no explicit account of tradition as the medium through history in which the "dynamic equiva-

---

13. Robert Schreiter, *Constructing Local Theologies*, p. 117.

14. Verging on such a privileging is Stephen Bevan's *Models of Contextual Theology* (Maryknoll, N.Y.: Orbis, 1992), where his "creation-centered orientation" (pp. 16-17) is characterized by the conviction that "culture and human experience are generally good," and that such a view should be contrasted with one characterized by sin and the need for redemption. About this latter alternative he says that "the Word of God might have to be adapted to differing and changing circumstances, but those circumstances could never be interpreted *as* Word of God." This sort of divorcing of one doctrinal commitment from another misunderstands the "webbed" nature of doctrines. And the notion of context *as* Word of God captures the priority of context, which identified here as a multifarious, hydra-like kind of "externalism."

lence" between Scripture and context is expressed. By contrast Schreiter offers a robust account of tradition as a doctrinally normed conversation between local theologies, and his use of the idea of grammar wants, from the point of view of this essay, only its material completion in the rule of final primacy. But both equally assume that the creative diversity of expressions of the faith is not stymied by, but rather made possible by, such a coherent process of ruled reflection over time. To be sure, there remain real differences between authors like Kraft and Schreiter, but in this one crucial respect they are, from the perspective of final primacy, more kindred than one might suppose. Though their circumstances and their tools are far different from Newman's, they are both in this one respect his heirs.

Theories in contextualization, then, need to see how tradition in fact is able to work, and so how final primacy can make possible a wide range of expression even as it maintains the identity boundaries important to both Kraft and Schreiter. To just such a demonstration of explanatory power in a "case-study" of the "local theology" called "African Christian theology" this chapter now turns.

A Test Case — African Christian Theology

The Crucial Category of "Before"

"Where does this [end of colonialism] leave the African Christian? Who is he? What is his past? A past is vital for us all — without it, like the amnesiac man, we cannot know who we are. The prime African theological quest at present is this: what is the past of the African Christian? What is the relationship between Africa's old religions and her new one?"[15] The question of the pre-Christian past, posed here by Andrew Walls, is the key one for African Christian theology. It is also a question most apposite for this study, in which the category of "before" plays a central role. To be sure, the "before" of African traditional religious practice has to do, for the Christian, not only with the history of Africa before European missionary contact, but also with contempo-

---

15. "Africa and Christian Identity" as quoted by Kwame Bediako in his *Theology and Identity* (Oxford: Regnum, 1999), pp. 238-39.

rary religious expressions insofar as they have to do with "the old life." With "before" in this wide sense, African Christian theology must come to terms.

It should also be noted that significant voices, particularly in South Africa, have insisted that the key question was the liberationist one, although this has remained for the most part a "minority report."[16] Even those who have placed the question of African traditional religion at the center have worried at the same time that such attention would be mistaken for an apology for a "fossil religion" accommodating itself to forms of religions now obsolete.[17] Still others suggest that the very notion of ATR (African Traditional Religions) is the product of contact with Christianity and the comparison implied therein. However, the evidence is that traditional practices have endured, in urban as well as rural areas. Furthermore they involve grooves of human thought and behavior that outlast the actual practices themselves. All these caveats have their own validity, but just the same, the question of identity looms large, and it continues to be posed in relation to the traditional "before."[18]

The relationship between the received Christian heritage and the surrounding host culture might be understood as a "zero sum game." When the issue is the African traditionalist past, it would often seem that the more European it looks and sounds, the more inauthentic and false it must be. The most egregious cases are assembled by one of the pioneers of African theology, Bolaji Idowu: "[The village catechist] can therefore wade through the ritual with the seriousness of one who is reciting an incantation, praying fervently in 1964 for Alexandra the Queen Mother . . . quite unconscious that Her Majesty has been dead for years. . . . For example it is not unusual for a Nigerian congregation to sing lustily, either in English or in translation, 'from Greenland's icy

16. See John Parratt, *Reinventing Christianity: African Theology Today* (Grand Rapids: Eerdmans, 1999), pp. 27ff.

17. John Pobee, *Toward an African Theology* (Nashville: Abingdon, 1979), p. 44.

18. Adrian Hastings, in a private conversation (Yale Divinity School, 1991), once commented that excessive interest in identity reminded him of the adolescent looking obsessively on him or herself in the mirror instead of getting on with life. While this is a good reminder that questions of identity are in a sense secondary to the actual object of theological reflection, at the same time such questions come quickly to have a direct bearing on how God, Christ, grace, etc. are conceived.

mountains/From India's coral strand, Where Africa's sunny fountains. . . . They call us to deliver/Their land from error's chain.'"[19]

The reasons for concern about postcolonial Africa are not hard to discern: Western guilt and African affront at the more proximate legacy of colonialism, and the more distant legacy of slavery. This is coupled with a sensitivity to cultural identity which is itself the product of diverse modern forces in both the West and the third world. But the assumption begins to break down if one considers worship in the West itself. Contemporary Anglicans in North America, after all, pray in seventeenth-century vestments according to liturgies rejiggered from the fourth century for various modern reasons, though this collage rarely faces a zero-sum ultimatum.

The past is painful, and the reasons understandable, but the "zero sum" assumption actually occludes accurate perception of the nature of the African church. The task of the following argument will be to show that inculturation of the gospel in Africa has been a more complex process than often acknowledged, a process in which African converts themselves play an active and discerning role. The thread running through what follows, and serving to tie it to the larger argument of this essay, is the formal assumption of a working tradition in whose light inculturation, both as historical process and theological project, may be understood in a deeper and subtler way.

Inculturation as a Threefold Generational Transaction

Contrary to the usual assumption, inculturation in Africa is not a single task, but rather a series of distinct transactions. For simplicity's sake they are called here "generational tasks," though this shorthand is not, strictly speaking, accurate, since each may take more than a single generation's span for its accomplishment. In the first generation, the first converts must hear the gospel, accept its challenge, and make the most demanding and clearest break with the old by becoming Christians. At the same time, their views of the world are most obviously in continuity with the pre-existing practices, the traditional reli-

19. See Bolaji Idowu, *Towards an Indigenous Church* (London: Oxford University Press, 1965), pp. 28, 32.

gious "before." In short, that first generation must break with the old, and its members are bound to do so for reasons couched in terms most closely related to the "before" itself. So at the level of acceptance of traditional ideas or practices, the earliest converts are the most rejectionist; for they are the ones who have been brought out of darkness into light. At the level of their own reasons why, they are least so.

The task of the second "generation" or phase in the life of the churches of Africa may be best illustrated by considering the Anglican Church in the Kingdom of Buganda. The first phase came to a crescendo in the martyrdom, warfare, and eventual victory of the Christian, and then Anglican forces. In 1878 Buganda became suddenly a Christian nation. But there followed a period of nearly a half century in which the church "limped between two opinions," in which many Christians struggled to assimilate the new commitment to Christ with the inherited shape of their life. The feeling of spiritual compromise and of helplessness to make one's life consonant with the new commitment finally found resolution in the great movement of renewal called the East African Revival, whose participants were the *Balokole*, "the saved."[20] One might say that the achievement of the second generation is consonance between the demand of the gospel and the particular circumstances of the context, which is another way to say "inculturation." Such consonance is often, though not necessarily, accomplished by means of revival.

The case of the *Balokole* movement is instructive, since it is difficult to say whether or not it is rejectionist toward the traditional religious "before." The adherents seemed vehemently so, and a central concern of the movement was the elimination of Christian hypocrisy in the continued involvement in traditional practices. At the same time the *Balokole* were equally adamant in their rejection of what they saw as inappropriate Western theological impositions, especially of a liberalizing sort. Meanwhile, the social form of the movement was so appealing because it represented "a remarkable recovery of the indigenous structure of the church which . . . consisted primarily of living Chris-

20. On the spiritual dimension of the movement known as a "reformation" of the "battleline" of the Spirit, see Max Warren's *Revival: An Inquiry* (London: SCM, 1954). The classic treatment of these transitions in Bugandan church history is John V. Taylor's *The Growth of the Church in Buganda* (London: SCM, 1955). On functional substitution, see Alan Tippett's *Introduction to Missiology* (Pasadena, Calif.: William Carey, 1987), ch. 15.

tian community groups, or clusters, around some natural head of a household."[21] Other scholars have seen in the Revival an echo of other traditional forms, for example the witchcraft eradication society, so that it may have served as what Tippett calls a "dynamic substitute."[22]

In short, no easy answer can be given to the question, "Is the Revival indigenous?" As a locally generated movement it obviously is so, and at many levels it served to recapitulate traditional forms and themes. At the same time it was (and still is) resolutely uncompromising with any involvement in or even valuation of traditional religious practice. The second task is just as much "inculturated" as the first, though its moment and its needs are different.

Where then does African theology as a self-conscious activity come into play? It constitutes a third task, namely that of the reappropriation of the past. For such a project presupposes the distance of a second-order discourse, and, practically, some advanced theological training in Western tradition. It also assumes that the past has become "past," something to be retrieved, as if across a ravine. Retrieval is classically a major aspect of the third task. One ought not to suppose that each successive task is somehow deeper or more authentic than its predecessors. Still, one might naturally turn a skeptical eye toward any "third task" construction that flies in the face, or takes no account of, the results of the first two. It ought be noted that concern for retrieval of the "before," and sympathy toward it, increases inversely as closeness to, and even familiarity with, that "before" decreases.[23]

A source of confirmation of this admittedly inexact model of the stages of inculturation may be found in Cyril Okorocha's study of conversion in Igboland.[24] There too the first converts were the most inimi-

---

21. Taylor, *The Growth of the Church in Buganda*, p. 102.

22. See both the treatment and the bibliography of Catherine Ellen Robins's *Tukutendereza: A Study of Social Change and Sectarian Withdrawal in the Balokole Revival in Uganda* (unpublished doctoral dissertation in political science, Columbia University, 1975).

23. At an anecdotal level, I can cite the occasional interest of younger Anglican ordinands in Tanzania in rethinking the church's rejection of polygamy, an interest that older priests attributed to their lack of any actual personal knowledge of what life in a polygamous household was like.

24. Cyril Okorocha, *The Meaning of Religious Conversion in Africa: The Case of the Igbo of Nigeria* (Aldershot: Avebury, 1987), esp. ch. 10.

cal to traditional practices, with a rationale most immersed in traditional ways of thinking. He calls this "two faiths in one mind: persistence of primal religious values," though it is found in early converts who make a decisive break with the old. Likewise the second task (what Okorocha, with more chronological accuracy, calls "the third generation") served to resolve tensions and inconsistencies. "[They] react against what they see as the syncretism of the second-generation Christians, and reject the eclecticism of the 'urban-man.'"[25] Yet Okorocha finds throughout these different generations, like a golden thread, a thoroughly Igbo interest in religion as power, equally evident in accommodationist and rejectionist believers. As for the concerns of the third task, they are represented eloquently by Okorocha himself, with his careful study of the continuity of the interest in power throughout manifold changes.

If one were to accept this more diachronic, variegated account of the relation between the practices of "before" and the converted, what conclusions can one draw? First of all, inculturation is shown to be a phenomenon more subtle and multidimensional than a "zero sum" criterion can take in. Clearly one can at once reject any compromise with traditional ideas and practices and still retain and assimilate the "before" in a variety of ways. Secondly, the perspectives of the first two tasks need to be taken into account in the offering of an African Christian theology, especially where the aim of such a construction is to render the lives of African Christians more consistent, or to make the faith make more sense or seem more compelling to them. The process of inculturation itself has a story, and the particular stories of conversion of individuals, their "before" and "after," have to be located within the stages of this larger story of the church coming to faith.

It follows, thirdly, that there exists an implicit level of inculturation, what will be called the "substratum." Here too one can argue that something analogous to the rule of final primacy is at work, although the object of consideration here is not theological concepts but rather, for the most part, particular practices of the church. Even where explicit, second-order African Christian theology is not present, Christians have found ways to transform the meaning of traditional ideas and practices as they are understood anew, now embedded within the Christian story.

---

25. Okorocha, *The Meaning of Religious Conversion in Africa*, p. 274.

Here illustrations will serve best to convey the meaning of implicit adherence to final primacy at the level of the "substratum." Consider first of all the most basic practice related to inculturation, the translation of the Scripture into the vernacular. Here the translators make a myriad of decisions about semantic equivalence, each of which is inexact, each of which represents a minuscule implicit act of theological inculturation. The study of the latter may best begin, not in abstractions, but in the detailed study of such gropings for words.[26] Consider for example the decision of the translators of the Bible into Kiswahili. The single decision to translate "to worship God" as *"kumwabudu Mungu"* carried with it a welter of connotations. The verb *kuabudu*, from the Arabic, invokes at once the more distant Hebrew cousin *Avodah*, "service" or "worship," even as it conjures up the preceding history of Islam (and so slavery) in east Africa. At the same time the use of the Bantu-derived *Mungu* for God sends thought upcountry and toward tribal connections. Thus the translation of that single phrase conjures, for good or ill, a complicated history before missionary contact, and places the acts of Jacob or Peter worshiping the God of Israel in the very midst of that history.

Most crucial of all for the direction of African evangelism, and eventually for African theology, was the decision to retain the local words for the high god in the translation of the name of the God of the Bible, in spite of the common (though sometimes disputed) perception that the traditional high gods were *dei otiosi*, uninvolved in daily affairs and hence not fitting subjects for sacrifice or intercession. For example, the use of the Bugandan name, *Katonda*, for the God of Israel caused the greatest surprise to the first hearers, who were amazed not by the coming of the Son, but rather at the awakened interest of the Father.[27] In narrative terms, though the earliest Bugandan Christians criticized traditional beliefs stringently, the use of *Katonda* served to splice the Bugandan story into the biblical one, which lies at the heart of the biblical template for final primacy as discussed in Chapter 1. Walls describes the effect of this stunning realization: ". . . in Buganda, as in most of Africa, God has a personal name, and that is a vernacular one.

---

26. So Hastings, *African Christianity: An Essay in Interpretation* (London: Chapman, 1976).

27. Taylor, *The Growth of the Church in Buganda*, pp. 252-53.

God is thus part of the African past; indeed as Katonda or Nyame or Olorun, he is part of the Ganda, the Akan, the Yoruba past."[28] In these key choices are implied powerful narratives of "before" and "after."

Another example comes from the noted phenomenologist of African traditional practice, John Mbiti, who studied the relationship between verb tenses in his native Akamba and the communication of the eschatological message of the Christian gospel. Mbiti argues that like most African peoples, the Akamba had only a sense of the generalized past, for which Mbiti used the Kiswahili word *"Zamani"* (long ago), and the *"Sasa"* (the present). The translation of the Bible meant a collision between Christianity's strong claims about the future, conveyed by the future tenses of the languages to be translated, and the assumed Akamba view of reality. While this introduction of the good news was inevitably surprising, its communication was made more difficult by narrow understandings of the African Inland Mission and an overly materialistic interpretation by the Akamba themselves. The point here is a simple one, that the sheer act of translating from Greek to Akamba inevitably carried with it enormous theological freight, loaded in this case into the very grammars of the languages.

The most penetrating analysis of the wider effects of translation has of course come from Lamin Sanneh.[29] The effect of translation is the prime example of the cunning of spiritual history, for its repercussions were quite independent of any intention on the part of the missionaries. The process of translation had the indirect effect of creating written languages, inducing pride in those languages, providing the means for cultural self-expression, and so building a bulwark against the erosion of individual tribal cultures. Far from eradicating local cultures, those early missionary Bible translators were effective agents of cultural renewal at the local, tribal level. Here one may note that the content and claim of the gospel as represented within the translation was unaltered, and the effect of cultural renaissance was ancillary.

After translation, a second practice worthy of special attention is church discipline, and in particular moral and ritual prohibitions.

---

28. Andrew Walls, *The Missionary Movement in Christian History: Studies in the Transmission of Faith* (Maryknoll, N.Y.: Orbis, 1996), p. 96.

29. See in particular *Translating the Message: The Missionary Impact on Culture* (Maryknoll, N.Y.: Orbis, 1989).

Here too a more recent generation of African church historians have "changed the subject" and focused attention on African converts as the primary actors in the drama of church and culture and the primary agents of implicit theological discernment. For example, John Karanja has shown how early Kikuyu Christians in Kenya set the direction for the church, and made decisive theological judgments as they determined which traditional rites of initiation they could and could not attend. Karanja offers a concrete example: "Mbatia (an early convert) refused to take part in the rite of circumcision . . . later he compromised on the condition that he would not be required to take part in sacrifices."[30] Mbatia made a judgment of practical theological reason about the relation of the gospel to traditional practice, one in which the implications of the uniqueness of Christ's sacrifice is the guiding principle, at the same time that he differentiated valid commitments of social and cultural solidarity from conflicting religious ties. Mbatia was an implicit theologian of inculturation in the Kikuyu context.

Likewise one finds in a number of African Protestant churches a strict moral code that often seems judgmental and legalistic to the outsider. To return to the example of the *Balokole,* their rejection of tobacco and alcohol may seem to be, from a "zero sum" perspective, an ill-advised importation of norms from the conservative English evangelicalism one might encounter at a Keswick Convention. But this would misunderstand the actual function of such norms in a relatively young church. Far from being a Pelagian retreat from the gospel, these rules serve to underline the distinctiveness of the Christian community, and hence its message, over against its pagan neighbors. In rural upcountry Tanzania, another *Balokole* stronghold, for example, beer or *pombe* is associated with the riotous living of the old life, and its prohibition serves to demarcate the decisiveness of conversion.[31]

One more dimension of this seeming legalism may be found where it is reminiscent of the Old Testament. Consider the life of Jacob: a pastoral existence in relation to the fathers, the clan, a need for material blessing, a life illumined by dreams, shows a compelling similarity

---

30. John Karanja, *Founding an African Faith: Kikuyu Anglican Christianity, 1900-1945* (Nairobi: Uzima, 1999), p. 25.

31. This is based on personal conversations held by the author while a missionary in Tanzania.

to the traditional life in many parts of Africa.[32] Kwesi Dickson has suggested that this "cultural continuity" with the Old Testament offers an entree into interpretation more promising than Western criticism of the sort often taught by missionaries in African seminaries.[33] The strongly Hebraic quality of Ethiopian Christianity, and its reverberation in the Zionist Churches of South Africa point in the same direction, though, as Dickson points out, these parallels may also serve to muffle the message of grace in the New Testament. Where the latter happened, the "before" nature of African tradition in its similarity to the Old Testament has been lost, and the kinds of Christianity sometimes seen in the independent churches come to offer, not an implicitly grammatical expression of the Christian faith, but rather a "bridge" back to the old life.[34]

Here, as elsewhere, the independent churches in their diversity act as a kind of margin or border for the field of varied, inculturated expressions of the grammar of faith in Africa. As churches born of the mainline denominations, their distinguishing beliefs and practices point to key, often neuralgic, issues that have been somehow misunderstood or underplayed by the mainlines. These distinguishing beliefs serve as sites either for the communication of the gospel to the surrounding environment or else for its corruption. One such practice is healing,[35] whereby the power of Christ is demonstrated in the domain of everyday life, that middle range whose neglect by the missionaries created an "excluded middle" that made the genesis of independent churches more likely.[36] Closely related to this issue has been, more generally, the emphasis on the role of the Holy Spirit; the danger has been that some attention to healing in independent churches has

32. Sundkler in his magisterial *A History of the Church in Africa* (Cambridge: Cambridge University Press, 2000), ch. 5, offers the Fang people of west Africa as a vivid example of this "cultural continuity" with the Old Testament.

33. Kwesi Dickson, *Theology in Africa* (London: Darton, Long & Todd, 1984), ch. 6.

34. Bengt Sundkler, *Bantu Prophets of South Africa* (London: Oxford University Press, 1948), conclusion.

35. On the centrality of healing, see especially Richard Gray's *Black Christians and White Missionaries* (New Haven: Yale University Press, 1990), ch. 5, "Christianity and Concepts of Evil."

36. Paul Hiebert, "The Flaw of the 'Excluded Middle,'" *Missiology: An International Review* 10 (1983): 35-47.

led to an exclusive focus on the Spirit to the detriment of any significant role for Christ himself.[37]

The third practice, implying a narrative and so a "before," is
ecclesiological, the design and maintenance of appropriate social
structures for the Family of God. How is the communal life of the
Body of Christ organized? It has already been observed that the structure of the community in the case of the Anglican *Balokole* communities of Buganda mirrored those of the clan or *bataka* system. Here too
one can imagine the pre-existing culture to be reconceived and
brought into new relationship with the gospel story, not in ideas or
words, but rather in the actual form of the community. One could give
many more examples whereby the pre-existing form was recapitulated
within the new context of the church, and thereby given a new significance. The Crio, Christian tradeswomen originally based in Sierra Le-
one, whose business eventually took them throughout West Africa,
lent the market structure to the task of the gospel; they thus became at
once successful purveyors of both goods and the Good News.[38] The
structure of their enterprise involved a borrowing from the culture of
"before," as subtle as it was uncontrived.

This is not to suggest that there have not been deliberate and explicitly confected adaptations that have proved to be successful and appropriate, but even in these cases, the reasons for the success have not been
predictable. Here contemporary church historians properly redirect attention to the primacy of the agency of African church leaders. One carefully documented case is the adaptation of male circumcision to the sacrament of confirmation by Anglo-Catholics in the Diocese of Masasi in
southern Tanzania. Circumcision was of course the great moment when
the young man was taught about and made accountable to the great "before," the tradition delivered from the ancestors and represented by the
clan authorities. Of the relating of this moment to the Christian past and
the forebears in faith Bishop Vincent Lucas was seemingly the prime ar-
chitect, but the revised rite only came to be accepted and effective as local clan chiefs, the *Mamwenye*, now Christian, exerted their authority
and lent their approval to the practice (after a good deal of jockeying for
power!). Again a traditional social structure was incorporated into, and

---

37. Sundkler on *Umoya* and on the black messiah in *Bantu Prophets*, ch. 7.
38. See Sundkler and Steed, *A History of the Church in Africa*, ch. 14.

so a pre-existing institution graciously "taken captive" for the sake of, the sacramental life of the Christian community.[39]

The fourth and final set of practices illustrating the implicit forms of final primacy in the African church comprises the calling of and preaching by ordained ministers. Here too it is not a matter of the actual reappearance of traditional beliefs and practices, but rather the recapitulation and transformation of the inherited themes. Bengt Sundkler's *The Christian Ministry in Africa* identifies several recurrent leitmotifs in the preaching that he heard over a lifetime of ministry in South Africa and Tanzania. He puts the matter this way: ". . . African theological encounter is an ellipse with two foci — the Links with the Beginning and the Links with the Living and the Dead, held together by a particular understanding of the Church." The last point he fills out as follows: "The great Biblical terms for the church — the People of God, the Body of Christ, the Household or Family of God — find a vibrant sounding-board in the structure of African social patterns particularly of the clan. "[40] Sundkler argues that these themes are not limited to more catholic traditions, but may be found in some form even in preachers of the most evangelical sort. The homily may hearken back to Abraham, or Peter, or one's faithful grandmother, or the first missionaries, but the desire to find that linkage is the common element. Likewise the linkage to the Dead may be in the functionally equivalent form of the "cloud of witnesses" or "communion of saints," regardless of one's explicit theology of the saints.[41]

This brings the argument full circle, back to the need to overcome

39. In his "Missionary Adaptation of African Religious Institutions: The Masasi Case," in *The Historical Study of African Religion,* ed. T. Ranger and I. N. Kimambo (Berkeley: University of California Press, 1974), Terence Ranger offers this concluding assessment: ". . . it was not Lucas' enthusiasm alone which turned the *Jando* [male circumcision] into an institution with its own vitality and dynamics of development. This happened because the Christianized initiation turned out to be the focus of many different interests and aspirations. In this way the *Jando* came to be a key point of *interaction* between Christian and 'traditional' ideas, between modern and traditional roles, rather than merely an experiment in adaptation" (p. 247). This chapter suggests, to use this essay's terms, that implicit final primacy is an appropriate way to describe the shape of that interaction.

40. Bengt Sundkler, *The Christian Ministry in Africa* (London: SCM, 1962), pp. 117, 119.

41. For an eloquent case for this functional substitution see Harry Sawyer's *Creative Evangelism* (London: Lutterworth, 1968), ch. 5, "A Fresh Liturgical Approach."

"zero sum" assumptions. The author once had a conversation with the elderly Dean of the Anglican Cathedral in Morogoro, Tanzania. The priest was decrying the spiritual vapidity of the new liturgies, and insisting that such innovations involving consciously "African" themes or references were misguided. "Our spiritual fathers, the first missionaries, were holy men. They prayed before they came to bring us the gospel. It is a precious treasure, and we must guard it carefully so as to pass it on to our grandchildren." The content of the Dean's point was adamantly conservative and anti-accommodationist, but *how* he thinks about the process of the appropriation of tradition is deeply east African. One might say that the first missionaries here serve as functional equivalents of the "eponymous ancestors."[42]

This focus on inculturation as it can be found in the very attitude toward tradition, as well as in the mode of its transmission, opens a rich vein in the substratum of implicit and practical final primacy. It corresponds to a view of culture not only as an assemblage of assorted ideas and practices, but also as the particular mode in which a particular people constantly renegotiates the terms of their life with various influences new and old. What MacIntyre has called an "epistemological crisis" would amount to a moment of renegotiation. A rupture or discord has appeared in the self-understanding of a culture, or in its confidence vis-à-vis its neighbors. Final primacy would represent, for a Christian community, the grammar governing the substance of the renegotiated settlement, and the particular attitude toward tradition might affect the style of that settlement as well. Such a view of ongoing local Christian culture as renegotiation is consistent with recent anthropological views about ritual process and the "cobbled-together" quality of cultures themselves.[43] An assumption of cultural homogeneity found within "zero sum" thinking is thus dislodged, and a way to see a culture as fully Christian and fully local is opened up.

A study of the relation between church practices and key themes of

42. Such is the argument in Philip Turner's "The Wisdom of the Fathers and the Gospel of Christ: Some Notes on the Question of Christian Adaptation in Africa," *Journal of Religion in Africa* 4 (1971-72): 45-68.

43. On the former see especially Victor Turner's *The Ritual Process: Structure and Anti-Structure* (Ithaca, N.Y.: Cornell University Press, 1977) and on the latter see James Clifford's *The Predicament of Culture: 20th Century Ethnography, Literature, and Art* (Cambridge, Mass.: Harvard University Press, 1988).

the "before" of African culture confirms the importance of the formal principle of a working tradition for the understanding of inculturation. A consideration of key practices such as translating, fencing and organizing the community, healing, and preaching has shown that there exists a substratum where final primacy, the setting of traditional elements in a new tacit narrative, is acted out implicitly. Always bearing this substratum in mind as a "tacit dimension," one can now turn to the explicit articulation of African Christian theologies.

How should one understand such theologies actually to work? The perspective of final primacy raises questions about several projects from the outset. Formally the assumption of a working tradition casts in doubt all efforts somehow to theologize from a position "upstream" of the polluting historical arrival of the gospel with the missionaries.[44] One finds such a method at work, quite explicitly and with a flourish, in Vincent Donovan's celebrated *Christianity Rediscovered*.[45] To be sure, his views were doubtless colored by the particular difficulty of the evangelization of the Maasai, but still he does not shrink from judging all African Christianity as "unadapted," producing a "subservient, dependent people" as a result of the "void" of missionary reflection.[46] Donovan courageously but naïvely set himself the task of "cutting [him]self off from the schools and the hospital [in order to] just go and talk to them about God and the Christian message,"[47] as if all the going and talking that had preceded in Catholic missionary and African Christian history to date could be disregarded. From such an assumption one might justifiably draw the deeply flawed conclusion that the community of faith in each place confects its own church according to its own needs.

The truth of the matter is, of course, that Donovan was himself necessarily bringing a wide array of theological assumptions to bear on his work of primary evangelism. When he sought to argue that the distant high God of the Maasai, *Engai*, had drawn close in Christ, he was following the royal road of African evangelism.[48] When he argued

44. Eboussi Boulaga, *Christianity without Fetishes: An African Critique and Recapture of Christianity* (Maryknoll, N.Y.: Orbis, 1984), p. 85.
45. (Maryknoll, N.Y.: Orbis, 1982).
46. Donovan, *Christianity Rediscovered*, pp. 9-10.
47. Donovan, *Christianity Rediscovered*, p. 15.
48. Donovan, *Christianity Rediscovered*, pp. 113-14.

that the newly baptized community must work out for itself what being church shall look like, so long as they "go forth in the Spirit to witness to this good news and to Jesus," he has spoken well, but in so doing he has already assumed much.[49] Indeed, his own intentions notwithstanding, some of his assumptions are derived from intellectual battles in the West. For example, his contrast between Maasai community and Western church organization smacks of the social scientific contrast between *Gemeinschaft* and *Gesellschaft*, and his borrowing of Paul Tillich's definition of church as "a group of people who express a new reality"[50] reflects a vein of Western liberal thought quite alien to African thought. In spite of himself, Donovan points toward the way in which African Christian theology as tradition really works.

Visiting the African Sites

A tradition, conflicted and contentious, coming to terms with a claim or practice of another tradition, must articulate its own claims anew as it takes into account the external challenge. This requires that the tradition muster its own resources, construe its contemporary debates, and find a fitting point of debate — what this essay has called a "receptor site" — for its newly articulated claim. It is just so with African Christian theology. Located as they are in the wider tradition of the church catholic, they will inevitably offer, first of all, some opinion, in consent or dissent, on the question of revelation in African traditional religions (which will often tend to follow the well-worn paths of *Logos*, nature/grace, or law/gospel thinking). Second, they will offer their proposal in some relation, acknowledged or implied, to a contemporary movement or strain of Western Christian theology. Third, they will bring these resources to bear as they address one of the "receptor sites," one of the small set of salient features of the "before" that suggest themselves for comparison.

These classic sites are the following: (a) The transcendent God of the Bible is the same as the high God. This understanding was, as already discussed above, the work of both missionary translators and

49. Donovan, *Christianity Rediscovered*, p. 82.
50. Donovan, *Christianity Rediscovered*, p. 84

native hearers, together forming the most basic organizing narrative of African evangelization: the God who was once far has drawn near. An author like Donovan would emphasize that this high God is now known to be the God of all, while Idowu would emphasize that he is more active and concerned than previously supposed. In both cases the traditional view of the high God, held "before," has been edited, and this editing has assumed a new narrative assimilated to the salvation history culminating in Christ.

(b) Christ is as the Great chief, medicine man, ancestor, etc. Working from the same analogy one might argue, alternately, that (c) the saints are an ancestor-like cloud of witnesses. As will be discussed below, this second classic move stands in tension with the first, since the prominence of these figures stood in contrast to the inactivity of the high God. These figures, fixed in one great, interconnected hierarchy of being, were traditionally understood as conduits through which the *élan vital* suffusing the universe was available to human beings.[51] The task of Christian reflection is to differentiate the being and work of God from this essentially monistic cosmology, in a manner comparable to the "overcoming" of Greek metaphysics in the Patristic period. Christ must as a result be shown to be "qualitatively" and not only "quantitatively" greater than human forebears or healers.

In each case one must place the perceived similarity in relation to a prior Christological norm. Care must be taken to show both the similarity and the yet greater dissimilarity, and to hold both together in a single account, integrated by a single underlying narrative. For example, one may consider John Pobee's Christology. When he uses the analogy of the medicine-man/healer, then the distinction between Christ and these other figures seems to be one of degree only: "The difference between Jesus and the healers would be the unprecedented scale on which he was 'ensouled' with God: Jesus was in a perpetual state of holiness, perpetually ensouled with God so much so that the divine power was like a continuously flowing electric power in him, unlike the traditional healer, who has the occasional experience of it."[52] Here the uniqueness of the God-man might seem imperiled, in a

---

51. Especially see Placide Tempels, *Bantu Philosophy* (Paris: Présence Africaine, 1969), ch. 1.

52. Pobee, *Toward an African Theology*, p. 93.

way similar to some Antiochene Christological projects. In fairness, however, one must note how, when Pobee treats Christ by analogy to a chief, he states that Jesus' priesthood was, as the author of Hebrews insists, operating on a level altogether unique, for it mediated between humanity and God himself.[53] Here Pobee's account must be read as a whole for the cumulative effect of his treatment of a number of analogies, serving to mitigate worry over one particular case.

(d) The human person is essentially relational (as exemplified in tribal life). This move is epitomized by John Pobee in his *"cognatus sum, ergo sum."*[54] As the imitation of Descartes suggests, this move implies a critique of the modern individualism that was an unfortunate by-product of the missionary message. From treatment of this receptor site spin off a number of other ancillary conclusions, for example that sin may be understood as isolation from the community, the prime example being the anti-social and selfish activity of witchcraft. Conversely the church may now be understood as the New Clan in a manner consistent with the Vatican II emphasis on the biblical theme of the church as the People of God.[55]

Finally, (e) the Holy Spirit is victorious over the spiritual powers. Here one may identify several strands, the first of which is the emphasis on power or life-force itself as the central metaphysical category in the African worldview, an emphasis going back to Tempels's pioneering work. This life-force is hierarchically articulated in a wide array of entities, including spirits and the ancestors, in relation to whom stand those presently alive, particularly figures like chiefs and diviners, while malevolently outside that hierarchy may be found witches. In such a climate the Holy Spirit comes quickly to be understood in relationship to power, and in turn conversion to be the overcoming of the danger posed by evil spirits. Here, on the subject of power, it may be noted that the study of conversion in the missionary churches on the one hand and splintering off of independent churches on the other converge, for both see the categories of power, and its victorious spiritual exercise, as central. Likewise, the supposed divergence between

53. Pobee, *Toward an African Theology,* p. 96.
54. Pobee, *Toward an African Theology,* pp. 50ff.
55. A good working out of this tack from a Protestant perspective is Josiah Kibira's *Church, Clan, and the World* (Lund, Sweden: Gleerup, 1974) and its treatment of Haya culture.

traditionalist and liberationist theologies might be overcome by attention to their shared interest in victory over evil, in the first case through the instrumentality of healing, and in the latter through political struggle.[56] Here one cannot help but wonder if the topic that is so far conspicuous by its absence in African theology is not the doctrine of the atonement. It could be that its development, in conjunction with the equally Patristic theme of the harrowing of hell (which will be treated below), is a crucial *agendum*.

Most African Christian theological proposals develop one of these comparisons. The stuff of each analogy resides in the "before" of traditional life, although some process of filtering or abstraction, itself employing imported tools, has taken place. No medicine man ever claimed that "the human being is essentially relational," though a wide array of actual prayers and rites might support this. One can point to the *oeuvre* of John Mbiti, bringing the tools of phenomenology to bear on that wide array, as a life's work aimed precisely at making such abstracting philosophical generalizations available to properly theological projects.[57]

African Christian theology is a tradition whose dynamics have been described above. Within this tradition explicit theological proposals should abide by the norm of final primacy, although here, as with Western theologies of other religions, some constructions evince a nuanced externalism contrary to the orthodox rule. A clear example of such nonconformity to the rule is Eboussi Boulaga's *Christianity without Fetishes*. The work opens in the following way, leaving little doubt what use the author has for any doctrinal norm in Christianity: "Claims rising in a self-definition of Christianity are expressions devoid of content."[58] Shortly thereafter he proceeds to decry the "imperialist, totalitarian, and sectarian potentialities of the incarnation."[59] This harsh critique is ostensibly in the service of the elimination of for-

56. See here Richard Gray's *Black Christians and White Missionaries*, ch. 5, "Christianity and Concepts of Evil," pp. 100ff. Here one may see how some treatments of healing in terms of wholeness and power, such as will be considered later in this chapter, may miss the mark by leaving out this element of battle against an alien force.

57. One may point most famously to Mbiti's *African Religions and Philosophies* (London: Heinemann, 1969).

58. Boulaga, *Christianity without Fetishes*, p. 1.

59. Boulaga, *Christianity without Fetishes*, p. 10.

eign and alien Western influences on the African church. The irony however, is that the proposal Eboussi then offers is equally Western, one part phenomenology and one part liberation theology. For Eboussi would bring a historicist consciousness of the human producing his or her own meaning to the African intellectual scene,[60] a quintessentially modernist project. Such a consciousness is something Africans of the "before" didn't have. Eboussi's project amounts to a form of nuanced externalism.

There are other theologians, however, who evince creative conformity to final primacy as they offer explicit proposals for a self-consciously African Christian theology. This chapter has already provided some scattered examples as it considered the key receptor sites, whose use constitute the "classic moves" in African Christian theology. But it will be helpful to study more carefully one cluster of proposals, built in this case on traditional African beliefs about the ancestors. As will become clear, these proposals do serve to illumine the gospel in a distinctively African mode, and so are successful, to varying degrees, as efforts in inculturation. Still, the argument that has proceeded in this section ought to offer a caveat for the theologian seeking a Christian concept of the ancestors. The lesson of the first and second tasks of inculturation serves as a warning lest the proposal fly in the face of earlier work and come to communicate, not Christ's gracious dominion over the ancestors, but rather the recrudescence of the old life. For the traditional view of the ancestors involved sacrifice to them, in some case to mollify a returning ill spirit, and some of this practice was motivated by fear. To restore favor to such beliefs would communicate the opposite of the gospel.

A second caveat, having to do with practice, follows on the first. Is the reader to understand that these new proposals are accompanied by a continued rejection of participation in such pagan rites? In other words, are the proposals operating at the level of better ways to understand what is happening in Christian prayer? The answer to such questions needs to be clarified if the real import of such proposals is to be rightly understood. At this very point, as insightful a theologian as the Tanzanian Catholic Charles Nyamiti seems to hesitate, at one moment advocating the design of and participation in new, purified an-

60. Boulaga, *Christianity without Fetishes*, pp. 192-96.

cestral rites of a Christian kind, and another warning of the risk in any such practice: "One can hardly emphasize too much the need of careful and assiduous preparation of the faithful before one allows them to practice ancestral worship in its Christianized version."[61] Other authors hesitate to sally forth into these deep waters at all.

Charles Nyamiti and Benezet Bujo are two prominent and articulate proponents of use of this site of entree and debate with traditional practice. They and others who focus on this receptor site agree that ancestorship is at the heart of the traditional African's *Weltanschauung*. They would insist that it involves not so much one distinct subject, but rather the way that traditional Africans understood what a human is, what the tribe is, what the cosmos is like. To engage the issue is not optional; to avoid the issue is to refuse to preach to the African person in his or her world.

One can extract from final primacy, and from the preceding treatment of the African church situation, some common criteria for the treatment of the theme of ancestorship, what may be retained and what needs to be transformed. First of all, the ancestors are, as discussed above, part of a larger cosmological picture, of which the unifying reality is power. While this relates humans effectively to the divine, such a monistic vision fails to differentiate them sufficiently, and the rites of sacrifice imply the manipulation of the divine. Somehow or other, each construction must find a way to show God as the distinctive and prime agent in and over the cosmos.

Secondly, and for African traditional thought surprisingly, Christ as "proto-Ancestor" must be identified with this divine Agent. This identification is, after all, exactly what traditional religions did not effect, since they emphasized middle-range beings and entities quite distinct from the uninvolved high God. This involves a transformation of the traditional worldview as radical as the transformation of Greek thought that required five centuries of intellectual labor. If strategies at the receptor site of ancestors hope to render the gospel more readily acceptable or appealing, they will disappoint. This does not disallow the concept, since a receptor site is apt as much because it communicates the affront as the attraction of the gospel.

61. Charles Nyamiti, *Christ Our Ancestor: Christology from an African Perspective* (Gweru, Zimbabwe: Mambo, 1984), p. 140.

How, where, and when does this proto-Ancestor Christ act? Thirdly, and perhaps most obviously, he does only good, unlike the ancestors in traditional belief. Furthermore, fourthly, he must be conceived as the Ancestor of all the saints and all the faithful in the whole world. Each construction must effect this universalization. Fifthly and finally, in light of the witness of the book of Hebrews, mediumship and the sacrificial role related to ancestor belief are at an end. More generally, it means that each theology must have some way, both conceptually and practically, of marking the decisive turning of the ages that Christ brings. Here one returns to the very heart of final primacy. For such constructions as those exploring the ancestorship are aimed at narrative continuity to the traditional "before." But that continuity, in the grammar of final primacy, is always predicated on a prior discontinuity tied inseparably to his person and work.

Charles Nyamiti's *Christ Our Ancestor* is a strong example of the nature-grace school.[62] Human beings have a natural desire for redemption, and through their appeal to the ancestors they reach out for spiritual fellowship beyond the bounds of death. These natural features are taken to a higher and wider level by the supernatural nature and work of Christ. They are made effectual, and given a source of power beyond themselves. In other words, nature is lifted up by the supernature of Christ.

Of course we are both creatures and sinners, needing of God both elevation and redemption to attain eternal life. Nyamiti is well aware that the practice of traditional ancestor worship was corrupted and flawed, but still his treatment gives greater emphasis to our need to be raised than our need for the forgiveness of sins.[63] For example, in a carefully delineated series of distinctions between human ancestors and Christ as ancestor, Nyamiti lists (in chapter 2) a number of ways in which human ancestorship needs to be changed: it must be expanded

62. This is consistent with John Parratt's judgment in *Reinventing Christianity*, pp. 38-39, that "Nyamiti's approach has its roots firmly in the traditional bases of Catholicism." Parratt cites Bujo, who sees Nyamiti's work as a kind of "African scholasticism" (p. 127).

63. This is particularly clear where traditional views of ancestorship understood immortality to be granted through death, while Christians understand death to be the "last enemy" because of sin, and God's forgiving grace to be required to defeat it. See, for example, Parratt's *Reinventing Christianity*, p. 35.

beyond mere consanguinity, it must be given an inner dynamic surpassing its own power, it must be encouraged to seek spiritual as well as material goods, etc. An optimistic presentation of the nature-grace model persists throughout Nyamiti's proposal.

To understand how nature and grace function in his proposal is not the end of the task, for Nyamiti offers a complex argument in which ancestorship serves simultaneously as the governing analogy for a number of relationships, that between humanity and the divine, between the church and Christ, and between the very persons of the Son and the Father in the Godhead. Where the same analogy is used at one and the same time for the creature-Creator relationship with its absolute difference, as well as the hypostatic union, with the "distinction without separation" and the "subsistent relations" of the very Godhead, one should not be surprised that problems of opposite sorts result. In each case the analogy remains helpful as this limit is identified and safeguarded with the help of doctrine, but difficulties arise when the limits of the analogy are stretched, sometimes in opposite directions at the same time. Such analogies call for modesty and a lightness of touch.[64]

Christ is able to play a mediating role between humanity and God, for he plays the role of the link between the two, being at once the Descendant of the Father, the divine Ancestor, as well as the Ancestor to human beings who are his Descendants through grace. But such a ladder presents the same sorts of problems for Nyamiti as did the *Logos* as mediator for a thinker like Origen. Here too one must worry about a latent subordinationism. As in the third century, so now, one needs to show how the Descendant is "eternally begotten," how the divine relationship may be distinguished from human begetting, with its temporal beginning and dependency, and how the relationship may be understood as truly reciprocal.

In the case of the relationship of Christ to the church, Nyamiti rightly understands the life-force to be granted continually to the church through the risen Christ. But a perennial danger of ecclesiologies that see the church as a sacrament of Christ in the world is that they fail to distinguish sufficiently between the two, and just such a

64. See the discussion of Augustine on the psychological analogy for the Trinity in Chapter 4.

worry is appropriate to Nyamiti's proposal. He speaks of the continually life-giving power of the Eucharist, and of the ancestral role of the saints. Both ideas can be perfectly grammatical, but both have at times been subject, in the history of Catholic doctrine, to excessive claims. The analogy of Christ as ancestor can conduce to just the blurring of agency that leads to such problems. The grammar of final primacy requires the Christian theologian to make it repeatedly clear that while Christ and the church are one, he is the vine who grants the church to be the branches (John 15:1ff.).

The practice of ancestor worship was, as has already been mentioned, closely connected to a pervasive emphasis on the life-force. It is also related to the office of the chief as the one charged to observe the necessary rites. Such themes form a *Gestalt,* and so it should be no surprise that a "theology of Christ as proto-ancestor" appeals to these attendant categories. A good example of such an approach is Benezet Bujo's *African Theology in Social Context.*[65] This *Gestalt* shows how Bujo's project actually works. As has already been stated, traditional rituals do not lend themselves to second-order reflection without some mediating thematization. For Bujo, in the tradition of Tempels, this is accomplished through the abstracting of the theme of the life-force. His theology of the "proto-Ancestor" is in fact shorthand for a theology of the life-force and its accompanying qualities.

With the emphasis on life goes the vision of unity,[66] between those who are present and those who lived in the past, and between all the different members of society. The goal of the traditional view was wholeness, of body and spirit in the individual, of one member of the group with another, of the social with the spiritual. So Bujo also abstracts this vision, essentially "anthropocentric,"[67] from traditional practice as its essence, and he cites the ancestors as its exemplars and guarantors. Thus Bujo accomplishes a number of theological goals, among them to overcome the unfortunate division between African theologies with traditionalist and liberationist interests. In the category of wholeness Bujo believes he has a tool with which to mend the rift.[68]

---

65. (Maryknoll: Orbis, 1992).
66. Bujo, *African Theology in Social Context,* pp. 21ff.
67. Bujo, *African Theology in Social Context,* p. 32.
68. So Parratt, *Reinventing Christianity,* pp. 122-23.

This is not to say that traditional life in the presence of the ancestors was faultless. Power was hierarchically arranged; the shunning of the barren was cruel; some ancestors did evil; society is plagued by corruption; tribes are bound within the narrow constraints of their own lineages. So Bujo agrees that "the history of the Crucified One must be subversive for the customs and practices of both traditional and modern Africa."[69]

One must consider how Bujo brings his ruling vision of the life-force and wholeness into relation with the revelation through the scriptures of Jesus Christ. African theology as a tradition involves not only the identification of a receptor site, in this case ancestorship, but taking a position vis-à-vis the inherited tradition, and in particular its Western expressions. So Bujo borrows the modern notion of Christology "from below." Jesus touched to restore to wholeness, threw out evil spirits, served as he washed the disciples' feet, educated at the Last Supper for those to follow after. For Bujo "Jesus manifested precisely all those qualities and virtues which Africans like to attribute to their ancestors and which lead them to invoke the ancestors in daily life."[70] To be sure, Jesus, as the perfect embodiment of these qualities, surpasses the ancestors and corrects their views, so that in relation to him they are "forerunners," who anticipated him in "many and various ways" (Heb. 1:1).[71] Still Jesus plays only an exemplary role, as the one who shows preeminently those qualities and virtues conducing to wholeness of life.

Here the question of practice serves as an apt litmus test: What does Bujo make of the continued involvement of Christians with traditional rites of invocation of the ancestors? Can one assume baldly that whatever furthers the wholeness and the life-force, purified and universalized by the liberating model of Christ, is necessarily to be encouraged? Bujo's approach can provide only a vague answer, since his approach does not focus on the specific practices of distinct communities of religious observance. Rather he moves in the orbit of a general vision based on the abstract category of power; and specific communities, traditional or Christian, are relevant insofar as they further the appropriate "virtues and qualities" toward this end.

69. Parratt, *Reinventing Christianity*, p. 90.
70. Parratt, *Reinventing Christianity*, p. 80.
71. Parratt, *Reinventing Christianity*, p. 83.

Into what family ought one to place such a proposal? If one begins with power for wholeness, and sees Jesus as its perfect exemplar, then one can see African traditional views of ancestorship as a partial understanding of that same truth, not yet made visible in Jesus. Bujo's project would seem closest to the modern family of narratives of self-consciousness, of movement from latent to patent. In Bujo one finds, not surprisingly, the same problems that characterize this family of solutions generally. Where Christ is a "model for our life which makes us creative for a future . . . ,"[72] unless some account is given how he himself is the necessary agent in this "making creative," Christ becomes a dispensable illustration of that life-force.

How then does Bujo fare when measured by the criteria enumerated above for the "classic move" of ancestorship? He would clearly insist that ancestorship must be universalized, and this is one of the prime features of Jesus' perfect modeling, who also should serve to eliminate unworthy aspects of ancestorship. But judged by the criteria related to the core Christian doctrines of God and Christ, Bujo's proposal raises more questions. In his attempt to correlate traditional "anthropocentrism" and Christology "from below," what room is there for a claim about Jesus' divine nature? At the end of the day, the unique decisiveness of Jesus is thrown in question.

While both Nyamiti's and Bujo's proposals have their weaknesses, both constructions are grammatical, for they assume an underlying narrative in which Christ is seen to be sovereign over the ancestors, as he takes over or transforms tasks and roles they previously held. At the same time each assumes a narrative with a temporal "before" for the ancestors, understood to reside in the domain of death until the coming of Christ, who now presides in that domain in this new chapter of the story. Final primacy has helped to show the orthodox intent as well as the outstanding issues for such proposals. It has provided a criterion by which to consider the appropriation of a theme from "before," here the role of the ancestors, into Christian theological discourse, so that the theological tradition at this location on the body might have a distinctively African feature.

If one steps back and considers the goal of distinctive Africanness a final time, one may see a way in which the theme of ancestorship has a

72. Parratt, *Reinventing Christianity*, p. 83.

further contribution to make. At the heart of this classical move is the intent to lay continued claim to the ancestors, to render them contemporaneous, in a way fully consistent with Christ as Victor. The *locus classicus* for such a move is of course the tradition of Christ's *descensus* and his "harrowing of hell," with the underlying scriptural narrative derived from 1 Peter 3:20.[73] The passage is important for it suggests, however elusively, a narrative framework for such proposals within Scripture itself. Several of the authors cite or allude to the passage, and John V. Taylor makes the theme central to his treatment of ancestorship. He cites Bengt Sundkler, who in turn cites a Zulu Lutheran student of his: "As the missionaries preached this Christ, they missed the gate [by not appealing to the harrowing] . . . they did not encourage and tell them that the Bible itself says that the deceased are not dead but are living and resting. . . ."[74] Whatever other traditional arguments are adduced in the aid of ancestorship arguments, the harrowing tradition is present, explicitly or implicitly, to such an extent that one is tempted to suggest it as another family of narratives, conforming to final primacy and particularly suited to contexts like Africa.

What has been shown about final primacy with respect to African Christian theology? It has accomplished a number of goals successfully. It has related the implicit theology of practice to self-conscious proposals. It can draw a boundary for proposals outside of orthodoxy (e.g., Eboussi). It makes theological sense of the urge to affirm the traditional "before." Final primacy has shown the deeper structures diverse proposals share, as well as their stress-points (e.g., Nyamiti and Bujo). Last of all, it can place a family of proposals like ancestorship, new though it be, in a longer lineage of the history of theology (i.e., the "harrowing" tradition). Final primacy is confirmed by its usefulness in all these respects.

73. For references on the harrowing of hell, see Hans Urs von Balthasar, *Mysterium Paschale* (Grand Rapids: Eerdmans, 1990), ch. 4, "Going Down to the Dead: Holy Saturday."

74. John Taylor, *The Primal Vision: Christian Presence and African Religion* (London: SCM, 1963), p. 157, citing Sundkler's *The Christian Ministry in Africa*, p. 290.

Conclusion

Any Objections?

This essay is an extended exercise in analysis. As such, the essay may invite the following question: What are the real-life implications of its argument for the practice of dialogue? "Dialogue" is the watchword, and so the moral imperative, of contemporary work in this field. The contention of this conclusion is that final primacy is friendly to dialogue, though it redefines dialogue even as it promotes it. Implied by this new definition is a different sort of relationship to disagreement, and so to the religions themselves.

Imagine what the objections might be to this argument from the proponents of dialogue. "Why can't the Muslim and the Christian, for example, meet at the level of their common humanity?" The answer is that of course they can, though not as Lessing's *blosse Menschen,* "naked or sheer humans," for who humans are may not be divorced from their histories, beliefs, commitments, and bodily practices. It is by virtue of these that we are who we are. Still, the practice of neighborliness described in Chapter 2 carries with it this sense of shared creatureliness.

"But shouldn't we be radically open to the other, and doesn't that require that we as Christians bracket or lay aside our commitments for the time of the conversation?" There is no reason to resist such a temporary laying aside of assumptions for the sake of exploration, in the form of a thought experiment, since the Christian spirit is not one of fear. But at the end of the day, on the far side of the answering bracket, the Christian must give some account of what she or he has learned, and that account ought to follow the pattern proposed here. One hopes that the thoughts there expressed will exhibit openness, but that quality ought not to be conceived, so argues this essay, to lie in antithesis to the grounding of Christian faith.[1]

The word in question, "dialogue," is itself fraught with its own assumptions. While the practitioner may intend no allusion to Buber or Gadamer, the assumptions originating with such idealist and romanticist authors may still be at work. Too often the term connotes an emphasis on process over content; too often it soft-pedals conflicts between traditions in the face of a universal or future horizon of mystery. By contrast, one can imagine a more modest definition, consisting simply of the willingness to listen and talk with adherents of other traditions. One can imagine a use of "dialogue" built merely on the assumption that one does not yet understand what they believe and the expectation that by such hearing one will profit.

This minimal definition alone will not suffice, especially in light of the distinctive practices of witnessing, narrating, and serving, understood in relation to the theological virtues, as we described in Chapter 2. The give-and-take of dialogue cannot be abstracted from this thicker description of the Christian relating to his or her counterpart in another tradition. At the same time one would not wish to return to the sheer polemics and deep suspicion forming much of the history of relations between the traditions. One should highlight the motive of concern out of which one witnesses, like one beggar telling another where there is food (as the great Indian preacher D. T. Niles once said). One would also highlight the charity of renarrating and the solidarity of neighborliness. Furthermore, the burden of this whole essay has been that the task of making oneself understood across lines of traditions is difficult, and so humility is required as well.

One seeks a way to speak of conversation that, honoring and taking seriously one's interlocutor, does not shy away from the real conflict and clash of claims, even as it demonstrates at the same time the

---

1. So Bishop Michael Ingham is right to advocate "grounded openness" in his *Mansions of the Spirit: The Gospel in a Multi-faith World* (Toronto: Anglican Book Centre, 1997). The problem arises when the openness is what one reaches as one moves mystically beyond the grounding.

virtues described above. How is one to describe this sharper and more honest sort of dialogue, and where might its historical precedents be found?

From Dialogue to Disputation

This essay began with the help of the moral philosopher Alasdair MacIntyre, and so it shall end. In *Three Rival Versions of Moral Enquiry*, he employs the analogy between the desired form of the university today and that of the thirteenth-century University of Paris. Education in the latter centered on the *disputatio*, in which rival schools, for example the Franciscans and the Dominicans, would contend over a common question. One may see the literary evidence of this form in Aquinas's writings, where assertion of one's argument requires overcoming one's opponents' arguments, stated as potently as possible, in the *sed contra*, which recasts and subsumes those arguments into one's own case. MacIntyre emphasizes, and this essay has concurred, that such strong disagreement presupposes an equally strong, tacitly agreed set of assumptions, beliefs, practices, and virtues. These become the boundaries for a common arena of conflict.

Those Dominicans and Franciscans had at it, and then adjourned together to chapel to break bread and hear the Scripture, whose interpretation had just been in dispute. MacIntyre believes that the postliberal university should be a "place of constrained disagreement, of imposed participation in conflict, in which a central responsibility of higher education would be to initiate students into conflict."[2] Christians who share the grammar of final primacy should be invited into an ongoing argument, one with another, about what to make of the claims of others. One could call this dialogue a disputation in the proper sense.

MacIntyre, one should recall, also emphasizes that traditions, as they engage in these struggles, especially in moments of epistemological crisis, seek to come to terms with the challenge of external

---

2. *Three Rival Versions of Moral Enquiry: Encyclopedia, Genealogy, and Tradition: Being Gifford Lectures Delivered in the University of Edinburgh in 1988* (Notre Dame: University of Notre Dame Press, 1990), pp. 230-31.

claims, articulated as fully and as robustly as possible. The theologian is aware, of course, that here disagreement will be interminable and misunderstanding rife. So there must also be charitable disputation *ad extra*, accompanied by the practices and virtues this essay has detailed. But here matters become murkier, for it has also been a goal of this essay to highlight how Christians themselves disagree in a more fundamental way over the evaluation of the claims of other traditions, contesting, implicitly, the very grammar of final primacy itself. In other words, Christians may share the bread and Scripture, and then engage in a fractured conversation, in talk with their own brothers and sisters that moves *across* the traditions of orthodoxy and pluralism. Here Christians working from the assumption of final primacy must engage in dialogue as disputation in the improper (but no less real) sense, as they attempt to assimilate pluralist challenges and so put the nuance in what we have called "nuanced internalism." This debate between estranged sibling Christian "traditions" will surely tax most the mandate of charity.

Only now does one come to dialogue between the orthodox Christian and the adherent of another tradition, which one may call dialogue as disputation in the extended sense. This conversation, especially in comparison to disputation in the improper sense, turns out in many cases to be more cordial than one might have imagined. First of all, the adherent too wants to make a strong case for the truth of his or her belief, and so may prove more comfortable in charitable disputation than in dialogue with the pluralist who retranslates the other's claim in a more concealed fashion. Secondly, because one is aware of the epistemic distance between the participants, the conversation must proceed in a more tentative, exploratory, necessarily *ad hoc*[3] fashion appropriate to the nature of the interchange itself.

The heart then of dialogue as disputation in the extended sense is modesty, an awareness of limits, and readiness for surprise. In these arts the Gospels say the best tutors are children, and psychologists in turn tell us that toddlers can be at once together and apart in "parallel play."[4] While this overstates the case, one may imagine conversation

---

3. William Werpehowski, "*Ad Hoc* Apologetics," *Journal of Religion* 66 (1986): 282-301.

4. The metaphor overstates the matter, since one can imagine such children's games

between the Christian and the adherent of a different tradition in an analogous way. Each endeavors to listen and respond in the immediacy of the conversation. At the same time the Christian participant must attempt to make sense of those claims by forming narratives of the sort this essay has described, thereby stretching and testing one's own "ancillary" beliefs.[5] But understanding will be partial, and so the constructions tentative, ever subject to correction and expansion in light of what is learned from the interlocutor.

One particularly suggestive way to imagine this "parallel play" being conducted might be called "midrashic." Each participant brings to the table a "textured" world, one literally formed by and into a text, one into which outside claims and practices are to be absorbed. But if we follow this metaphor out, one may imagine the account of the interlocutor with his or her claim in the margins of the sacred text. Francis Clooney[6] has suggested just this picture for Hindu advocates of Advaita Vedanta, who are better understood not to be offering abstract metaphysical theories but rather philosophical commentary on the Vedic text. The advantage of this image for both interlocutors in the disputatious dialogue is that it ties the understanding of the other to the internally authoritative text whence the evaluation flows. The interlocutors debate, conflicts and even agreements arise, as each labors in a parallel motion to inscribe these tentative results in the "midrashic" margins of their scripturally derived tradition.

The possibility of conversion endures, lending the requisite seriousness to the proceedings, though the difficulty of this cataclysmic outcome must also be borne in mind. The Christian, from within his or her own doctrinal resources, is reminded that such conversion de-

---

merging and overflowing often and in unpredictable ways. The metaphor reminds us, in philosophical terms, of the implication for dialogue of the fact that religions are incommensurable, but still comparable. On this distinction see Garrett Green's *Theology, Hermeneutics, and Imagination: The Crisis of Interpretation at the End of Modernity* (Cambridge: Cambridge University Press, 1988), pp. 72-73, where he relies on Richard Bernstein's *Beyond Objectivism and Relativism: Science, Hermeneutics, and Praxis* (Philadelphia: University of Pennsylvania, 1985), pp. 79-108.

5. See Nancey Murphy, *Theology in the Age of Scientific Reasoning* (Ithaca, N.Y.: Cornell University Press, 1990).

6. *After Vedanta: An Experiment in Comparative Theology* (Albany: State University of New York, 1993).

pends not on clever argumentation, but on grace. The sting of enmity is dulled by the awareness that each side must interpret what is heard within his or her own tradition. From time to time, nonetheless, as when the eye spies a shaft of light through breaking clouds, unexpectedly shared terrain is illumined. This gives courage to the hope the Christian participant may have, for reasons of his or her own, that the conversation partner too might perhaps receive some light from Christ, which in the end he or she owns by being found by him.

One would have to admit that such moments of generous, tentative, fecund dialogue as disputation have been rare episodes in the history of the interaction of the religions. Lest the reader despair of its possibility one example may be proffered. Ninth-century Baghdad[7] delighted, albeit under the constraints of the medieval Islamic laws of *dhimmi*, in disputations between the faiths in its house of wisdom, the host faith being, one may reckon, confident enough of its cultural and intellectual vigor and divine sanction to listen to challenges with a benevolent ear. In dialogue as disputation in the extended sense one hopes for this same security, though (and here is the rub), without the sanction of the caliphate.

The security in question comes only from God, and cannot then rely upon any other bulwark, political, cultural, epistemological. Shaken by a crisis of conscience, Luther found the only fortress to be the grace that justified, though he had no claim in himself to merit it. Likewise, the Christian is today shaken by the crisis of the claim of the Hindu or Buddhist or Muslim at his or her very hand, and can thank that neighbor for clarifying anew the sole source of security of the sort that strips away all claim the Christian might make to superiority or merit. But as Luther also learned, that grace which is Christ's, final and primary, is not only the end of the story, but its beginning too. The Wittenberg professor of the promises of the old dispensation had found not the end of his disputing, but rather the fire of love that could stoke it aright. He had found the end of striving, yes, but only the beginning of the fruit of good works, only the beginning of the proclaiming to and serving the flesh-and-blood neighbor, fellow sinner, fellow child of the image, at his right hand. So it is for all Christians, constrained in loving obedience to the One who is Alpha and Omega.

7. R. W. Southern, *Western Views of Islam in the Middle Ages* (Cambridge, Mass.: Harvard University Press, 1962).

Index